THE ART OF JAPANESE GARDENS

One of the "Turtle Islands" in the Gold Pavilion garden lake. From
a painting by Samuel Newsom.

THE ART OF
JAPANESE
GARDENS

by Loraine E. Kuck

THE JOHN DAY COMPANY, NEW YORK

COPYRIGHT, 1940, BY LORAINE E. KUCK

Designed by Robert Josephy

PRINTED IN THE UNITED STATES OF AMERICA

ACKNOWLEDGMENTS

Quotations have been used from *Japan, A Short Cultural History*, by G. B. Sansom, and from *China, A Short Cultural History*, by C. P. Fitzgerald, through the courtesy of the Cresset Press, London, and of D. Appleton-Century Co., New York. Excerpts from Arthur Waley's translation of the *Genji Monogatari*, published as *The Tale of Genji* by Houghton Mifflin Co., have been used through permission of the translator.

STYLE NOTE

Except in the Foreword, all names of persons in Japanese are placed in their native order, the family name first, the given name following.

Also, different words are used in Japanese to designate a Buddhist and a Shinto building. Foreigners follow this custom by reserving the word "temple" exclusively for Buddhist and "shrine" exclusively for Shinto edifices. This custom is followed here.

To make clear the meaning of words to those who do not understand Japanese, I have not hesitated to resort to redundancies, repeating often as English words, syllables which stand as suffixes in Japanese names: for example, "Nanzen*ji* temple," "Koho-*an* temple," even "Mount Hiei-*zan*." Inconsistencies in hyphenating Japanese names were deliberate, being used at times to show division into syllables where doubt might exist. Inconsistencies in marking the long "o" were also deliberate, the marks being omitted in commonly known words such as Tokyo and Kyoto.

L. E. K.

Contents

CONTENTS

Illustrations

ILLUSTRATIONS

ILLUSTRATIONS

ILLUSTRATIONS

ILLUSTRATIONS

ILLUSTRATIONS

LINE ENGRAVINGS

Foreword

A FEW WRITERS have begun to make clear the fact that Far Eastern gardens sometimes hold a meaning, a symbolism, much deeper than appears outwardly in their small hills and ponds. But heretofore, I think, no one has made it plain that many of these gardens are not only works of symbolism but of fine art as well. The West has been led to think of them too often as merely quaint and pretty toys which somehow sound as if they were rather like enlarged topographical maps. It has not been emphasized that many of these gardens were created as serious works of art and are far indeed from toys, deserving rather to be classed along with the great Oriental landscape paintings to which they are closely related in spirit.

The art which has gone into making Far Eastern gardens is one entirely unknown in the West. It is an art which, in spirit and subject, comes closest, as said, to the landscape paintings; but in form it is more like sculpture than any other Western art form. Yet, it is really quite different, a unique art, built on the technique of choosing and arranging natural stones so as to make, first of all, a creation esthetically satisfying through their own intrinsic forms, and, secondly, to suggest some aspect of nature, a small scene or a great panorama.

Such art is obviously in no way akin to the making of a "rockery" in an Occidental garden, where the display of flowers against stones is the primary interest. When a rockery is to be made, if stones do not already exist on the site, they are brought in from anywhere and dumped down, more or less helter skelter; they are sometimes made into a wall. Frequently there is dependence on plants to cover up the inartistic result. "It will look better when the vines have grown over it," we say. To arrange stones so they make by themselves forms of balanced and harmonious beauty, and which re-create, furthermore, a suggestion of nature, is quite outside the artistic knowledge of the West.

In discussing this art it is necessary to speak of it as existing in Far Eastern gardens rather than those of China or Japan, for, while considerable difference exists today between the gardens of these two countries, it was not always so. It has been known, of course, that the gardens of Japan stemmed originally from those of China, but it has not been recognized heretofore that the differences now visible have arisen in China rather than in Japan. In gathering the facts about the Japanese gardens into a coherent story and fitting them into their background, it has become increasingly evident to me that, not only in the beginning, but right down the centuries, the gardens of Japan have reflected those of China. Sometimes, indeed, they appear to have been made by exiled Chinese garden craftsmen. In other words, the naturalistic gardens still found in Japan were also those of China up to the Ming period; it was not until after that time, when landscape painting went into a decline and Chinese gardens with it, that strong differences began to develop. Even Japanese students of the gardens have not realized this up to now, for their attention has been concentrated on gathering the facts in their own field.

As yet the history of Chinese gardens is only sketchily known. No pre-Ming gardens survive in China as far as we are aware, and very little search has been made through the documents for facts. However, many gardens made in the earlier centuries still remain in Japan, so that it is there that the early garden art of both nations must be studied. When experts, well grounded in the earlier techniques as revealed in Japan, can begin a search in China, many fragments of earlier Chinese gardens probably will come to light among later reconstructions. Until that is done, however, and the old documents are combed for corroborating facts, the full story of Chinese gardens cannot be written. When the time comes, it

is my hope to write it, as I have told here the story of the Japanese gardens, giving as far as possible, by inference, something of their Chinese background.

The true story of the Japanese gardens, their art, their meaning, and the way in which they expressed their times and the personalities who made them, has proved a fascinating tale to trace and put together. It has not, heretofore, been made into a coherent account in any language including the Japanese. The pageant of garden makers is a long and brilliant one, starting with the sixth century Japanese Empress who found a Korean craftsman able to build for her a garden something like the one her ambassador had recently seen at the court of the Chinese ruler, and including, down the centuries, other emperors and nobles, military conquerors, priests, artists, and common folk. Even the obscure laborers who did the actual work of handling rocks and plants must be included, for occasionally they rose to great heights, revealing that even in them glowed the spark of artistic genius.

In portraying these personalities, which are often but hazily sketched in the documents, I have drawn on my knowledge of the Japanese people as a whole to round out the picture. Customs and modes of thought of the nation have changed but little compared to other countries and these have necessarily been quite as much a part of the garden study as facts bearing more directly on the subject. For only by knowing the people and the times which produced a work of art can we hope to understand it. The background of events has, therefore, been painted in, including the political happenings which conditioned the development of culture and the arts in general. Certain arts, such as painting, architecture, and the tea ceremony, which are closely connected with gardening, have also had to be outlined.

The full and true story of the gardens could only have been written within the last year or two, for only just now have all the facts become known. Tales and traditions there have been in plenty, most of them still popularly accepted in Japan; the material I have incorporated here is still known to but a few specialists, even in that country. The Japanese people

have always had a better intuitive understanding of their art than a passion for the facts about it, so, while they have loved their gardens and understood them emotionally, they have known or cared little who made them or why. Only since Western scientific scholarship has begun to make some headway in the country have the gardens been studied objectively. Lately, by going directly to the obscure and difficult documents which were contemporary with the gardens themselves instead of carelessly taking the word of someone who was writing two or three hundred years afterward, have the facts become known.

To the scholars who have laboriously unearthed the material I use here, I make full acknowledgment; to Dr. Tatsui and Dr. Tamura, pioneers in the subject; to Mr. Toyama, whose standards of scholarship must benefit the whole field of research in Japan, and to Mr. Shigemori, whose monumental work, in twenty-six volumes, on the history of the gardens was only completed this year.

Their material, however, I have handled in a way which is highly unorthodox from the traditional Japanese standpoint, a fact which I hope will be understood and condoned in that country; for I have written it for and from the Western viewpoint. I have discarded much of the accepted vocabulary and invented many terms of my own, such as the expression "painting gardens." All this in the attempt to make the story understandable to those who know little or nothing about the subject. I have had to be very obvious, to the Japanese mind, and, moreover, I have had to run the risk of making errors, for I have tried to put into words—English words which necessarily limit and define—that vague feeling of understanding about art and nature which the Oriental mind absorbs from the first year of life and which it never feels the need of setting apart and studying objectively.

In organizing the story into a sequential account, there have developed, here and there, what have seemed to me certain inevitable conclusions; such, for instance, as the one already mentioned about Chinese and Japanese gardens being alike up to the Ming period. For these surmises the Jap-

anese scholars, who have stayed very close to the documentary facts, are not to be held accountable. In setting down both facts and surmises, I have tried to make very clear which was which, so that no one need accept my conclusions unknowingly.

Even handling the documentary facts, however, has not been simple. The Japanese language can be, and often is, so obscure that the exact meaning of a sentence is in doubt even to the most learned. I have tried to sift out the definite facts, but no one can realize better than I the great possibility for error which exists in an attempt of this sort. I hope I have not made too many. Since I am no linguist, I owe everything in this respect to my two faithful translators and interpreters, Mr. Masaru (Victor) Otake and Mr. Kazuomi Yanagisawa, who have worked painstakingly over every line for me. Without their wide understanding of both languages, my task would have been an impossible one. I owe, besides, to the special English ability of Mr. Otake (known to many at the University of Syracuse) all the quoted translations used, including the poems, when they are not otherwise accredited in the text. And to the fine understanding of Buddhism and Japanese culture possessed by Mr. Yanagisawa, I owe much of general background and understanding, for, with a few words, it was often possible for him to clear up an obscure reference which I might never otherwise have understood.

To acknowledge and give proper thanks to all the many others who have assisted me is, as usual in a work of this kind, quite impossible. The people of Japan, everywhere and always and as a matter of course, have gone out of their way to be helpful. A few names, however, I must mention, of persons who gave me special aid; I owe particular thanks to Dr. Tsuyoshi Tamura, Professor of Landscape Architecture in the Imperial University of Tokyo; to Mr. Eitaro Sekiguchi, his one-time student, now head of the same department in the Kyoto Imperial University; to Dr. Jiro Harada, of the Imperial Household Museum, who was the first of his countrymen to write an authentic book in English on the gardens; to Dr. Daisetz T. Suzuki, noted Zen scholar, who greatly aided my understanding of that difficult philosophy; to Mr. Ryusaku Tsunoda of Columbia University, who threw light on many angles of Japanese history; to Mr. Tsutomu Ema, authority on the ancient background of Kyoto, who secured for me the scroll picture reproduced here. Finally, to Mr. Mirei Shigemori I owe special thanks for the hours of his time he spent in amplifying for me facts from his great historical work on the gardens.

I must mention, too, a number of organizations which extended courteous help; the Imperial Palace Bureau in Kyoto which allowed me to study the imperial estates and Mr. Tsumizani Nori, its head; the library staff of Kyoto Imperial University; the municipality of Kyoto and Mr. Tye Harada, head of its tourist department, who supplied many pictures and secured entry into many gardens; the Japan Welcome Society; the Board of Tourist Industry and the Japan Tourist Bureau, which gave me many photographs and on numberless occasions was helpful.

Finally, I must also express the appreciation I feel to my foreign friends in Kyoto, who have always been kind and helpful. The permanent residents have welcomed me to their circle, and a number of them have been my hosts during the years I lived among them. Others who were making studies of Japanese cultural subjects were always willing to contribute from their specialized fields. These include Jon Carter Covell, Alexander Soper, William Acker, P. D. Perkins, and Samuel Newsom. The latter, who has been making a study of the craft and technique of the gardens at the same time I have been delving into their esthetics and history, has made for me the drawing of the turtle island used in the frontispiece. For this I am especially grateful.

Loraine E. Kuck

Kyoto, 1939
Honolulu, 1940

THE ART OF JAPANESE GARDENS

I. *The Ancient Chinese Prototype*

AFTER man had given up his pastoral life and settled down to tilling the soil—or letting his woman do it for him—he noticed one day that she was digging in the grass at the edge of their clearing. When she rose, she held in her hand a bit of earth in which were the roots of a little plant, bright with flowers. She crossed to their hut and stopping near the doorway, scooped a hole with her finger and carefully put the plant back in the ground. Watching her, the man thought she might better be at her hoeing and grunted. But the woman looked at the flower and smiled. The first ornamental garden in the world had been made.

Later, when man began to huddle in villages for protection and into cities for trade, he found he could not stifle a deep-lying love of green forests and growing things. He longed for a sight of the wild flowers and the smell of grass. So behind the wall of his house, where it would be hidden from the crowded ugliness of the town, he planted a tree and made a little garden of flowers.

Trees and flowers are all that we, who have a European background, think of when we think of gardens, for to us garden making means little more than the cultivation of plants. But in the Orient it has not remained so simple. There, when men remembered nature, they remembered it in its entirety, the hills and streams and rocks as well as the trees and blossoms. So, when a garden was built, they put into it stones and water as well as plants, suggesting the whole outdoor picture.

It is interesting to trace the reason for this difference. Our European ancestors, as we know, had little use for nature in the rough. Before the time of Wordsworth, they considered crags, cataracts, and wild moors only deplorable conditions in a world of hard facts. Certainly they had no desire to seek out such things merely for the dubious pleasure of looking at them. Green trees and flowers, of course, were quite a different matter; they were tender and lovely and worthy of cultivation.

This European aversion to wild nature was based, I think, not on any innate dislike of nature in its virile moods—for consider how we, the descendents, flock today to stand breathless before the great scenery of the world. It was based, instead, on a fear association which had come down from an even more simple and primitive ancestry. Someone has suggested that an adequate police force is the first requirement for appreciation of the wilds; that it was fear of robbers and bandits that made Europeans shun lonely places before the eighteenth century.

This can hardly have been the whole reason, however. Bandits and brigands have infested lonely spots in the Orient quite as often as in the Occident, yet this fact has never prevented the Oriental from going into the wilds when he desired. Europeans, moreover, have never been really afraid of *men*. But they have become cowering and fearful before the creations of their own imaginations, that host of beings—usually inimical to men—who in the mind of the primitive European peopled the forest, moors, and ravines. Trolls, hobgoblins, pixies, water and tree spirits, kobolds, dwarfs and gnomes, to say nothing of ghouls, ghosts, and vampires haunted the wild and forgotten places of Europe, ready to do harm to any lonely traveler who should venture there. We can feel the shuddering fear of such beings in the tale of the Erl King, for instance, of the water sprite, Undine, and we hear it in Grieg's "Dance of the Trolls." It runs like a shiver through all the folk literature of Europe. When our forebears sought quiet and peace, they had no desire to go where such beings could harm them; they preferred to stay snugly behind the walls of their castles or their cottages, growing perhaps a few flowers, but certainly with nothing else to remind them of gloomy ravines, menacing peaks, and dark trees haunted by such fearful creatures.

4

THE ANCIENT CHINESE PROTOTYPE

In the Orient the imaginations of men have created another host of demons, jinn, and devils, but these evil genii are seen to be more menacing in the cities than in the empty outdoors. Oriental demons do not haunt rocks and streams and trees; there is, rather, a feeling that rocks and trees are themselves, in some dim way, sentient beings and possess a sort of kinship to humanity. No Oriental, therefore, fears nature itself. Instead of wishing to escape from it, there has been, rather, a yearning to fly to it when life becomes too pressing. Many scholars in China actually have become mountain recluses, happy in the simplicity, even the poverty, of their lives if they could have natural beauty around them, leisure to enjoy it, to think and write about it, and sometimes to discuss it with their cronies as we often see them doing in the traditional paintings. It follows that from the beginning, men in that part of the world have had a different feeling toward the things that remind them of nature; and when they built gardens, they put into them the things that would aid this remembrance.

We do not know how long there have been gardens in China, but certainly for several thousand years. We are quite sure, however, they have been following their characteristic pattern of rocks, hills, lakes, and islands for well over two milleniums and probably much longer. Ancient writings reveal quite clearly how the gardens came to have this pattern, how they were expanded merely from places where plants grow into reproductions of nature.

Sages writing twenty-five hundred years ago make it plain that, even in that age, men were tired of cities and muddy fields and longed to get away from their dirt and confusion to the quiet beauty of the hills. Because some of those who did escape were seeking the way of understanding, the way to the most complete fulfillment of man's nature, they were called Seekers of the Way, that is, Taoists, *tao* meaning the way or the road. They formulated the most ancient school of Chinese philosophy, whose leader is regarded as Lao Tse, but there were many others. They taught that activity is useless, that the only reality is inward, that man must return often to the quietude and beauty of nature if he is to know the reason

5

for his being and his relationship to the world around him and to the Infinite.

The Taoists were, of course, crystallizing a very deep human instinct found all over the world. The Hebrew poet sang, "I will lift up mine eyes unto the hills from whence cometh my strength." The Greeks created the myth of the giant who renewed his strength each time he touched the earth. Europe and America have produced their philosophers and poets who have expressed it—Emerson, Thoreau, and Rousseau, Wordsworth, Blake, and Whitman. The feeling that man is but a phase of his environment, a brother to the winds and rocks and clouds as well as to the plants and animals, has found words in the West more often, perhaps, than we realize. Thomas Edward Brown followed the Hebrew imagery when he wrote the well known lines:

Not God! in gardens! when the eve is cool?
Nay, but I have a sign;
'Tis very sure God walks in mine.

He came nearer to the Far Eastern form of the same thought when he exclaimed:

—do ye not understand
How the great Mother mixes all our bloods?
O breeze! O swaying buds!
O lambs, O primroses, O floods!

Down the ages there have been many Chinese scholars who might also have liked to lead a simple life in the hills, but for one reason or another could not give up their conventional homes and their families and probably their official positions to do so. These scholars did the next best thing; they brought the mountains to their own courtyards, at least in imagination, by arranging rocks and trees to suggest hills and water to remind them of lakes. Shut away in the quiet seclusion of these gardens, they could believe they were really sitting in some mountain retreat, a place to ponder on nature and beauty and the universe and man's relation to it all.

Since scholars were usually officials and, hence, often influential at court, it is not surprising to find their ideas reflected in the development of the large imperial estates where landscape gardening on a grand scale first appeared in China. Such men as these were also the literati of their generations, not only as writers and poets, but often as painters. In consequence, poems and pictures as well as descriptions of the gardens have been preserved. And since the Chinese have always respected tradition and deferred to literary and artistic precedents, the early gardens became models for later ones, even though the new builders might be neither philosophers nor artists. Thus the traditional style of the Chinese garden was fixed in the suggested image of nature, thus it was handed down the centuries, and so it remains to this day.

Of course this naturalistic pattern would not have persisted down the ages, in spite of the respect for tradition, had there not been something about it fundamentally congenial to the Chinese mind. It would have been just as congenial to the Occidental mind, no doubt, had the latter been freed from superstitions. But perhaps it is this very crystallization by the Taoist philosophers that has made the feeling for nature so conscious in the East. There man has not generally conceived himself as in conflict with nature; his efforts have been to bring himself into harmony with it. In the West man has constantly seen himself battling natural forces, first in conquering the wilderness; later, through science, bending the forces of nature to his own ends.

But although the Taoists were the first in China to express man's harmony with nature, they were not the only ones to put it into concrete form. The same idea appears as a basic concept of Buddhism, in which man is conceived as but one of the manifestations of nature and his return to the cosmic element as the end and object of his world-strife. Buddhism began filtering into China from India in the first century after Christ, and its tenets proved so acceptable to Chinese thought that for over a millenium it was a dominant force in Chinese culture and history. From China it spread to Japan. Indeed, it was certain sects of Buddhism which continued to emphasize the basic feeling of harmony with nature when the later Taoists diverged from their first high philosophy to follow a path of pseudo-science, the pursuit of immortality and alchemy. The Ch'an branch of Buddhism clung to the ancient feeling for nature and worked out a technique of meditation by which man could sense his unity with the cosmos and glimpse its truths.

The first large gardens of China, as we have said, were constructed as expressions of imperial power and wealth. They developed from vast hunting preserves which included natural hills and lakes, forests and streams, and they were stocked with animals and birds to improve the sport. We read[1] of Liu Wu, the son of a Han emperor, who lived in the second century before Christ.

"At one time he built the T'u-yuan, or Rabbit Park. Within it was the Hill of a Hundred Supernatural Beings: on the hill were Fu-ts'un Rock, the Lo-yuan Grotto and the Dragon's Peak. At the foot of the hill was a goose pond; within the pond stood Crane Islet and Bird Bank." The chronicle adds, "The Prince would spend his day with his courtiers and favored guests, hunting and fishing in it."

The earliest record of islands artificially constructed in a garden lake dates back also to the Han empire and a belief in the Isles of the Immortals. The tale of the three Magic Isles which lay in the Eastern Ocean, not far from the coast, was a part of earliest Chinese folklore. Formerly, it was said, men had been able to reach the Magic Isles, but in later days, whenever a boat approached, it was driven away by storms. Only those personages in Chinese mythology who had learned the secret of immortality might go and live on them. These Immortals, or *Sennin,* were not disembodied spirits but living men and women of great wisdom who had learned the secret of postponing death. They flew about wherever they liked on the backs of cranes, as we often see them depicted in Chinese paintings. It is this association of the crane with the Immortals and the fact that the bird is long lived, that has made it one of the important symbols of longevity in the

[1] See Note A, p. 289.

8

Orient. Both the turtle and the crane have been curiously interwoven into Oriental garden art and its symbolism, as we shall see.

Of the mystic Isles on which the Immortals lived, there had originally been five, all floating gently in the sea. The Immortals, however, didn't like their movement and complained to the Son of Heaven, who thereupon ordered great turtles to stabilize them. This worked very well until one day a giant waded out and caught some of the turtles. Without their support, two of the islands drifted away and were lost in the void. The names of the three remaining were P'eng-lai, Fang-chang, and Ying-chou. The name P'eng-lai is rendered in Japanese as Hōrai, and garden islands, which trace their origin to this tale are called Hōrai-jima. Down the ages, the concept of these fair, celestial isles, where care and death never enter, has stimulated the imaginations of poets and painters. Even today we often find them depicted, usually as distant, lofty, purple peaks rising from the sea to the clouds. Misty verdure trails down their slopes, and the blue valleys between are deeply shadowed. On high plateaus on the slopes of these peaks dwell the Happy Ones who do not die.

The earliest historic record of artificial islands based on this tale states that the Emperor Wu (141-87 B.C.), who seriously believed in the Isles, sought to send an expedition to them that he might learn for himself the secret of immortality. To insure success, he resorted to sympathetic magic, constructing replicas of the Isles in his garden lake.[2] Probably he hoped to lure some of the Immortals to a spot so similar to their own realm and so learn the secret from them.

In the next centuries, the naturalistic garden pattern was developed and standardized in China. Where no natural hills and lakes existed, they were constructed artificially. About 500 A.D. Ju Hao "who was a subtle craftsman . . . fashioned a hill west of T'ien Yuan Ch'ih. He chose fine rocks from the quarries of Ping-mang, transplanted bamboo from Ju and Ying, directed the construction of two-storied pavilions set in order, above and

---

[2] *T'ien-Hsia Monthly,* October, 1936.

below, and laid out trees and plants, all to give the impression of rustic wildness."

Sometime during the period when islands were becoming a standard part of Chinese garden design, a new form developed. It was obviously inspired by those based on the Immortals' Isles but derived from Buddhism instead of Taoism. Buddhism had become important in China about the 4th century A.D. and often was at odds with Taoism and Confucianism. It is not hard to picture Buddhist monks objecting to the construction of islands founded on a Taoist myth in their temple gardens and deciding, instead, to build their own Buddhist islands. They chose to represent Mount Sumeru which, in Buddhist literature, is an attempt to visualize the universe. It is described as a vast peak of almost inconceivable height, rising from an illimitable ocean. It is four-sided, broader at the top and bottom than in the center, so that illustrations in Buddhist books make it appear like a squat, square goblet on a thick base. It is the central axis of the universe around which all heavenly bodies revolve. Rising out of the sea to heaven, it is surrounded by seven concentric rings of rocky mountains which inclose circular seas. These have given rise to the descriptive name, "Nine Mountains and Eight Seas," by which representations were sometimes later known.

One of the earliest references to a reproduction of this mountain says: [3] "Within the temple Mount Sumeru was built. Its four faces were of sublime rocks and austere precipices. Pearly birds and rare beasts, trees and plants of exquisite beauty grew upon it. There were images of Immortals and Buddhas. It was something people had never heard of before and was regarded as miraculous."

The pearly birds and images of Buddhas were probably made of porcelain. In that period, and doubtless for some time after, the graphic description of Mount Sumeru as given in the Buddhist scriptures was probably followed rather closely in island construction, with its central peak and the surrounding rings of rocky mountains. When the form was transferred

[3] See Note B, p. 289.

to Japan, the name was rendered *shumi-sen*. We have no way of telling what the earliest form was like, but later the *shumi-sen* arrangement was made with a central pointed rock, slanting a little, rising from lesser rocks about its base.

At the end of the 6th century, Yang Ti, second emperor of the Sui dynasty (589-617 A.D.) built such extensive parks that his extravagance and preoccupation with this project brought about the downfall of his dynasty. Even in the present day of large undertakings the tremendous size of his gardens is impressive.

"To create his Western Park the ground was broken over an area some sixty miles in circuit and the labor of a million men was required, on the average. Within, the park was divided into sixteen courts; earth and rock were brought to make hills and the ground was excavated for the Five Lakes and Four Seas. . . . In the center of each, earth and rock were piled to form a hilly island, with arbors and pavilions built upon it. With the lake shore bending and turning and the broad expanse of the water, there were a thousand prospects and a variegated beauty unequaled in the world of men. . . .

"Also was excavated the Northern Sea, some thirteen miles in circuit. Within it were three island peaks, in imitation of P'eng-lai, Fang-chang and Ying-chou, the Isles of the Immortals. Upon each were terraces, arbors and cloisters. The depth of the water being many feet, canals were used to connect the Five Lakes and the Four Seas so that dragon and phoenix barges might go back and forth over the whole system of waterways."

It is interesting to note here that, by the time of Yang Ti, the Isles of the Immortals were well established as a garden form. They had become pleasure isles holding terraces and pavilions and were reached by the many-colored barges which had models of a dragon or a phoenix for a figurehead.

After the fall of Yang Ti came the great T'ang dynasty (618-906 A.D.) often called the Golden Age of China. This period is one of the most important to our story of Chinese garden prototypes, for Japanese civilization stemmed directly from it. The two great cities of the period were Ch'ang-an[4] and Lo-yang. Ch'ang-an served in the 8th century as the model for Nara, the first important capital of Japan, and for Kyoto in the 9th. The gardens of these Chinese cities were undoubtedly copied as nearly as possible in Japan during those centuries.

Sir George Sansom[5] pictures cosmopolitan Ch'ang-an at the time of its greatest glory. "Along the streets of Ch'ang-an there passed in those days Buddhist monks from India, envoys from Kashgar, Samarkand, Persia, Tonkin, Constantinople, chieftains of nomadic tribes from Siberian plains, officials and students from Korea and, in now increasing numbers, from Japan. It is easy to imagine the effect upon the eyes and minds of these last, of a capital so rich in interest and excitement, their despair at the sight of such profusion, their proud resolve to rival it, if industry and courage and restless ambition could eke out their country's material shortcomings. No doubt, with that tireless curiosity and patient attention to detail which characterized their study of other alien civilizations with which they later came in contact . . . the Japanese set themselves to observe and report on every aspect of Chinese life, and to consider what features they might profitably adopt in their own country."

Many descriptions survive of Ch'ang-an and Lo-yang gardens. There was, for instance, the one built for the Imperial Princess, An-lo, by the Minister of Agriculture, Chao Li-wu. "He created the Pool of Ting K'un, a mile in length and breadth; he had rocks heaped together to form the Hill of Flowers, setting stone steps and plank bridges at unexpected angles. There was a ninefold whirlpool and a rock spring, leading the clear torrent through fissures so that the sound of water rushing down was like that of a cataract."

There are also descriptions of two gardens belonging to the Grand Secretary, Li Te-yu, who had a town house in Ch'ang-an and a country villa near Lo-yang. The former was, "at the southeast corner of Anse Ward on a road lined with mulberries so luxuriant that it was given the name of the

[4] Present day Hsian-fu.
[5] In *Japan, a Short Cultural History*.

Jade Bowl. Although his lodgings were not spacious or imposing, their ordering showed a rare ingenuity. The courts were lined with curious stones, unusual pines, other fine trees and fragrant plants, all as if seen in a painting."

Also, "Li Te-yu's Quiet Springs Villa possessed a great number of unusual rocks of all sorts, of which most have gone into strengthening the city wall of Lo-yang. Today, there are only the Li-star stone and the Lion cub stone which have been moved to the garden of the Liang villa and set up to give pleasure to scholars."

Of all the Chinese garden records which I have seen, the most revealing and appealing, the most human and understandable, is that of an official of the later T'ang dynasty named Po Chü-i. He was an inveterate garden maker and one of the greatest poets China has produced. Down the eleven centuries which separate our time from his, the record of this poet-official's gardening reaches us and finds deep response in anyone who shares the love of garden making.

The career of Po Chü-i, like that of most Chinese officials, was a series of ups and downs, of high position in times of favor and of virtual banishment in times of disfavor. But wherever he went, he built gardens. When he was an important official, he caused large works to be carried out; as a private individual, in times of retirement, he built a cottage garden for himself. Often enough, it would seem, he worked with his own hands, for he speaks with the authentic voice of the dirt gardener when he says of himself:

"From youth to old age, the whitewashed cottage of poverty or the vermilion gates of affluence have each lasted but a day or two in turn. But to build up a hillock with dirt spilled from a basket, to pile up a hill with rocks carried in the hands, to make a pool of water borne in a dipper—joy in such things has completely obsessed me always."

During one of his periods of banishment, he chose to live near the famous sacred mountain, Lu-shan. This district, it is recorded, "in strange beauty has no equal under the heavens. There are mountains and mountains. To the north is a peak known as the Peak of the Fragrant Censer; the northern temple is called the Temple of Lost Desires; between these lies a place of surpassing excellence, the first in all Lu-shan."

In the autumn of 816 A.D. the poet, passing by as a traveler, saw and fell in love with this district and there he built himself a cottage and a garden. Of the cottage the record says:

"The wood was hewn but not painted; the walls were plastered but not given a white finish; steps were of stone, windows covered with paper, screens were of bamboo and hangings of homespun, all in keeping.[6] In the cottage were placed four wooden couches, two plain screens, a lacquered lute, and of books, Confucian, Taoist and Buddhist, two or three scrolls each.

"Since then the poet has come to set these things first of all: To lift up his eyes and see the mountains, to lower them and listen to the stream; to look about him at bamboos, willows, clouds and rocks."

Whimsically the record adds, "It is proper to attend to one's business, without leisure time and without whims; yet here things conspire to entice one outdoors and indoors at the same time."

The description of the cottage garden is as graphic and minute as one could hope to find. It was only a small garden but complete. We could almost duplicate it from this description although, evidently, much of it was the natural setting, but little changed.

"In front there is a level area some 117 feet in length and breadth. From this there rises a flat terrace, covering almost half the area: south of the terrace and something under twice its size lies a square pool. Surrounding the water is a profusion of mountain bamboo and wild herbs; in it grow white lotus and white fish.

"On its south side one comes to a rocky torrent narrowed by the projection of ancient pines and old firs, almost eighteen spans in circumference and I know not how many hundreds of feet in height, their tall heads touching the clouds, their branches drooping over the water below like

[6] This would be a fairly accurate description of a present-day Japanese house.

hanging streamers, like an umbrella or like dragon snakes. Under these conifers winds a dense growth of vine, through whose interwoven shade the light of the sun and moon cannot penetrate to earth and under which the winds of summer at full tide blow cool as autumn. Through this copse runs a path of white pebbles.

"Five paces north of the cottage the clearing ends with the stepped rise of the cliff, piles of stone, a gully, abandoned anthills and a confused debris of wood, with some strange vegetation growing over all. . . .

"East of the cottage is a cascade. Dropping some forty-three feet, the water flows over ledges, around corners and passes off down a stone gutter. At dusk and dawn, and at midnight, like an artful beauty, it becomes the sound of girdle ornaments tinkling accompaniment to the lute and zither.

"On the west, the cottage backs against the western base of the northern precipice to whose top leads a scaffolded stairway of split bamboo. A spring, dividing into thin veins of water, runs down to drip from the eaves and trickle over the ledges, the drops bound together and intermingling like strung pearls, like falling dewdrops; then, as fine mist, drifting and scattering far in the breeze.

"In these four directions, staff and sandal, ear and eye may win [to such scenes as these]: In spring the variegated embroidery of valley flowers; in summer, clouds and a torrent rushing through a rocky defile; in autumn the Tiger Ravine under the moon; in winter the snow-capped Fragrant Censer Peak, cold and gleaming in obscurity. Dusk and dawn cherish and display a thousand changes, a myriad appearances, never to be wholly caught in words. . . ."

Yet the words of this poet do bridge for us the thousand years that have intervened, revealing for us the spirit of the age and its love of natural beauty. It is no wonder that the Japanese, with their own deep love of such beauty, should have thrilled to discover this spirit and the forms of loveliness which it produced.

II. *The Modern Chinese Prototype*

WE ARE fortunate in having preserved for us a splendid example of the traditional great Chinese garden landscape, similar, no doubt, to the vast gardens of the early centuries when Japan was learning from China. Evidence points to the fact that the present garden of the Forbidden City in Peking stems directly from the same T'ang gardens which served also as prototypes for those in Japan. Peking was laid out on the plan of Ch'ang-an, just as were Nara and Kyoto, and we can trace a close similarity in their forms. Likewise, we can see, in the existing Imperial Garden in Peking, just such a great, artificially constructed garden landscape as served as a model for those of Japan. While present-day Peking was built only five hundred years ago by the Mings, there had been a city on the site many centuries before.

The principal feature of this imperial landscape park is three large lakes, lying north and west of the inclosed Forbidden City. This park would hardly fit the Western conception of a garden for it covers scores of acres in which are not only these lakes, their islands, a hill of almost natural size, but roads, bridges, pavilions, minor palaces, and temples. All of this has been created by man, however, for there is no rising ground, hardly any water, on the flat dry plain around Peking. But some miles away a bountiful spring, now called the Jade Fountain, bubbles up in an imperial hunting preserve. Its waters were conducted to the city, and the chain of three lakes dug. The excavated material was piled into two hills.

The first to build these lakes, apparently, were the Kins, a northern tribe of barbarians which had conquered the country around the city in the

12th century. Like all primitive peoples who have come in contact with Chinese civilization—including the Japanese—the Kins quickly adopted and adapted themselves to it. In making these lakes they were but following a custom, already old, that the palace park of the ruler should have such bodies of water in it.

The Peking lakes are magnificent in size, each many acres in extent. In winter they are used for skating and in summer they become vast seas of lotus, over which pass strange and baffling blue-green shadows when breezes stir the great cupped leaves. Many of the leaf stems extend a full six feet above the water while the pointed flower buds push up even higher. To cross this jungle of water plants, a small boat must wind through dim green waterways which have been purposely kept clear, or the boat could not move at all. It is quite impossible to see out over the forest of tall leaves and stems on either side.

Until the fall of the Manchu dynasty in 1912, imperial boating parties took place on these lakes quite regularly. Princess Der Ling[1] tells of going with other court ladies to accompany the old Empress Dowager in gaily ornamented barges, poled by eunuchs. Boating, indeed, had been a principal diversion on such imperial lakes from earliest times. In the 6th century, Yang Ti's great Western Park, it will be recalled, had a system of waterways "so that the dragon and phoenix boats might go back and forth" over it. Pleasure seekers, courtly poets, musicians, and dancers went out in them to seek inspiration. Boats of a similar type had been taken to Japan in the T'ang period and by the time the Peking lakes were dug, they had long been sailing on the large garden lakes of those islands.

Soil taken from the Peking lakes was used to form the only two hillocks in all the flat plain, one the Coal Hill, the other a hilly island in the lake. The Coal Hill is so unromantically named because it was supposed to hold coal in case of siege. It is a fair-sized hillock, covered with trees and draped with a chain of five similar pavilions, one at the top and two symmetrically on either side. Although these pavilions date only from the 16th century

[1] *Two Years in the Forbidden City.*

17

and so are much newer than the hillock itself, they are an excellent example of that Chinese love of symmetrical balance which seems to go back to earliest times.

Among those who later improved the Peking lakes were the Mongols. They paid particular attention to the large hilly island in the northern lake. This island, which covers many acres, is now bowered in trees and crowned by the most conspicuous object in Peking, the tall white *dagoba*. Below, on the slopes of the island, brightly colored pavilions and halls of entertainment look out over the quiet water. It was on this very island, if we may judge by Marco Polo's account, that Kubla Khan decreed the "stately pleasure dome" which inspired Coleridge's opium dream after he had been reading Polo— or rather its Chinese-Mongolian reality, which almost certainly was *not* domed. Peking was then called Cambulac or Khanbylac, the City of the Khans, for it had been conquered by Jengis Khan of the Mongols. Like the Kins before them, these later barbarians were rapidly adopting Chinese civilization. In building up this large island with its magnificent entertainment hall, they, too, were but following an old Chinese tradition of what an imperial estate should be like.

To the Western world, probably the most familiar of all Chinese gardens is that shown in the blue "willow pattern" design on dishes. From aristocratic Wedgwood to modern Woolworth this quaintly fantastic lake garden has proved so enticing that few people in America and England can have failed to see it. Many persons, probably, have looked at the curious little islands, the arched bridges, and fantastic pavilions and thought they could be only charming creations of the imagination. Yet the willow tree itself is quite recognizable, and if we will make due allowance for the style of the drawing, we can get a very good idea of some of the gardens which still border beautiful old West Lake, Hsi Hu, near the city of Hangchow— gardens whose predecessors were the inspiration for this very design and for dozens of others on chinaware which the West has never seen.

From earliest times Hangchow has been a great silk weaving center as it is today. And from earliest times, too, villas and gardens must have crowded the lake's edge, doubling in the mirrored flood the tiptilted corners of their little pavilion roofs, the azure, turquoise, and rose of their tiled walls, and the long, drooping, jade-green of their willow trees. It was in the late T'ang period that the imperial governor of this district was no other than that lover of gardens, the poet-official Po Chü-i. Between the years 821 and 824 he was in one of the periods of official favor when he lived behind "the vermilion gates of affluence." We can imagine how the beauty of this district must have delighted him, and with what pleasure he went floating to the gardens around the lake. In his capacity of governor he carried out what has been, ever since, the most distinctive feature of all West Lake, a long earthen causeway across the water leading to the imperial island.[2] It lies today like a silvery thread, fringed with green willows, frequently interrupted by arches to allow boats to pass under. The arches are half-moon, completing their dark circles in the water below. If we had no other evidence than this causeway of Po Chü-i's artistry, we should know him for a great landscape architect. He turned the whole lake into a landscape garden with it, intensifying and unifying the silvery beauty of the water, the receding circles of hills, and the little green islands. Eight hundred years after him we find the causeway copied in garden portraits of the beauty spots of China, made by the Japanese.

Hangchow reached its greatest peak when it become the capital of the Southern Sung dynasty in the 12th century. Sung civilization was the most urbane, peace loving, and civilized in all Chinese history. Its painting, esthetics, and philosophy have never been excelled. Because it practiced pacifism, this civilization fell easily before the savage Mongol hordes, but Hangchow itself largely escaped destruction by surrendering. Marco Polo,[3]

[2] Fitch: *Hangchow-Chekiang Itineraries.*

[3] This Venetian gentleman-trader who wandered all across Asia in pursuit of business became an official of Kubla Khan's Mongolian empire, since the Mongols welcomed competent outsiders, not trusting their conquered Chinese subjects and being themselves only soldiers. Although he saw only the ruins of Sung civilization, the China he described on his return was so much greater than anything in 13th century Europe, that his account was long put down as a tale of the imagination. Hangchow he calls Quinsay or Kinsay, meaning the Capital.

visiting it a few years later, was unbounded in his admiration. But he wrote only with the dull, factual mind of the business man, as we realize with a shock when we turn to his pages seeking romance. To quote:

"Inside the city there is a lake . . . and all around it are erected beautiful palaces and mansions of the richest and most exquisite structure that you can imagine, belonging to the nobles of the city. . . .

"On the lake there are numbers of boats and barges of all sizes for parties of pleasure . . . these barges are always found completely furnished with tables and chairs and all the other apparatus for a feast. The roof forms a level deck on which the crew stand and pole the boat along wherever may be desired, for the lake is not more than two paces in depth. The inside is covered with ornamental painting in gay colors, with windows all around that can be shut or opened, so that the party at table can enjoy all the beauty and variety of the prospects on both sides as they pass along. And truly a trip on this lake is a much more charming recreation than can be enjoyed on land. For on the one side lies the city in its entire length, so that the spectators in the barges from the distance at which they stand, take in the whole prospect in its full beauty and grandeur, with its numberless palaces, temples, monasteries and gardens, full of lofty trees sloping to the shore."

About two hundred years after Messer Marco, Hangchow was visited by the Japanese painter, Sesshū, avid to see and paint its beauties and hoping he might still find an artist who could teach him some of the greatness of Sung art. But these artists had departed, and it was Sesshū himself who drew for us a picture of West Lake at that time with the city wall of Hangchow in the foreground, Po Chü-i's causeway arching across the lake to the islands, and the fantastic pagoda-crowned hills in the background.

Today we can still float about on West Lake in little high-prowed boats and feel that we have grown down to the size of the figures on the Willow Pattern plate. Cloud shadows race across the sky, and slender pagodas on the inclosing hills stand up like curious rabbits with pointed ears. The gleaming walls and curving roofs of villas and gardens are still doubled in the dark water that ripples against their foundations. Little islands are hazy

A Chinese landscape garden in the traditional grand manner still
survives in the Imperial Palace park in Peking. The large, hilly
island shown here, crowned by the Mongolian dagoba and reached
by a marble bridge across a sea of lotus, is the island on which
Kublai Khan decreed his "stately pleasure dome"—or rather, its
Chinese-Mongolian reality.

West Lake, in front of Hangchow, from a painting attributed to the Japanese artist, Sesshū, in the fifteenth century. This picture shows clearly the earthen causeway, broken by arches, which was built by the poet-official Po Chü-i in the T'ang period, and the fantastic pagoda-crowned hills around the lake. (Painting now in the possession of Mr. Hatakeyama of Tokyo.)

"Heaven above, Hangchow below," runs the Chinese saying. Villas and gardens like this one of the Liu family still border lovely old West Lake. Such villas were the originals of the quaint garden shown on the willow pattern plate. (Photo by R. C. Tongg.)

The courtyard of the Liu family villa at Hangchow looks out across West Lake; the willow-draped causeway is dimly visible between the pillars. (Photo by R. C. Tongg.)

through a rain of green willow branches. We stop at one and find that it holds a lake within the lake—the Three Pools of the Moon's Reflection. Across this inner pool, a bridge zigzags to a vermilion summer house. Its latticed walls make intricate use of the ancient swastika motif, creating a pavilion more delightful than any of those in the Willow Pattern garden itself. Nearby a huge fantastic rock stands up starkly, with many grotesque curves and angles. Dorothy Graham[4] tells us the Chinese sometimes regarded rocks as the earthly counterpart of clouds; this rock looks like a solidified fragment of cloud.

Rock and stone have always been indispensable to Chinese gardens, outwardly because they are a necessary part of nature, inwardly, perhaps, because as Chiun Tung says[5] "stone in general has that quality of unchangeable solidity which the human character so often lacks." Earliest Chinese pictures show stones set up in Chinese gardens as ornaments. We see them, for instance, in a scroll, the original of which was probably made in Wei times (386-577 A.D.) although now only an 8th century copy exists.[6] The written text of this scroll is one of the Buddhist scriptures telling of Guatama Buddha and his kingly father. The pictures illustrate the text. Like the Renaissance painters who drew Biblical characters as if they were contemporaries, the Chinese artist here depicted these Indian gentlemen as Chinese rulers. Several scenes show them in spots that are naturally scenic, and others show them in a garden. All the rocks, both those in nature and those obviously set up as garden ornaments, are strangely shaped, twisted, and pierced with holes. They form very early evidence of the Chinese taste for such stones.

This preference, both in painting and as garden ornaments, is probably the result of the Chinese landscape itself and its effect on the Chinese temperament. In many parts of China the mountains and gorges are almost unbelievably grotesque.[7] We must remember, moreover, that Oriental

[4] *Chinese Gardens.*
[5] *T'ien Hsia Monthly,* October, 1936.
[6] The *Kako Genzai Inga Kyō* belonging to Prince Kuni of Tokyo.
[7] See for instance the *Illustrated London News,* January 4, 1936.

painters do not draw directly and photographically from nature but reproduce with their ink and brush the emotional impression which nature makes
on them. Sensitive to the forms they see and alive to their implications, they
have often painted peaks and valleys, cascades and rocks in such exaggerated forms that to Western eyes they appear to have little relation to
reality.

The artistic grouping of stones seems to go back to very early times in
China. Little direct evidence of it remains there, but at least one rock arrangement, dating from T'ang times, still exists in Japan, which would
seem to have been made under direct Chinese influence. Other very early
gardens in Japan were in too advanced a stage of stone artistry to have come
into being without some prototype.

There is every reason to think that Chinese rock artistry reached its
greatest perfection in the Sung period. The first of the splendid gardens
devoted to this artistry was made, apparently, by the Emperor Hui Tsung,
last ruler of the Northern Sung dynasty. This sovereign, like Po Chü-i, is
regarded as one of the greatest artists which China has produced, for he was
not only a patron of the fine arts, but a painter himself, one of the best of
the great Sung period. He was, in fact, so absorbed in art and the cultural
amenities of that civilized period that he disregarded the threat of the
Mongols on the northern border and eventually lost half his empire to
them and died as their captive.

But before this happened he built in his capital city of K'ai-fêng, between 1117 and 1122 A.D., a rock garden known as Ken Yu. The imperial rock commissioner, we are told, was sent far and wide to find suitable
stones for it. This is as we would imagine it to be; an artist like Hui Tsung,
we can be sure, would have made his garden just as artistic a creation as his
paintings, and he probably put into it the same qualities of outward form
and inward meaning that the paintings possessed. We do not know more
in detail, at present, of what Ken Yu was like but we can find a hint of its
form, I think, in certain gardens made a little later in Japan, probably by
Chinese craftsmen who had learned the technique perfected in the imperial

estates. These Japanese gardens really do contain rock forms which reproduce the pinnacles and spires, the rugged cliffs and giant crags of the Sung landscape paintings, and we know that they held the same esoteric significance as the pictures. Ken Yu was probably much larger and finer than anything surviving in Japan, but everything points to its having a form quite different from modern Chinese gardens.

Evidence points also to the gradual decline of Chinese stone artistry after the Sung Period. Painting then became pedantic and formal, and the gardens lost inspiration also. This has been going on right down to the present day. There is discernible a very distinct difference, for instance, in the quality of the stone work found in some of the older Ming gardens in Soochow and later ones. The best surviving Ming rock work is less forced and fantastically awkward, more harmonious and naturalistic than the later work.

Modern Chinese rockeries indeed have little of harmony, rhythm, and proportion; pieces of rock are placed together with an apparently studied disregard of naturalism—flat pieces across uprights, like monstrous mushrooms, or sharp chunks stuck together at impossible angles. In some recently made gardens around Shanghai these rock forms have even been executed in cement, a material which lends itself to almost insane contortions. The first impression on entering such a garden is that it has become a repository for whale skeletons. Nothing of this sort appears in older Chinese gardens or in other forms of graphic Chinese art. We can only conclude that quite recently this ancient form of artistry has failed entirely to be understood and has become completely decadent.

III. *Earliest Japanese Gardens*

IT IS not hard to picture Japan before man had made his mark on it, for to this day his hand is light. The folk of Japan love the natural outdoors and take no pleasure in desecrating it. Large parts of the country which are too hilly for rice culture are still naturally beautiful, and the seashore is but little changed.

Japanese civilization developed mostly on the Pacific side of the islands, sheltered from the northern cold by a central chain of mountains. On this protected side, the climate is mild and pleasant, very similar it seems, to that of South Carolina, as the azaleas indicate. The old cities of Nara and Kyoto grew up in these sheltered provinces, and Japanese culture, developing in them, was profoundly influenced by the beauty of their surroundings and by the gentleness of nature. We must know what this beauty is in order to understand the garden art which reflected it and which it endowed.

The low hills are always green with pines and broad-leaved evergreens. Under the light snows of winter it seems as if a giant sifter had dusted flour over their dull green. The snow is never powdery cold, but wet and clinging so that it wraps itself even around the slender branches of the willows making them hang whitely over the cold green of streams.

The year is ushered in with a long spring, surging with the excitement of blooming flowers—plum blossoms and camellias in February and March, cherries in April, wisteria and azaleas in May. Summers are lushly tropical, vivid with emerald growth and shrill with the voice of cicadas. In autumn, long weeks of mellow quiet mark the declining season. The warm haze of Indian summer hangs over the hills where wild chrysanthemums bloom, and sumach and maple turn the ravines into rich brocades of gold and scarlet against their perennial green.

Nowhere in the country is a plain so wide and flat but that a rim of hills is visible—green near at hand, blue and purple in the distance. Peaked volcanic cones stand up oddly, pointedly, among the hills—most of them conical mounds of green, forested with age. The newest and greatest of these cones, vast Fuji-no-yama, rises bare, smooth, and grey above its forest skirts, its lines almost unbelievably smooth and simple.

Gentle rains fall at any season, causing springs to seep from mossy hillsides and little crystal streams to flow down small valleys. Large mountain lakes mirror the reflection of green peaks around them. In the hills, frantic little rivers have cut rocky gorges and now dash whitely among the boulders at the bottom. These boulders, volcanic in origin, are often beautifully molded and twisted from nature's crucible. Many have been partly smoothed by the water; others after centuries of quiescence are painted with lichens and moss.

The dashing streams tumble frequently into waterfalls, tall plumes of white falling against granite cliffs or short broad cascades sliding glassily over smooth rocks. Some are thin high threads; others complex and leaping. The rocky canyon walls down which they fall are draped in ferns and greenery and made mossy by the spray. The torrent is sometimes partly veiled by a single lacy branch of maple. It has become a garden tradition to train such a branch across the waterfall.

When the rivers reach the coastal plains, they become meandering channels of dark water in broad beds of yellow sand. Water is drawn from them for the rice fields which make the level lands into a mosaic. The earliest people to arrive here probably had been rice cultivators even before their migrations brought them to these islands; so these coastal plains have doubtless presented the same appearance since time immemorial. Farmers still stand knee-deep in the fields, bending to tend the young plants. Their primitive houses are raised above the flood, probably always in small groups as we see them today.

THE ART OF JAPANESE GARDENS

The Inland Sea, a great channel of blue water between the larger islands, has been a highway since prehistoric times. Large and small islets rise from its blue floor, and the yellow sails of small junks cut across it now, as they must have been doing for ages past. The Japanese seacoast is particularly beautiful—a series of small sandy bays curving between pine-covered headlands; islets, often a single great rock, rise in these bays; clinging to the islets may be a twisted weather-beaten pine, incredibly picturesque.

In a land of such natural beauty, it is inevitable that the love of beauty should be a part of the people. The feeling of pleasure in nature, a sense of close relationship with it, has been and is still, I think, one of the most profound and fundamental traits of Japanese personality, influencing all cultural expressions.

The earliest religion was the worship of nature spirits. Feeling for nature has given direction to the development of culture by its emphasis on emotional reaction to beauty; it has made art the pre-eminent product of this culture. The native philosophy has been not a logical system but an intuitive emotion. Truth has been reached by flashes of insight, rather than by processes of reason. The West has sought truth through the intellect, paying little attention to the technique and power of intuitive and emotional understanding. As a consequence, the genius of the West has appeared largely in great thinkers and scientists. In Japan, with an opposite system, genius has appeared mostly in great artists. It is no wonder that the naturalistic gardens of China, when they became known in Japan, fitted the Japanese temperament perfectly.

The earliest gardens of the Japanese were the natural groves—as these are still the environment of the little shrines which house the native Shinto gods. The feeling persists today, as always, dimly but strongly, that these ancient spirits prefer the quiet of trees to the stately temples built for the alien Buddhist deities. There is a legend about the founding of the main shrine to the Sun Goddess, the Imperial Ancestress, which indicates that the first cultivated gardens may have been of herbs, probably for dyeing and medicinal purposes. The story relates that the Heavenly Princess, Yamato Hime no Mikoto Seiki, was sent to earth to find a suitable spot for a shrine to the Sun Goddess. At Ise she met an old man who had a large garden of herbs. He promised to turn it over to her if she would locate the shrine nearby, an offer which she accepted.

This shrine at Ise to the Sun Goddess is today the holiest spot in the Japanese empire. It is a simple wooden building with a bark roof—just such a building as prehistoric chieftains probably lived in and, at death, dedicated to their gods, thus preserving its form down the ages. The Ise shrine stands in the midst of a magnificent natural forest, near a small river—a spot sacred for long ages. Modern civilization is checked at the edge of this forest; the people come quietly along its graveled paths to bow the head before the outer gates of the shrine buildings. On their return they linger to enjoy the beauty of great trees, the glossy green of low undergrowth, the glimmering vistas of the river. This enjoyment of beauty is undoubtedly a real, if unrecognized, part of the worship.

The Japanese have been not only lovers of trees and streams but lovers of the sea, and good sailors. Indeed, the people of these Eastern Islands all had seafaring ancestors who first had to reach them in boats, either by following up that chain of southern islands, including the Philippines, which forms a series of stepping stones from southeastern Asia to Kyūshū; or by crossing the narrow straits in the north which divide the islands from Siberia or by coming over from the tip of the Korean peninsula. Because the inward swing of the Asiatic continent made direct crossing from the Chinese coast to Japan comparatively difficult, few Chinese found their way to the Eastern Islands in earliest days. The Chinese and Japanese people are, therefore, of quite different racial stocks and temperament. In the Japanese a warm volatile southern temperament is mingled with ancient proto-Caucasic elements from the north.

Korea had been settled as a Chinese colony in the first century before the Christian era and Chinese culture took root there as did English culture in the Thirteen Colonies. The primitive people of the Eastern Islands early learned that by making the short voyage to the tip of the Korean peninsula and following its coastline, they could obtain—either by trading or raiding—many articles that appealed to them. Among such articles were metal swords and polished bronze mirrors which were so greatly prized they were often placed in the tombs of chieftains, where modern excavators have found them.

Thus the first Japanese contact with Chinese civilization came through this indirect Korean intercourse. As time went on, however, there grew up definite political relations with the small kingdoms which had developed out of the original Korean colonies. By the middle of the 6th century, many chieftains of Japan must have had a fair idea of the outward aspects of Chinese civilization as reflected in Korean towns. Perhaps some of this was adopted earlier than 550 A.D. After that time, approximately, Chinese learning and art were definitely sought by the Japanese, at first slowly, then with an increasing enthusiasm which reached its peak when direct contact was made with China itself.

The first official embassy sent by Japan to China was headed by one Ono no Imoko, a member of the imperial family.[1] He went to the court of the Sui dynasty in 607 A.D. to find out as much as possible about Chinese civilization and the glories it had produced. The Sui Emperor at that time was that Yang Ti who, it will be recalled, was engaged in building the stupendous landscape estate of lakes, hills, and pavilioned islands called the Western Park, which was sixty miles in circuit and which, before the decade was out, was to cause, indirectly, the fall of his dynasty. Any such undertaking as this Western Park would certainly have been a chief topic of conversation, not to say of scandal, in the Sui capital and we may be sure that the Japanese ambassador, all eyes and ears to learn as much as possible, would have heard a good deal about it, may even have seen a part of it. At any rate, it was shortly after his return, about as soon as opportunity offered, that we find mentioned the first landscape garden built in Japan.

[1] Later he became the founder of the art of flower arrangement which he had learned in China.

Japanese garden art reflects nature in Japan. The piney isles of Matsushima might be the prototype of many garden islets. (Photo from Board of Tourist Industry.)

A long tree-covered spit, called the "Bridge of the Gods," or Ama-no-hashi-date, is sometimes reproduced in Japanese gardens. (Photo by Board of Tourist Industry.)

EARLIEST JAPANESE GARDENS

The record of this garden is found in the ancient chronicle called the *Nihongi*, under date of 612 A.D., when the Empress Suiko was on the throne, and the enlightened Prince Shōtoku was regent and virtual ruler. In that year, says the Nihongi, there arrived in Japan a man from Korea, named Michikō, whose face was blotched with white. (He may have been a leper.) His appearance was not pleasing to the Japanese, who threatened to banish him to a distant island—often their way of getting rid of an undesirable. This Korean, however, seems to have been a man of spirit and humor, for he protested sturdily that if they were going to banish him on account of his looks, they should banish all the spotted cattle also. He added, craftily, that as he knew how to build "mountain shapes," he was a person who could ill be spared from an up-and-coming country like Japan.

"Mountain shapes" obviously referred to the rocky artificial hillocks of a Chinese garden. It was suddenly realized that this stranger was someone who could build a garden for the Empress like those which were the glory of the Chinese capital. The Korean's appearance, therefore, was overlooked and he was ordered to construct a "Chinese bridge" and a *shumi-sen* in the southern courtyard of the Imperial Palace. Thereafter, the chronicle adds, he was known as Michikō, the Ugly Artisan.

From his claim to know how to build "mountain shapes" it is assumed that this Michikō was a regular garden craftsman, skilled in all branches of the art. He would have known how to lay out a pond and construct hillocks behind it from the excavated material, how to build an island and bridges, and how to plant trees and shrubs. But most of all he would have had skill in the artistic arrangement of rocks.

It is clear that, around the palace, the Japanese had already made some attempt to build a Chinese landscape garden, the presence of a pond being unmistakably implied. They could have done this through their skill in rice field terracing and from descriptions of the foreign gardens. But the finer details would have been unknown to them, hence the willingness to employ the Ugly Artisan to build the Chinese bridge and the *shumi-sen*.

The bridge, if we may judge by later examples, was built of wood, arched into a high half-moon, and lacquered vermilion, its upright posts decorated with pointed bronze knobs. The *shumi-sen,* however, was an example of stone artistry, a rocky island in the pond, its four faces suggesting the "sublime rocks and austere precipices" of towering Mount Sumeru in the Buddhist scriptures. The representation of this mythical mountain rising from illimitable seas was probably a standard feature of Chinese garden design at that time, a fact known to the Japanese and desired in their own gardens.

The importance of such island rock forms is clearly revealed in the *Nihongi* a few years later when it tells of an island built for Soga no Umako. This created such wonder that its owner was sometimes spoken of as Lord of the Island. After the death of Prince Shōtoku, Umako became the most powerful man in the country, dictator and ruler in all but name. His family had been interested (for purely political reasons) in introducing Buddhism from Korea, and the first Buddhist temple in Japan had been a Soga chapel. After Umako attained supreme power, he caused many other temples to be built and did everything possible to foster the new religion. It is easily understood why he might have wished to possess a fine garden, perhaps even better than that of the Imperial Palace, and why he might put into it a symbol of Buddhist piety. Umako is first mentioned in the record as Lord of the Island in 620 A.D., doubtless the year the garden was completed, but we must look ahead to the notice of his death to find the definite explanation. In his obituary notice, it says, after fulsome tribute has been paid:

"He possessed a house by the Asuka river where he built a garden with a small pond, and in the pond an island. Therefore he was often spoken of as 'Lord of the Island.' "

This island must have possessed outstanding merit to have been considered so important. Undoubtedly it was a splendid piece of rock artistry, fully appreciated by the people of the court who saw it. It is evident, too, that, even at that time, rock artistry held a high place in popular opinion. Probably Umako's garden was built by Michikō, the Korean, for it was

made only eight years after he had done the one in the southern courtyard
of the palace. It is interesting to note that Umako was the first of a long line
of *de facto* rulers of Japan who have diverted themselves, after achieving
power, by building fine gardens. And it is also significant that, for long
after, the word used to designate gardens was "island," that is *shima,* or
jima when used as a suffix.

No garden remnants have come down to us from this earliest period,
but probably Bacon's observation about nations building stately before they
garden finely was, in general, true of Japan. The very importance accorded
these gardens indicates how exceptional they were. Architecture at that
time was in an advanced state compared to what it had been. Strangely,
there have survived, during the thirteen hundred years since, a group of
wooden buildings put up in 608 A.D., the buildings of Hōryūji monastery
founded by Prince Shōtoku. While this institution's first buildings may
have been burned and replaced about a hundred years later, those which
stand today are undoubtedly the oldest wooden buildings in the world.
These splendid old Korean-Chinese structures, with their curving tiled roofs,
white plaster walls set between red pillars, and with complicated eaves, are
a far cry from the simple, bark-thatched shrine of the Sun Goddess at Ise,
representing the best of the prehistoric dwellings. One of Hōryūji's smaller
buildings is supposed to have been part of the dwelling of Prince Shōtoku's
mother, and we may safely surmise that the palaces of the Emperor and
nobles were sufficiently like these structures to give us a picture of them.

Before 710 A.D. it was customary to change the location of the imperial residence on the death of each sovereign, for death was considered a
defilement. This change had not presented difficulties when houses were in
simple style of wood and thatch, but grand Chinese palaces like those of
Hōryūji could not be so lightly abandoned. They managed, therefore, to
get around the custom and when Nara became the seat of the imperial
residence in 710 A.D., it remained so for seven reigns.

The city that rose from the rice fields of Yamato during those years was
unlike anything the Japanese had ever seen. The imperial palace, govern-

ment halls, great monasteries, and mansions of the nobility made it a place of wonder and awe to the country folk. I cannot do better than quote Sir George Sansom's description of Nara at that time.

"Nara was a copy, but it was more splendid than anything that had ever been known before in Japan. Even today, a visitor to its ancient site can, with but little effort of the imagination, reconstruct its vanished glories from the remains of its great temples and their treasures, peopling its palaces with courtiers in ceremonial robes, its holy edifices with priests who chanted litanies in a strange tongue, its workshops with artists from China and Korea and their eager Japanese pupils, who wrought the exquisite shapes of gods in bronze and wood and lacquer. . . .

"It is difficult to imagine how complete a revolution was effected in all departments of life in the capital. Life in the country went on as before. Peasants grew their rice, fed their silkworms, grudged their taxes, and worshipped their native gods. But in the city all was new, all was foreign. The very architecture of the palaces and temples was Chinese . . . the costumes of the courtiers, their etiquette, their ranks and appellations were borrowed from China. . . . It is hard to find a parallel for this curious phenomenon of a small society, busily digesting and assimilating a superior foreign culture, not imposed from without by conquest or proximity, but voluntarily, even enthusiastically adopted. It numbered probably not more than twenty thousand people and the total population of Japan is estimated at six million."

We get fascinating glimpses of Nara's gardens in the poems of the period—those brief poems of thirty-one syllables, called *waka*, which catch fleetingly a mood or sentiment epitomized or reflected in some beauty of nature. In the anthology of such poems, called the *Manyōshū*, which was collected at the end of the 8th century, we catch here and there the sparkle of a garden lake, the reflection of an island rock, the green aura of young willows, or the fragrance of plum and wisteria.

On a March day in the year 785 a group of highborn gentlemen sat in a garden in Nara. They were delighting in the early coming of spring, as evidenced in the blooming of the Andromeda shrub, and were expressing their feeling by writing short poems. The Andromeda (*Pieris japonica*) whose dainty clusters of white flowers are shaped like lilies-of-the-valley is one of the earliest blossoms of spring to appear in Japan. Even today it is the commonest shrub to be seen in Nara, for the herd of tame deer wandering through the park will not touch it. Of the poems written by the gentlemen on this occasion, three were later considered good enough to put in the *Manyōshū* anthology.

Wrote Ōtomo no Yaka-mochi,[2] mentioning the pond:

> *The pond water reflects*
> *Even the shadows*
> *Of blooming Andromeda—*
> *Let me take it carefully*
> *In my sleeve.*

Another, Ikako no Mabito, saw in the fleeting beauty of the flowers the Buddhist teaching that all things are ephemeral. He lets us know there were rocks near the pond:[3]

> *Under the rocks*
> *The transparent pond water*
> *Has become the bright color*
> *Of young Andromeda leaves.*
> *Must these things die?*

[2] *Ike mizu ni*
Kage saye miyete
Saki niou
Ashibi no hana wo
Sode ni kokirena

[3] *Iso kage no*
Miyuru ike-mizu
Teru made ni
Sakeru ashibi no
Chira ma ku oshi mo

But we get our clearest picture of this garden from the poem of Prince Mikata no Ohogime who mentions the island:[4]

> *In this, your island*
> *Home of the mandarin duck—*
> *I see today also*
> *The Andromeda*
> *Blooming.*

The quaint little mandarin ducks, more like brightly painted toys than real birds, still come wild in winter to some of the quiet old ponds in Japan. They are the symbol of conjugal felicity in both China and Japan; perhaps the writer of this poem was paying a graceful compliment to the domestic happiness of his host.

Other poems in the *Manyōshū* mention violets, orange blossoms, plums, cherries, azaleas, wisteria, and the green of young willows. The two following are Aston's translations:[5]

> *The rippling wisteria*
> *That I planted by my house*
> *As a memento*
> *Of thee whom I love*
> *Is at length in blossom.*

Also:

> *Before the wind of spring*
> *Has tangled the fine threads*
> *Of the green willow—*
> *Now I would show it*
> *To my love.*

[4] *Oshi no sumu*
Kimi ga kono shima
Kyō mireba
Ashibi no hana mo
Saki ni keru kamo.
[5] W. G. Aston: *A History of Japanese Literature.*

EARLIEST JAPANESE GARDENS

In a second anthology[6] of the Nara period, made up of poems written in the fashionable Chinese language, are other delightful pictures of Nara gardens, giving us additional details. At another spring garden party, given this time by the Minister of the Left, Nagaya Ohogimi, one of the guests, Otsu Renju, was inspired to compose this whimsical poem:

> *Sunlight sparkles on the dancing water*
> *Spring warms the garden wall,*
> *Plum buds smile like red lips—*
> *But the gate-willow has not yet*
> *Grown its eyebrows.*

In still another of these poems we have definite mention of the pleasure boats which floated around the islands of the garden lake. This is by Ishikawa Sekusaku:

> *Clear and deep-brimming is the pond,*
> *Fresh is the garden with opening blossoms,*
> *Frolicking birds skim the waves—and scatter—*
> *Pleasure boats wander among the isles.*

Additional details may be picked up in single lines of other poems from the *Manyōshū*. "Pearly pebbles on the seashore, where the pine shadow is sharp" does not refer to the real seashore but to a garden in Nara thirty miles from the coast. "Garden stones glowing in the mellow light of autumn" reveals that keen appreciation of the beauty of stones which has come straight down the centuries since.

It is just such a group of actual stones which constitutes the earliest concrete remnants of a garden in Japan. This group of stones apparently dates back to the years when the capital was being moved from place to place with each reign. Between 667 and 672 A.D. the Emperor Tenchi had his simple dwelling at Ōtsu, on the shore of beautiful Lake Biwa. It is recorded that the Crown Prince Ōtomo, at the Emperor's suggestion, built a Buddhist chapel near his residence, calling it Onjōji, or the Garden Palace Temple. Before it was fully completed, however, the Emperor died and the

---

[6] *Kaifūsō*. Transliteration of these Japanized Chinese poems is impossible.

Crown Prince, after briefly succeeding him on the throne, was killed in a revolt. The uncle who thus made himself Emperor instead, moved the court back to the Asuka district (where Soga no Umako had built his garden) and in time the temple of Onjōji assumed control of the Prince's estate.

This temple grew into one of the largest and most powerful institutions in the country. It is popularly known as Mii-dera, the Temple of Three Wells, because of a spring near it where three imperial infants were said to have been bathed. The remnants of this spring, surrounded by a few rocks, still exist beside the present main hall of Mii-dera temple, greatly revered because of their antiquity and association. But it has remained for Mr. Mirei Shigemori, one of the foremost garden experts of Japan, to identify these stones as the probable remnants of Prince Ōtomo's original garden, corroborating their history by old documents.[7] That this spot is the site of the original estate is indicated by roof tiles of the Nara period which have been dug up on it. Whether these stones actually date back to the original garden built by Prince Ōtomo or were arranged somewhat later, cannot now be determined. But from the study of their type and style Mr. Shigemori has little doubt but that they are one of the earliest remnants of gardens in Japan.

At present, the stones around the spring itself give little indication of their original grouping; a well-house, which still stands, was built over them several hundred years ago, and other stones were moved in beside them at that time. Now they all are decorated with the rice-straw rope of holiness. But a few feet away, outside the house, are several other stones, notably a group of three, which show very definite artistic arrangement. There is no possibility that these three could have just happened to exist as they do or have been carelessly thrown there. The central stone, tall and narrow, stands upright; in front and somewhat to one side of it is a flat broad stone; at the other side is one of middle height, roundly pointed. Together they illustrate perfectly that form of occult balance based on the triangle, which is

[7] See his *Nihon Teienshi Zukan*. Vol. I.

36

found throughout Japanese art; when it is used in flower arrangement, its three basic lines are popularly called Heaven, Earth, and Man.

The Mii-dera temple stones, those under the house as well as those outside it, seem once to have formed the border of a pond. Probably the water of the spring flowed more abundantly in early days than now. The suggested pond is the only indication of what the original garden may have been like, but the artistry of this stone grouping shows that a high degree of skill had been attained in Japan even in that early day. The nation was then only beginning its Chinese tutelage, and very little original, creative work had been undertaken. The artistic skill displayed in these stones was undoubtedly of direct Chinese origin, in all probability the same as that taught by Michikō, the Korean. If he had lived a normal lifetime, this artisan would have been dead but a few years at the time this garden was made. Very likely, it was the work of men who had learned the stonecraft from him. It proves concretely that his claim to know how to make "mountain shapes" was well founded and that the *shumi-sen* he built for the Empress Suiko in the lake south of the palace was probably a thoroughly artistic piece of work.

IV. *Gardens of Heian*

WHY the grand new city of Nara, only seventy-five years old, should have been abandoned as the capital, is still something of a mystery. The most probable explanation is that undue influence on secular affairs was beginning to be exerted by the great Buddhist institutions in Nara. At any rate, it was decided to move the location of the Imperial Palace, and a site some thirty miles away was selected.

The new situation was, and still is, particularly beautiful. The city lies in a round valley inclosed on three sides by hills which rise on the northeast to a notched green peak. A monastery had recently been built on this peak at that time, and its holy influence, it was believed, would ward off evils expected from that quarter. Two rivers meander over the gently sloping floor of the bowl-shaped valley, and the city lies between them. The valley floor is still a mosaic of dyked fields, each little patch a-blossom in spring with a crop of a different color. In summer the dykes disappear under the even green of the young rice; in autumn the land is golden with harvest; in winter the empty brown fields are spiked with conical straw ricks and touched white with frost.

The city built in this beautiful spot was first named Heian-kyō, the Capital of Peace and Tranquillity. Poets have since called it the City of Purple Mountains and Crystal Streams from the circle of hills and the many little waterways that course through the town. The literary have delighted to call it Raku-Yō[1] after its great Chinese contemporary, Lo-yang, the later

[1] The Japanese, Raku-yō, is derived from the old Chinese pronunciation of Lo-yang, which was Lok-yang.

T'ang capital. During a thousand years of history it was usually spoken of simply as The Capital—Miyako. Today it is called Kyoto.

Like Nara, the plan of the new city was inspired by Ch'ang-an. It was laid out as a large square, some three miles in each direction, divided into square wards and smaller blocks by wide straight avenues and cross streets. To this day the streets of Kyoto run at right angles, north and south, east and west. Within the northern boundary of the city was set apart a second square forming the inner imperial inclosure, similar to the Forbidden City of Peking. This inclosure was something under a mile square, and within it were all the imperial buildings, the great hall of state where the enthronements took place, government offices and shrines as well as the Palace of the Emperor and apartments for palace ladies. As in Peking's Forbidden City, the great hall of state stood behind an impressive sequence of gates and lesser buildings. We can judge the magnificence of this great hall and its main gate by replicas of them now standing in Kyoto, constructed not many years ago to celebrate the eleven-hundredth anniversary of the city. The hall is gay and splendid, with red pillars, white plaster walls, latticed windows, complex eaves, and blue-green roof tiles, crowned with dolphin finials of gold.

There was no space for a large park within the imperial inclosure, but just south of it was built an immense pleasure garden suggestive of the extensive lake garden which lies outside the square of the Forbidden City in Peking. This garden was called Shinsen-en, meaning Divine Spring Garden.[2] It was laid out in 800 A.D., shortly after the city was built, and for long was the greatest and finest garden in the capital. Many poems and references scattered through the old records testify to its beauty, but actual descriptions are vague. We know, however, it covered some thirty-three acres and contained a large lake, a spring, a hill, and a large pavilion. Maples, willows, and cherry trees grew in it.

We get a brief picture of Shinsen-sen in the record called *Keikokushū*.

[2] The translation of this name and many details of the garden following are taken from Mr. Ponsonby Fane's scholarly work, *The History of Kyoto and its Vicissitudes*.

39

"The honorable path is clean swept and shadows of willows lie long across it. . . . A sandy white beach winds around the lake. All is calm and clear. The eye catches a pure spring bubbling up, to run off in a narrow streamlet. If we climb the low hill we may often catch sight of birds among the trees. When we work our way through the undergrowth we startle the wood doves. . . . In the dragon-pond glimmer the sun, moon and stars. . . ."

Says another, the *Honchō Bunsui;* "The red-leaved grove is wide. In the pond the water brims deeply, even at the edges—it seems like a small River Wu. . . . Clerks from the court often steal away secretly from their duties to visit it. . . . Fishing is prohibited. One cannot look at this garden long enough for its beauties are ineffable. Darkness always seems to drive one home before one is ready. . . ."

The Emperor and court came often to visit this garden, and all manner of entertainments were given in it—banquets, poem parties, wrestling matches, and military exercises. To accommodate the guests a large pavilion was built, called the Kenrin-kaku, or Pavilion of the Imperial Seat. This was apparently of typical form with a red lacquered balustrade, dolphin finials, and smaller wing pavilions overhanging the lake. In it was a special seat for the Emperor, and others for the Crown Prince, princes of the blood, and ministers.

A little pond on a quiet side street in Kyoto is all that remains today of Shinsen-en, the once glorious, first imperial pleasure garden of the capital. The bit of pond, only a fraction of its original size, is now a public park; a few fine trees grow on its banks, and children play around the water, while a temple on its banks brings the devout to say a prayer. But few know the romantic history of this bit of water.

The palace and other buildings of the imperial inclosure were swept by fire many times in the centuries that followed the founding of the city. During rebuilding, the emperors had often to live outside for long periods, and finally they made their permanent residences in outside palaces. But for long they returned to the great hall of state for their enthronement ceremonies. Finally this hall, too, was burned again and not rebuilt, for difficult times had come to the country. The imperial inclosure and Shinsen-en garden nearby became a neglected wilderness during the period of wars, and only in comparatively recent times has the bit of remaining pond been identified as the old imperial garden.

The delight of the court in such outdoor entertainments as those held in Shinsen-en greatly influenced the style of gardens in this period. They were designed largely to serve as the setting for these entertainments and to form an outlook for the residence. House and garden were closely associated, the buildings clustering around one end of the lake. A person sitting in the main hall had a charming view over the silvery water and green islands, with the natural landscape beyond the rim of bordering trees like a backdrop. But no one view was of greater importance than another, for pleasure boats floated about the lake, the people in them enjoying the view from every direction. The buildings themselves became part of this picture from the boat. Because the view was such an important part, the estates were always situated in the most scenic spots possible. Within the city itself, of course, not a great deal could be expected, although the river and the surrounding hills were always to be counted on. But the country villas of the court nobles were invariably placed in some charming spot. The first of these villas whose outlines we can trace with any certainty is the estate to which the Emperor Saga retired in 823 when he abdicated and took holy orders.

Such retirement on the part of a Japanese Emperor or other high personage has never meant that he became a recluse practicing austerities in a monastic cell. Such persons have, rather, only given up the public and ceremonious part of their duties to become quiet country gentlemen with leisure to pursue their hobbies and devotions. Often, indeed, such a man has continued to exercise the real power of his office from this retirement while his nominal successor was occupied with its ceremonies and complicated etiquette. The retreats in which such persons have taken up their residence were not temples or monasteries but country estates endowed, perhaps, with special chapels. Down the ages garden making has been consistently a popular diversion of such persons, so that many of the greatest gardens in the nation have come into being under such circumstances. Umako's garden was the first instance we hear of, but the Emperor Saga's estate is the earliest to have survived.

Today, some eleven hundred years after its construction, this estate consists of a large old pond holding a couple of small half-drowned islands and a rocky islet on which the turtles sun themselves. The pond, called Ozawa-ike, serves today as a reservoir for the neighboring rice fields. It owes its preservation largely to the fact that the estate was early turned into a temple, called Daikakuji, whose buildings stand at one side of it.

The estate was originally called Saga-no-in, the Villa of the Emperor Saga. It was located in one of the most picturesque spots near Kyoto, on a low flank of the hills, with spreading rice lands stretching away below. The hills encircling the spot extend protecting wings on either side, their green forests always beautiful under the snows of winter or the hazy heat of summer. The villa buildings with their red pillars and graceful roofs stood on the north side of the lake, with their backs to these hills. The countryside fell away below the edge of the lake, its rice fields glimmering with the tender young shoots in spring or dusty gold in the level sun of autumn.

Today, cherry and maple trees border the large old pond. When clouds of pink petals or tiny, bright maple leaves drift down to the ancient green water, the path around the lake becomes a favorite rendezvous with Kyoto people. A pleasant melancholy hangs over the scene, sprung from its quietude and the awareness of passing centuries. This feeling is still perfectly expressed in a poem written about four hundred years after the garden was built, when it had been neglected but was still beautiful.

GARDENS OF HEIAN

Although the scene
At Ozawa-ike be old;
The same bright autumn moon
Casts down its tranquil light.[3]

Even earlier, another poet wrote:

While the sound of the cascade
Long since has ceased,
We still hear the murmur
Of its name.[4]

This cascade, so sentimentally bemoaned in its ruin, has lately been re-discovered.[5] It lies back of the lake, behind a bamboo grove, and consists of a few large old stones buried in a grassy slope. Yet they are still so undisturbed that it appears to experts—whatever the poets may have thought as they viewed its ruins—as if it never did contain water; that it was, in fact, a "dry" cascade in which the presence of water was suggested merely by the graphic arrangement of stones.

Before the remains of this cascade was found, it had not been realized that the Japanese practiced this "dry" technique so early. At the time this garden was built, in the early part of the 9th century, Japan was still avidly copying China. The Emperor Saga himself is known to history as one of the three "Learned Emperors" whose devotion to Chinese studies brought the sinocization of the Japanese court to its highest point. We may assume

[3] *Ozawa no*
Ike no keshiki wa
Furi yuke do
Kawarazu sumeru
Aki no yo no tsuki.
        By Fujiwara no Shunzei
[4] *Taki n'oto wa*
Tayete hisashiku
Nari nuredo
Nakoso nagarete
Nao kikoye kere.
        By Fujiwara no Kinto
[5] By Mr. Shigemori.

43

that this garden was as close an imitation of those in the T'ang capital as the Japanese could make it. And we must conclude that the dry-landscape technique exemplified in this cascade was something that had been learned in China and has, perhaps, been since forgotten there.

Under the Emperor Saga, ceremonies, pastimes, and etiquette of the court were all Chinese. Thus, the large lake was used for boating as in the garden lakes of China. Today, in the old pond we can visualize the brightly colored dragon-headed barges filled with courtiers in gay costumes, some playing the flute, others composing poems on the beauty of the spring and autumn landscape. Finally we see the boats poled to the island where those on board get off to write down their poems in bold Chinese characters on long strips of colored paper, afterward reading them aloud.

The islands in the lake doubtless also followed a Chinese pattern. The larger one is long and pointed, the small one round, and lying off the point of the larger island. Perhaps what is now a peninsula in line with the opposite end of the large island was once a third island. All of these, no doubt, represented the mythical Isles of the Immortals, P'eng-lai, Fang-chang, and Ying-chou, which floated in the Eastern Ocean supported by giant turtles. By the time this garden was built, garden islands derived from this tale were established as a traditional form, and the old story had become merely a pretty myth. The names of the islands pronounced in Japanese are Hōrai, Hakoya, and Eishu.

Stretching in a straight line along the shore of the large island and extending halfway to the smaller one is a row of five large boulders. Since the water level of the pond was considerably raised after it was turned into a reservoir, most of these stones have washed free and toppled out of line; only one now remains in its original position, but the others are unmistakable. This straight line of stones was evidently a standard design for it occurs in a number of other old gardens of the period. They are known as *yodo-mari*, night-mooring stones. They undoubtedly had some special significance, probably derived from China, but just what it was we do not know, although a number of possible meanings have been suggested.

44

The oldest example of arranged stones in Japan, perhaps in the whole Orient, are these near Mii-dera temple at Ōtsu. They date back, it is believed, to about 670 A.D. and were probably derived directly from Chinese stone artistry of the T'ang period. (Photo by the author.)

On a snowy morning in the eighth century, the enthronement hall of the first Imperial Palace in Kyoto might have looked like this, its modern replica—the arcade and end-pavilions of Heian shrine. (Photo from Kyoto Municipal Office.)

Present-day remnants of Shinsen-en, the first great imperial pleasure garden in Kyoto. (Photo by the author.)

Heian courtiers in one of their dragon-headed pleasure boats. This scene, so often a part of the early Japanese garden picture, is shown here as it is re-enacted at an annual festival of the literati of Kyoto. Those participating wear the old court costumes, play old music, and compose poems in the old manner. (Photo from Kyoto Municipal Office.)

One is that the stones may have represented a procession of boats attempting to reach the Mystic Isles. The name, *yodo-mari* suggests the idea that the stones might represent a line of treasure boats moored for the night in some haven. Anyone who has sailed in Oriental waters must have noticed with delight the stubby little cargo junks with picturesque sails, looking, probably, not so very different from the way they have since time immemorial. In early days, when navigation was precarious, these boats used to hug the shore and drop anchor for the night. This line of stones was, perhaps, intended to suggest such a convoy anchored for the night in a cove. Whatever the meaning, in this garden they were plainly put in primarily as ornaments.

These stones are not simply rocks dumped down on the pond bottom, and allowed to show above the surface as best they may; each islet is—or was—a carefully composed bit of rock arrangement planned to be as artistic as possible. The form of each may be seen in the one that survives, the slanting islet where the turtles sun themselves. In this arrangement the larger of two stones is placed upright, slanting a little and supported on its under side by a smaller stone. The whole arrangement creates a very pleasing shape of contrasted size and line forming the inevitable triangle.

The bottom of Ozawa pond is covered with tightly packed small stones in clay, a finish which has survived the centuries. Traces of a similar bottom finish often indicate whether or not other old lakes date from Heian times.

Estates as large and fine as this imperial villa must have been rare at the time it was made, but as the 9th century advanced, more and more of the courtiers built such gardens for themselves in the most picturesque spots they could find. A few of these have survived. There was, for instance, a famous estate called Kawara-no-in, or Riverbank Villa, built by the Minister of the Left. Descriptions of where this estate stood in the city make it seem to have been the original garden on the spot now occupied by Shosei-en, the garden of Higashi Honganji temple. The present garden occupies a large city block near the Kyoto railway station. It is set apart from the dirt and noise of the busy streets around it by a high wall over which rise its tall trees. Lying quietly behind this wall is a large lake with islands, and on the islands are remnants of stone arrangements with characteristics of those made in the Heian period.

In 872 the Minister of the Left—who built this estate—was Minamoto no Tōru. He had been born one of the numerous younger sons of the Emperor Saga, but, like most of his brothers, was reduced to the rank of subject and given the surname of Minamoto. From this he rose to be honorary chief minister, building for himself a magnificent villa and garden on the banks of the Kamo River that ran east of the town.

Part of this garden was laid out, it is said, to suggest the scenery around the town of Shiogama in the far north of Japan. The word *shio-gama* means salt-caldron, and tradition has it that this town was the first place in Japan where salt was made by boiling sea water. Shiogama is located on the beautiful bay of Matsushima in which rise hundreds of picturesque rocky islands. Often they are single vast boulders on which may grow a stunted pine tree, torn and twisted by the wind. The spot is counted today as one of three most picturesque areas in all Japan.

In the 9th century, however, this northern country was the frontier of the nation. The indigenous Ainu tribes were still fighting against the advance of the conquering Japanese. Forces from Kyoto were frequently sent against them but were often far from victorious. It is said that Minamoto no Tōru was once in Shiogama; if true, he probably went there as the honorary commander of such an expedition. At any rate, as already mentioned, he constructed in his Riverbank Villa a salt-boiling place, calling it Shiogama. He ordered gallons of sea water to be brought daily all the thirty miles from the coast to Kyoto. While it was being boiled, he could sit and watch the ever-changing flutter of the smoke banner across the sky and romantically imagine himself far away in the picturesque north country.

The authority for this whole story seems to rest chiefly on a poem and its note of explanation. The poet, Ki no Tsurayuki, states that after the death of the Minister of the Left he visited Kawara-no-in, saw the place called Shiogama, and felt moved to write:[6]

> *Departed the prince—*
> *Vanished the smoke*
> *Of Shiogama*
> *Lonely the beach*
> *Along its length—*

The chief interest of all this, I think, lies in its suggestion that by the end of the 9th century the Japanese were definitely thinking of garden making in terms of their own landscape and not as a Chinese copy. The esthetic appreciation of fluttering smoke was characteristic of the refined pastimes of the Heian court, and we find it mentioned in the *Tale of Genji*. But I cannot escape the feeling that it was the piney isles of Matsushima and not the salt boiling that gave Shiogama its ultimate appeal. If these islands did not serve as the models of those of Kawara-no-in, they easily could, at any rate, be the natural prototype of most of the islets of later date.

Another of these large estates survives as the garden of Kajūji temple east of the city. The original owner of this place chose a delightfully picturesque spot in the midst of a quiet, sunlit valley, with the hills forming a distant bowl-like rim; one small peak, nearer at hand, rises up as if purposely put across the lake to concentrate the vista. The original owner of this estate was a courtier named Miyamichi Iyamasa. His daughter married a member of the important Fujiwara family, and when their daughter became the youthful consort of the Emperor Uda, Miyamichi, the grandfather, was a man of wealth and power. He built this estate at the end of

[6] *Kokin Wakashū* (Songs of Pathos) Book 16.
   Kimi masa de
   Kemuri tae nishi
   Shiogama no
   Ura sabishiku mo
   Mie wataru kana

the 10th century, about the time his granddaughter became mother of the Prince who later was to be the Emperor Daigo.

This estate has maintained its original form better than any other of the period. There were five islands in the broad lake recalling the original five Mystic Isles and, as at Saga-no-in, a waterfall. The garden must always have been as quiet and lovely as it is today with long jade shadows stretching across the clear water and the song of birds in the stillness. In an old writing[7] is found a line of description;

"Mandarin ducks come to float on the precious jade pool of this garden, their purple and vermilion mantles spreading the hues of a thousand autumns."

Even yet, the priest tells us, these little ducks come to this pond as they must have been doing, literally, for a thousand autumns.

[7] *Engi.*

V. *The Glory of the Fujiwaras*

THE court of Heian reached the pinnacle of its glory about the year 1000 A.D. Since Nara days the affairs of this court and of the nation had been dominated by a single great family, named Fujiwara. The head of the Fujiwara clan held the hereditary office of regent and was all-powerful, with actual control over the throne.

Under him all high offices were filled by Fujiwara men and all the Empresses were Fujiwara ladies, usually the regent's own daughters. Maids of honor and ladies-in-waiting were other Fujiwara ladies of lower rank. One of these court ladies has given us a remarkable picture of the times in a novel which she wrote in her spare hours, depicting the life around her. It is called the *Genji Monogatari,* or *Tale of Genji;*[1] translated into English in recent years, by Mr. Arthur Waley of the British Museum, this work has been pronounced by modern critics one of the world's literary masterpieces.

The authoress belonged to one of the lesser branch families of the Fujiwara. Her given name we do not know, but she was nicknamed after the heroine of her story, Violet, or Murasaki. Left a young widow at about twenty-five, she was appointed a lady-in-waiting and tutoress to the Empress, a girl of only sixteen, who was the daughter of the regent, Fujiwara Michinaga. Murasaki had secretly learned a little of the Chinese language as a girl, an accomplishment supposed to turn a girl into a hopeless blue stocking, and her literary endeavors were a standard joke around the court. But that she was not unattractive is proved by the fact that her kinsman,

[1] Genji is pronounced with a hard "G" to rhyme with Benjy.

49

the regent, usually tried to make love to her when he came to visit his daughter, the Empress. From Murasaki's diary we gather he was not very successful in these overtures toward the pretty lady-in-waiting. This regent Michinaga had brought the fortunes of his family and of the court to the highest point they attained in history. In Murasaki's story the hero, Prince Genji, is modeled after Michinaga in position and importance, but her diary makes it very clear that the regent himself was not portrayed in the character of the Prince.

The era was one of luxury, elegance, and extravagance in which the court nobles vied with one another in building splendid houses and gardens and in giving magnificent entertainments. In the pages of Murasaki's story we find vivid pictures of this life, of the manners of the court, the thoughts and emotions of its ladies and gentlemen, and details of their diversions and occupations. We see a small group of romantic, sentimental, highly refined people for whom love and the appreciation of beauty and art were principal occupations. Nights were one romantic affair after the other; days a succession of esthetic pastimes. They played plaintive music in the moonlight, wrote tender little poems to each other, and wore some of the most magnificent costumes the world has ever seen. The refinement of their literary and artistic tastes was far superior to their political talent or moral sense, as Dr. Anesaki points out.[2]

Yet they were sensitively aware of every beauty and change of the outdoors. In them the inherent Japanese love of nature took its sunniest, gayest, and most open forms. They wore bright hues, loved flowers, and wrote their poems on charmingly tinted paper. They built their houses so they could practically sit outdoors in them and they designed their gardens to show nature in her brightest, happiest moods.

In the tale, when Prince Genji became all-powerful in the country, he built for himself a magnificent estate. So also had the real regent, Michinaga, who is noted in history for his extravagant mansions and gardens. Besides his magnificent town house, he had country villas, one at

[2] *Art, Life and Nature in Japan.*

Uji and one at Katsura. Murasaki's description of Genji's estates is doubtless compounded, and perhaps slightly idealized, from various of these gardens and others, which she had seen. Genji had been a great lady's man in his youth and in his maturity the ladies he had wooed had become his consorts. They lived, now, each in a special wing of his house. When he built his fine new mansion, he created around the apartments of each lady a garden designed to meet her special tastes and preferences. For the heroine, Murasaki, with whom he spent most of his time, he built a spring garden, since that season was specially liked by her. Of the construction of this garden it is written: [3]

"He effected great improvement in the appearance of the grounds by a judicious handling of knoll and lake, for though such features were already there in abundance, he found it necessary here to cut away a slope, there to dam a stream, that each occupant of the various quarters might look out of her windows upon such a prospect as pleased her best. To the southeast he raised the level of the ground and on this bank planted a profusion of early flowering trees. At the foot of this slope the lake curved with special beauty, and in the foreground just beneath the windows, he planted borders of cinquefoil, red-plum, cherry, winteris, kerria, rock-azalea and other such plants as are at their best in springtime; for he knew that Murasaki was an especial lover of the spring; while here and there, in places where they would not obstruct his main plan, autumn beds were cleverly interwoven with the rest."

The Lady Akikonomu preferred the autumn:

"Akikonomu's garden was full of such trees as in autumn-time turn to the deepest hue. The stream above the waterfall was cleared out and deepened to a considerable distance; and that the noise of the cascade might carry further, he set great boulders in mid-stream, against which the current crashed and broke. It so happened that, the season being far advanced, it was this part of the garden which was now seen at its best; here indeed,

---

[3] Waley's translation, Part III, "The Wreath of Cloud."

was such beauty as far eclipsed the autumn splendour even of the forests near Oi, so famous for their autumn tints."

A garden which would be most agreeable in summer was made for the "Lady from the Village of Falling Flowers."

"In the northeastern garden there was a cool spring, the neighborhood of which seemed likely to yield an agreeable refuge from the summer heat. In the borders near the house upon this side he planted Chinese bamboos and a little farther off, tall-stemmed forest-trees whose thick leaves roofed airy tunnels of shade, pleasant as those of the most lovely upland wood. This garden was fenced with hedges of the white deutzia flower, the orange tree 'whose scent awakes forgotten love,' the briar-rose and the giant peony; with many other sorts of bush and tall flower, so skillfully spread about among them that neither spring nor autumn would ever lack in bravery."

For the timid Lady of Akashi, mother of Genji's only daughter, he built a garden that would be most beautiful in winter:

"To the north of Lady Akashi's rooms rose a high embankment, behind which lay the storehouses and graneries, screened also by a close-set wall of pine-trees, planted there on purpose that she might have the pleasure of seeing them when their boughs were laden with snow; and for her delight in the earlier days of the winter there was a great bed of chrysanthemums which he pictured her enjoying on some morning when all the garden was white with frost. Then there was the mother oak [4] (for was she not a mother?) and, brought hither from wild and inaccessible places, a hundred other bushes and trees so seldom seen that no one knew what names to call them by."

In another part of the estate was a race course.

"On the east a great space was walled off, behind which rose the Racing Lodge; in front of it the race-course was marked off with ozier hurdles; and as he would be resident here during the sports of the fifth month [June] all along the stream at this point he planted the appropriate purple

[4] *Quercus dentata.*

irises. Opposite were the stables with stalls for his race-horses and quarters for the jockeys and grooms. Here were gathered together the most daring riders from every province in the kingdom."

The heroine's spring garden is more completely pictured a little later when the account of a boating party is given. It is interesting to notice the appreciation of the stone artistry discovered on the island. Only one who had herself taken part in such an excursion could have written this intimate description:

"Toward the end of the third month [April] when out in the country the orchards were no longer at their best and the song of the wild birds had lost its first freshness, Murasaki's Spring Garden seemed only to become every day more enchanting. The little wood on the hill beyond the lake, and the bridge that joined the two islands, the mossy banks that seemed to grow greener not every day but every hour—could anything have looked more tempting? 'If only one could get there,' sighed the young people of the household; and at last Genji decided that there must be boats on the lake. They were built in the Chinese style. Everyone was in such a hurry to get on board that very little time was spent in decorating them, and they were put into use almost as soon as they would float. On the day when they were launched the Water Music was played by musicians summoned from the Imperial Board of Song. . . .

"It was possible to go by water all the way to the Spring Garden, first rowing along the Southern Lake, then passing through a narrow channel straight toward a toy mountain which seemed to bar all further progress. But in reality there was a way round, and eventually the party found itself at the Fishing Pavilion [of the main lake]. Here they picked up Murasaki's ladies who were waiting at the Pavilion by appointment. The boats were carved with a dragon's head at the prow and painted with the image of an osprey at the stern, completely in the Chinese style; and the boys who manned them were all in Chinese costume, with their hair tied up with bright ribbons behind. The lake, as they now put out towards the middle of it, seemed immensely large and those on board, to whom the whole experience was new and deliciously exciting, could hardly believe they were not heading for some undiscovered land. At last, however, the rowers brought them close in under the rocky bank of the channel between two large islands, and on closer examination they discovered to their delight that the shape of every little ledge and crag of stone had been as carefully devised as if a painter had traced them with his brush. Here and there in the distance the topmost boughs of an orchard showed above the mist, so heavily laden with blossom that it looked as though a bright carpet were spread in mid-air. Faraway they could just catch sight of Murasaki's apartments, marked by the deeper green of the willow boughs that swept her courtyards, and by the shimmer of her flowering orchards which even at this distance, seemed to shed their fragrance amid the island and rocks. In the world outside the cherry blossom was almost over; but here it seemed to laugh at decay, and round the palace even the wisteria that ran along the covered alleys and porticos was all in bloom, but not a flower past its best; while here, where the boats were tied, mountain-kerria poured its yellow blossom over the rocky cliffs in a torrent of colour that was mirrored in the waters of the lake below. . . ."

When such boating parties were held at night, pine knot fires were kindled in iron baskets swung out over the prow of the barge. Other fires were also lighted in baskets hung from iron standards along the shore. The flare from these clear-burning lights threw golden reflections in the dark water and lighted the trees and foliage with a rich glow.

One of the estates belonging to to the Regent Michinaga was, as mentioned, on the Uji river. The spot is still a popular resort with Kyoto people, who love to go there at any season to see the river winding smoothly out of its sinuous green canyon, sparkling in its flight past the wooded hills inclosing the valley. Uji is at its best, perhaps, on June nights when mammoth fireflies make their nuptial flights, whirling above the dark water like glowing green flakes of phosphorescent snow. At Uji there remains today the only trace in the Kyoto district of Fujiwara architectural glory, a splendid old building called the Phoenix Hall, standing behind its pond.

THE GLORY OF THE FUJIWARAS

This part of the Uji river had early been recognized as a charming place for a villa by the owner of the salt-boiling caldrons of Riverbank Villa, Minamoto no Tōru. He had built a country place here which became, in time, the retiring estate of several Emperors. But a few years before Lady Murasaki went to court, this estate, called Uji-no-in, was bought by the Regent Michinaga who proceeded to improve it greatly. Various records tell of gay boating parties held on its pond with Michinaga and his son, Yorimichi, as hosts. At this time Uji became so popular that Murasaki lays the latter part of her tale in its vicinity.

On Michinaga's death his estates became the property of Yorimichi who continued to carry on the tradition of Fujiwara splendor. When this son was himself ready to retire in 1052, he constructed on the Uji estate a beautiful chapel and placed in it an image of Amida, Lord of Light, sixteen feet high and gleaming with gold.[5] This large figure occupied nearly the whole of the main building, which was not large, but its interior was richly and lavishly decorated with paintings of paradise.

This chapel, still with its image, is the building today called the Hōō-dō or Phoenix Hall of Byōdō-in temple. We view it across the small pond which lies in front, the water reflecting its weathered walls, its multiple, curving roofs, and its graceful old pillars. Once all these were lacquered red, but most of this has now worn off, leaving only patches of faded salmon against the warm brown of weathered wood. The central hall was balanced on either side by pillared arcades ending forward in small, graceful wing-pavilions. The total effect is of "a structure of such exquisite balance, that it looks almost as if it were some great bird poised for flight."[6] It is this effect, not the two images of the mythical Chinese *gekishu* seen in the act of alighting on the upper roof corners of the main hall, which has given the name of Phoenix Hall to the building.[7]

[5] *Fusō Ryakuki.*

[6] Sansom.

[7] The Chinese *gekishu* is not the phoenix of classical literature but a mythical bird which came to a country only when it was peaceful, prosperous, and happy; hence it was an omen of good fortune.

Of the garden which once surrounded the Phoenix Hall only traces now remain. While the golden image of Amida could lift its eyes from meditation and still behold in the pond the reflection of the green hills across the valley, all other remnants of the magnificent villa have disappeared. The land on which the chapel stood was an island with an arm of the pond curving around it. Today this is hardly more than a marsh, crowded in summer with the great leaves and tall pink buds of lotus. The shoreline in front of the building maintains its original sweep outward, as did those in front of mansions of the period. For although the Phoenix Hall was built as a chapel, it was constructed like the miniature hall of a mansion, designed to house the image in the most excellent and honorable manner possible.

This style of mansion developed by the Heian nobility, was called a *shinden*. It was not a single building, but a group, joined to each other by raised wooden arcades or bridges. Around the outside of each building ran a narrow porch or gallery, and large sections of the walls could be lifted by hinges at the top and hooked overhead, turning the house virtually into an outdoor pavilion. The main hall stood in the center of the group facing the garden, the other buildings beside and behind it. Arcaded wings extended from either side, outward and forward, inclosing a forecourt which extended down to the lake edge. Especially picturesque were the two pavilions at the tip of these arcaded wings. Usually they stood over the water and were called the Spring Hall and Fishing Hall. The lake shore swept in a graceful curve outward before the building and inward under these pavilions, as it does before the Phoenix Hall.

This court before the main hall, inclosed by the arcaded wings, was the most frequently used part of the garden. In a nobleman's house its width would be sixty or seventy feet "to accommodate the multitudes of people coming to make obeisance," as the *Sakuteiki* says. The central area was kept level and clear for this practical use but in the corners it was turned into a miniature landscape with a streamlet, a few rocks, some trees, and flowers.

THE GLORY OF THE FUJIWARAS

The streamlet rose somewhere behind the buildings, wandering around and among them before it entered the main courtyard. If there were a waterfall, it was often back among these buildings, perhaps in one of the small interior courtyard gardens which were laid out in spaces between the buildings. These little interior gardens called *tsubo* usually formed the outlook for the apartments of the ladies. Most often they were decorated with tubs of flowering plants in the Chinese manner—cherry, plum, or wisteria. The ladies who occupied these apartments were often known by the flower dominant in their courtyard. Readers of the *Tale of Genji* will recall Fuji-tsubo, the Lady of the Wisteria Courtyard, who is one of the principal characters of the story.

The streamlet entered the main forecourt under one of the corridor-bridges which connected the central hall with the buildings right and left of it. The rivulet then meandered across the courtyard to the lake; it was crossed where necessary by small bridges, some made of a single large flat stone, others made in the arched Chinese style and lacquered red.

The streamlet in the courtyard was often used for one of the most popular *divertissements* of the Heian court, the form of poetical contest called the winding-water banquet. Guests on such occasions were seated at intervals along the streambank and given a subject for their poems. Wooden trays holding cups of rice wine were set afloat, and the poem had to be composed before it reached them. Those who were successful rewarded themselves by reaching out and taking the winecup as it floated past. Murasaki gives us a description of such a party, held at the Katsura estate of Prince Genji.

"So many times the cups were set afloat and so steep were the banks of the stream that the game proved somewhat dangerous. But the wine made them reckless and they were still shouting out their couplets long after it grew dark."

In not one of the gardens has the little streamlet been able to resist the centuries, but we can still see it in certain contemporary paintings. In the one illustrated here we discover some important personages seated in the

Contemporary painting of a shinden *style courtyard garden showing the* yari-mizu *streamlet emerging from under the bridge which joins the main hall and its right-hand wing. It flows forward around stones to the lake, passing under an arched red-lacquered*

central hall, about to enjoy a cockfight. A marquee has been put up in the courtyard under a blooming plum tree and the attendants are bustling about in a great state of excitement and preparation. The streamlet can be seen entering the court under the arched arcade which joins the two buildings. It flows in artful curves around the edge of the courtyard, dividing at a rockey islet or whirling around the boulders on its bank. The red Chinese bridge crossing it is a colorful and conspicuous part of the scene.

The general pattern of the *shinden* garden as here outlined was followed not only for the mansions of nobles, but for residences of less important gentlemen. Another description in Genji gives us a picture of such a modest estate. The Prince was one time unexpectedly forced to spend the night in the home of one of his gentlemen retainers, Ki no Kami. The time was evidently early June from the mention of fireflies.

bridge. The original of this picture is believed to have been painted in the twelfth century by Mitsunaga; now only a copy exists in the Imperial Museum, Tokyo. It is known as the Calendar of Festivals, or Nenjūgyōji, this portion of it illustrating a cockfight.

The coming of the Prince caused a flurry of preparation in the house of Ki no Kami and we read:

"The eastern side of the *shinden* was opened and swept and an elevated mat hastily placed in it for the Prince. The garden streamlet had been designed unusually well [to suggest coolness]. The place was inclosed by a brushwood fence in country style, and the plantings in the forecourt had been carefully arranged. The murmur of insects was borne on the cool evening breeze, while the whirling of innumerable fireflies delighted the onlookers. The Prince and his attendants drank saké, seated where they could see the pond rippling under the eastern pavilion. . . . Ki no Kami was surprised and delighted [by the visit] thinking it a great honor to his streamlet."[8]

[8] Special translation by Victor Otaké.

It is interesting to note that this modest garden was inclosed by a brushwood fence "in country style." Just such fences may still be seen occasionally in Kyoto, especially in old tea gardens, where they are valued for their rustic appearance.

Details of the theory and construction of these Heian gardens have been preserved for us in a remarkable book written at this period. It is called the *Sakuteiki* or *Memoranda of Garden Making* and its author was probably Fujiwara no Yoshitsune who himself became the regent toward the end of the 12th century. By that time the glory of the Fujiwaras had waned, and uncouth military men were administering the actual government from Kamakura, although life in Kyoto went on, outwardly, much as always. We are warned by Dr. Tatsui that the text of the *Sakuteiki* may have been edited and added to in a way that is hard to detect, but, on the whole, the book seems to cover rather exactly the heritage left to garden art by the Heian court. Because all later generations of garden makers have read and followed it, it seems worth while to give a rather complete resumé.[9]

Regarding the arrangement of rocks along the streamlet, the *Sakuteiki* says: "Place them where the water turns, then it will run smoothly. Where the water curves it strikes against the shore and so a 'turning stone' should be put in at that point. Other stones should be laid here and there as if forgotten. But if too many stones are placed along the stream, while it may appear natural when you are close by, from a distance it will seem as if they were there for no purpose. . . ."

Regarding plants in the stream-bed it adds, "Don't put those which will grow too fast or too large, but rather use small wild flowers like the *kikyō, ominaeshi, waremoko* and *giboshi.*"[10]

When a bridge was built to the island, it was usually in the arched Chinese style. The picturesque form of these curving bridges had not

[9] See Note C, p. 289.

[10] *Platycoden grandiflorum, Patrinia scabiossaefolia, Poterium officinale, Hostea coerules.*

"A structure of such exquisite balance that it looks almost as if it were some great bird poised for flight"—The Phœnix Hall at Uji, built in 1052 to glorify the Fujiwara family, has cast its reflections into the quiet waters of its garden pond for almost nine hundred years. (Photo by Okamoto Toyo.)

The winding pool of Taira Shigemori's garden, made in the late Heian period and now known as Sekisui-in of Myōhō-in temple. It marks the beginning of a change in the old, open, boating style of lake. (Photo from Board of Tourist Industry.)

originated merely as ornament, but was based on the practical necessity of allowing boats to pass under. Regarding the artistic placement of the bridge, the *Sakuteiki* continues. "The foundations of the arched bridge should not be disclosed but hidden by rocks. In constructing this bridge across to the island it should not be set straight on the main axis but slightly aslant."

The greatest interest of the *Sakuteiki* lies, however, in its generalizations on the art of gardening. The emphasis is all on how to make the garden a reproduction of nature, differing in this greatly from later books which laid down rules without relation to nature. While we find in the pages of the *Sakuteiki* that love of nature which made hills and streams, lakes and valleys the only possible pattern for a garden, the book is no such poetic outpouring as was the description of Po Chü-i's retreat on Lu-shan. The *Sakuteiki* is a practical gardener's handbook; much of it applies specifically to the design of the *shinden* garden; some of it covers gardening superstitions, but most of it is devoted to general art theories.

In the very first sentence we come upon one of the most revealing phrases in the whole book. The author begins: "The following general points should be kept in mind when one is to arrange stones." Here the words "to arrange stones" is synonymous with garden design. It was, apparently, the ordinary phraseology of the day and indicates plainly that stones were considered then, as later, the most important element entering into garden composition and their arrangement the real essence of garden art.

The *Sakuteiki* continues: "The character of the terrain must be taken into consideration in laying out the pond. Special care must be taken to produce fine feeling at the points where the observer's eye is naturally directed. The design should be planned in such a way as to make the observer feel it could not possibly have been otherwise, that is, as if nature itself produced the garden. The designer should study the great gardens of the past. He should also take into consideration the wishes of the owner and to this add his own creative spirit."

61

All this has a curiously modern sound; it might almost be the opening paragraph of a recent textbook on professional landscape gardening.

The rest of the book is a series of notes with very little attempt at organization. Following is a brief outline with a quotation here and there. Islands, as might be expected, receive a considerable amount of attention. They are classified under ten styles as mountainous, flat, forested, coastal, cloud-shaped, misty, trefoil, single-sloped, tidal, and pine-bark.

Mountainous islands are exemplified by the familiar Hōrai-jima, the peaked Isles of the Immortals. Flat islands are intended to suggest a moor behind a sandy beach with only reeds and grasses growing among a few rocks. The forested style is flat also, but thickly planted with trees; its stones are small, scattered among low grass.

Coastal islands should suggest desolate rocks rising from the sea, beaten upon by the waves and carrying a few stunted pine trees. The cloud-shaped and the misty islands seem much alike, intended to suggest vague shapes on the horizon, either clouds or islands; they are of sand only, without rocks or trees.

The trefoil island is composed of three irregular parts, made of sand and small stones and a few small pines. The single-sloped style is regarded as rather monotonous, a straight slope as if worn by a stream. Tidal islets are partly submerged, holding a few rocks half under water and no trees. The pine-bark style refers to the grouping of scattered islets in the irregular but pleasing pattern created by the splitting bark of an old pine tree.

In this discussion of islands it would seem as if a good deal of hazy theorizing has been indulged in. If we are to judge by the old garden islands which remain, and by pictures, most of these ideas were never followed up by practical exemplification. Their chief interest to us lies in their proof of how closely nature was studied and how it was always kept consciously in mind as the prototype of the garden design.

The *Sakuteiki* classifies waterfalls under various forms: those in which the water drops over the middle of the cliff; in which it falls off one side of the cliff; in which it runs over irregularities in the rock face; in which it is divided into two parts at the top; in which the face of the cascade is seen at an angle from the *shinden* seat of honor; in which it falls in a smooth flow "like a piece of hanging cloth"; in which it is divided into many falling threads by numerous irregularities at the lip; in which it is compounded into several falls or steps.

To judge by existing waterfalls, more attention has been paid to this subject than to variation in garden island styles, for the waterfalls found at the present time are even more varied than these.

Considerable discussion is devoted to the most auspicious direction in which the streamlet should flow. Here superstition enters the subject of garden design. Various authorities are quoted, all tending to show that the stream should rise at the north and east and flow toward the south and west, thus carrying evil influences from the direction of the Green Dragon to that of the White Tiger. A quotation given from an unspecified Chinese classic says:

"A proper watercourse is one which travels from east to west, passing through the south, for this is the course of the sun. A watercourse flowing from west to east is wrong!"

The *Sakuteiki* points out that the streamlet therefore should rise on the east side of the main hall and, after flowing around the building, pass west and south across the courtyard to the lake. This left to right direction (as one sits in the central hall) has been largely preserved and may be seen frequently at the present time in modern gardens.

The important subject of rock placement is dealt with at length. In contrast to the formalized rules governing it at a later day, it is interesting to note that all the rules in the *Sakuteiki* are derived either from direct observations of nature, from esthetics, or, occasionally, from geomancy. Threat of good or bad fortune, it would seem, was sometimes used to reinforce a natural or esthetic law—as in this case:

"Do not set upright a stone which naturally was flat, and vice versa; violations of this will surely bring evil fortune."

Stones are not to be placed promiscuously, but should be useful, if possible, as well as artistic.

"The usual places to set out rocks are: where the stream emerges into the courtyard; where it curves around a hillock; where it empties into the pond; where it bends in passing around buildings. Other stones should be set out only after consideration, lest they spoil the effect.

"Within the stream itself the most suitable place for stones is at the bend, for two reasons: first, the esthetic effect, second, to prevent the point of land from being washed away. Elsewhere in the stream too many stones should not be laid. While these might look well enough from near at hand, from any distance an overabundance of rocks will make the course seem one of stone rather than of water."

Again:

"Rocks called 'side hanging stones' should be set up like a folding screen (imitating the latter's in and out line). Others should be laid like a flight of steps. Stones laid along the path at the foot of the hillocks should suggest lying dogs or running pigs or calves playing with their mother. In making these combinations, if one stone seems to be escaping from the rest, seven or eight others may be placed as if following it."

In discussing trees for the garden, the emphasis is almost entirely on tradition and omen. The subject of plants was then, as now, evidently considered of slight importance compared to the foundation structure of hills, stones, and water.

"Trees should be planted on the four sides of the house so it may have the protection of the Gods of the Four Directions."

A "Man of Old" is quoted as saying:

"Flowering trees should be planted on the east (associated with the spring) and red maples on the west (associated with the autumn)."

The tradition of planting willows by the gate is mentioned, and directions given to put willows and pines on the islands. Other trees mentioned are Japanese species of catalpa, cypress, sophora, cercidiphyllum, and eurya.

All of these directions in the *Sakuteiki* are written as from one gentleman to another, for garden layout was a gentleman's task in those days as we have seen. Yet there must have been artisans, men who did the actual work, and, as legatees of the craft of Michikō, the Korean, were responsible for much of the artistry in stone placement. But the gentlemen-owners kept a close eye on the work. Prince Genji is described in one place as standing in his shirt sleeves directing the workmen cleaning out a spring. And a note in the *Sakuteiki* tells that the grand estate called Kaya-no-in, where the regent Yorimichi lived before he retired to Uji, was designed by himself. Down the centuries garden making remained the activity of other high personages, while the most gifted personalities, poets, painters, and mystics, have used it as a medium of expression.

VI. *Gardens of the Western Paradise*

FOR nearly three hundred years the city of Heian, Capital of Peace and Tranquillity, justified its name, but the gay, brilliant, and effeminate court depicted by Murasaki was its climax. Quarrels for land and power were beginning in distant provinces, even in her day, and the idyllic period was approaching its end. The sounds of this strife were scarcely heard in the gay city, and no echo of it reaches Murasaki's pages. Yet, in the next century armed conflict entered the capital itself, and a child emperor perished in a great battle on the Inland Sea.

To maintain order in the capital, the Fujiwaras had come to rely on two military families, the Taira and the Minamoto, since the imperial guards of which their sons were officers was a merely decorative organization. It was only a matter of time until these virile military men should realize it was they, not their effeminate employers, who held the real power. This came to pass in the second half of the 12th century when, by a series of adroit moves backed up by military force, the leader of the Tairas, Kiyomori, made himself the real master of Kyoto in place of the Fujiwara regent.

Autocratic and tyrannical, Kiyomori maintained a position in the capital rivaling in opulence that of the Fujiwaras. His great estate, which lay along the eastern bank of the river, was called the Rokuhara. All trace of it has disappeared, but just across the road, behind what is now the high, white wall of Myōhō-in temple, lies an old pond garden which has very recently been identified as that of his son, Taira Shigemori. This son has been made a Japanese hero in recent decades because he dared to restrain

66

his father when the sanctity of the Imperial House was threatened. A record of the time, the *Azuma Kagami,* mentions that his residence was located exactly where is now the garden of Sekisui-in, belonging to Myōhō-in temple. With its long, winding old pond, this neglected corner of the temple grounds has long lain almost forgotten behind the inclosing wall. But the pond is still charming, the tall trees that inclose it creating cool green vistas looking to the hills behind. The water is dappled in summer with lily pads and crowded at the edge with lush water grasses.

It has been supposed that this garden was made at a much later period, but it possesses unmistakable evidence of its greater age. The pond bottom is pebbled in the old style and there is a straight line of *yodo-mari* "night mooring" stones across it in the Heian manner. The winding shape of the water shows, however, a modification of the old boating style, for the *shin-den* mansion and its garden were undergoing changes by the end of the Heian period.

With the Tairas gathering up all the prizes of wealth and power, it was not to be expected that the Minamotos, the other military family, would stand quietly by. Although impotent for awhile, the Minamotos gathered together under their leader, Yoritomo, a man of genius, and attacked the Tairas. The civil war ended with the Minamotos victorious in a great sea battle in which perished the old Taira leader's small grandson, the little Antoku whom he had made into a child emperor. The victorious Yoritomo established what was termed a "camp government" in the city of Kamakura, three hundred miles east of Kyoto, this distant site being selected to escape the enervating court influences which had undermined his late rivals.

Yoritomo's vassals, the provincial barons, made virtues of frugality, simplicity, and hardihood. Luxurious living and fine estates were no part of their ambitions, at least in the early decades of military rule. In those years of the late 12th and early 13th centuries, the tramp of armored knights was heard on both sides of the world, for the Kamakura period in Japan was coincidental with the Third Crusade in Europe, and Yoritomo was a contemporary of England's Richard the Lionhearted. The small sea-side town of Kamakura bustled with activity in those days. On the broad, sandy beach mounted knights exercised their horses; on the archery ranges bowstrings twanged; the forges of the armorer and swordmaker glowed redly at night, and the sound of their hammers clanged an overtone by day.

Foot soldiers and followers, newly arrived in the train of some country knight, gazed with wonder and respect at the new red shrine of Hachiman, Deity of Warriors, for religion was flourishing as it often does in periods of turmoil and danger. The roofs of new Buddhist temples were rising above the trees of Kamakura; at the site of one of these temples was an unusual amount of activity, for a huge mold was being constructed in which was to be cast a bronze statue of Amida. This image would be known in later centuries as the Great Buddha of Kamakura. On street corners the militant monk Nichiren thundered against the abuses of the times, and the gentle monk Hōnen preached a new doctrine of salvation through faith for simple folk. And more and more, as time went on, were seen the monks of the new Buddhist sect, called Zen, in which so many of the warriors were becoming interested.

Occasionally, through this parade of military and churchly pomp would pass a figure in silken gown and small black cap, conspicuously of neither world—a courtier up from Kyoto. A number of such men, having realistic outlooks and no taste for empty office, took service under the Kamakura government. They did much to make the new rule an administrative success. And with them the courtly culture, hitherto closely confined to Kyoto, began to make some contacts with the population at large.

While Yoritomo held actual power, the civilian court continued its existence in Kyoto, outwardly much as always. Its offices were still filled with Fujiwaras who hoped for better times when the military upstarts should somehow be put back in their places. This never happened; nevertheless, down the centuries this court has continued to exist, usually almost without political power, often impoverished, but clinging to the prescribed pattern of its life with its refinements, its ceremonies, and its social distinctions. It has never lost a certain prestige which has made it the fountain-head of honors and titles eagerly sought and humbly acepted by the actual rulers.

The refining influence of this early court has subtly penetrated through-out the nation and colored the whole of its cultural fabric. Warriors, while despising courtly effeminacy, have again and again come to accept courtly manners and courtly traditions of art and esthetics. The warriors themselves contributed new and virile influences to the national culture, and, later, Zen Buddhism almost reoriented it; but there has remained always a certain fundamental pattern laid down by the Heian court. Founded upon T'ang culture, it was softened by the Japanese inherent love of beauty in nature and joined to a ceremonious refinement of manner and a tendency to view all things in terms of esthetic appreciation and art.

After Yoritomo had established himself in Kamakura, he had still to conquer one branch of the Fujiwara family which had not submitted to him. A hundred years before, this branch had come into possession of vast estates in the far northern end of the country; their territory included the lovely bay of Matsushima with its piney isles and Shiogama of the ancient salt-boiling caldrons. Not many miles from this spot, near what is now the village of Hiraizumi, these Fujiwaras built their mansion and family tem-ples, reproducing in them some of the capital's magnificence. Today, around Kyoto, nothing remains which surpasses in faded splendor one of their sur-viving old temple buildings, the Golden Hall of Chūsonji.

Another of their temples, called Mōetsuji, possessed a chapel modeled after the Phoenix Hall at Uji and, like that, set in a large landscape garden with a lake.

It was inevitable that Yoritomo should attack this northern Fujiwara stronghold, conquer and annex its riches; but he could not foresee that the conqueror would be conquered by the beauty and magnificence of Mōetsuji temple and its garden. But on his return to Kamakura he ordered the con-struction of a similar building and a fine garden, which became Eifukuji temple.

Remnants survive of both the Mōetsuji garden in the far north and its Kamakura copy. The broad Mōetsuji lake with its islands and surrounding trees must have been a breath-taking sight as Yoritomo first came upon it. Flung across the wide lake to an island was the low arch of a red lacquer bridge, its posts capped with pointed bronze knobs. A smaller bridge continued the line across the water to the shore before the building which stood, colorful and graceful, among tall trees. Its vermilion pillars and small curving roofs were reflected in the water while right and left, connected by arcades, stood a bell tower and a drum tower, taking the place of the usual end-pavilions. From the central island rose a small pagoda, its slender lines doubled in the clear lake.

Today the old pond of Mōetsuji lies dreaming, long tree shadows still floating on its mirror surface. The bridge and the gay red buildings have vanished, although their foundation stones may yet be found. The stonework on the shore and island remains, however, in better condition than in any other garden of the early period. The cascade by the side of the lake was of the dry type. The typical straight line of "night-mooring" islets leads across the pond. Everywhere, the stone groupings show the technique of the period, large upright stones leaning slightly over and supported by lesser ones as at Saga-no-in; others in the balanced three-stone arrangement of Mii-dera's spring.

Although Yoritomo advocated simplicity in living, he lavished large sums on religious institutions; in erecting Eifukuji, the copy of Mōetsuji temple, no expense seems to have been spared. Eifukuji stood for over two hundred years, but in the turbulent middle ages it was burned and not rebuilt. Gradually its garden and pond slipped back into rice fields, and only recently has excavation begun to reveal its old shape. Except for the fine hills around it, the site, today, holds little of beauty; there exists only a recently dug pond in which water weeds are springing, a modern island, and a few stones. Continued excavations are likely to reveal more of the stonework and, probably, the foundations of the buildings, while time will restore the trees and shrubs. But until this takes place, we shall have to rely on literary sources to learn of its beauties.

Fortunately, a better record exists of this garden than of any other made previously; and, indeed, few of the gardens which come after it are so well documented. The story of Eifukuji is found in the *Azuma Kagami*, the Mirror of the East, a detailed chronicle kept between 1180 and 1266. Scattered through its entries may be found the story of Eifukuji's rise and fall. In this record we have the first complete picture of the construction of such a large estate. With this information, supplemented by present-day technique of garden making—for the continuity of this technique has been virtually unbroken—it is possible for us to visualize, as plainly as in a moving picture, the making of one of these great pond gardens eight hundred years ago.

First mention of Eifukuji in the *Azuma Kagami* tells of Yoritomo's determination to duplicate the hall of Mōetsuji. Work on this new undertaking was begun the very year he returned from the northern campaign, 1189. Nearly three years, however, were required for the buildings to be sufficiently finished to justify intensive work on the garden. This period may also have been required to gather together the necessary stones, for we learn that they came from many provinces, evidently as the contributions of vassals. By the time work was ready to begin, we read of huge stones "piled up like hills" around the edge of the garden, waiting to be put into place.[1]

[1] Today, stone merchants send men far afield to search for boulders of fine shape and surface texture. When proper stones are located, they are brought to the cities, usually in an oxcart, the trip often requiring weeks or even months. Extreme care is taken not to injure the weathered surface of the rock nor to scratch any lichens or moss growing on it. Dr. Jirō Harada tells of seeing men who were transporting such stones carefully water the moss during the journey. Stones too large to handle are broken into parts and reassembled after transportation, only small cracks indicating what has taken place. The stone merchant sets up his wares in a display yard where they can be inspected by prospective customers. The cost of good stones is obviously high, for they represent a considerable investment by the time they have been discovered, transported, and finally disposed of.

Finally, in 1192, under the date of the twenty-fourth day, eighth month—which would have been about the end of September—an entry reads: "Today excavating was begun on the pond of Nikai-dō (a popular name of the temple). Natural conditions around this site are very well suited to a landscape garden. Yoritomo has ordered each vassal in the neighboring provinces to send three men to work on it."

Another entry tells us the name of the landscape designer, the man who was arranging the stones, especially those on a rocky island in the pool. He was Seigen, a Tendai priest. His is the first name of a Japanese garden technician to come down to us. Doubtless he had learned this art as a gentlemanly accomplishment in Kyoto. Yoritomo himself took a keen interest in the construction of the garden, visiting it often to inspect its progress. While he despised the effeminacy of the courtiers in Kyoto, he accepted, apparently without question, their dictate that garden making was an occupation worthy of anyone. He evidently had very definite ideas on what he liked and didn't like, for while he approved, on his first visit, of the way that Seigen had been putting in rocks and lanterns, on a second visit he didn't like the position of some of the upright stones in the pond and asked Seigen to change them.

The *Azuma Kagami* does not mention specifically the transplanting of trees and shrubs into this garden, but we judge it must have been done, since, on its completion, in only three months the place was said to be like paradise. Such enthusiasm would hardly have been provoked had the trees and shrubs been small and meager. A later entry mentions the cherry and plum trees which grew around Eifukuji. Some decades after Yoritomo's death, when his temple was becoming neglected and the Hōjō family was wielding his power, a note in the *Azuma Kagami* says that plum and cherry trees were moved from Eifukuji to a Hōjō estate. By this we know also that the art of transplanting full-grown trees was practiced as early as the 12th century; in all likelihood it was much older, probably being something that had been learned from China.[2]

[2] Modern Japanese gardeners are extremely skillful in handling large trees, thinking

GARDENS OF THE WESTERN PARADISE

Mention of the huge stones "from many provinces" and the workmen levied from the neighboring vassals reveals the way in which all the great feudal estates were constructed. A lord or baron might almost measure his power by the number of men and amount of material he could command. In times of rebellion, if a vassal felt himself strong enough to refuse such a request he might do so. On the other hand, powerful leaders sometimes took this means of keeping their vassals too poor to consider rebellion. Many fine buildings resulted from this policy, among others, in later centuries, the Nikko temples.

With men and materials at last assembled, work on the Eifukuji garden could go ahead rapidly. One who has watched the making of a modern Japanese garden can visualize without difficulty this scene at Kamakura in the year 1192, for Japan in its isolation is a country in which many things have come down the centuries practically unchanged.[3] The greater part of the garden would be a wide, raw excavation covering the future lake. Swarming about everywhere would be the workmen, some digging the earth with their mattocks, others in pairs carrying it away in rope nets slung on a pole between them. Around the edge of the garden would loom the stones and in another corner the balled trees, like a forest, the dirt around their roots bound tightly in place by a network of rice-straw rope.

Standing in the midst of this activity, a quiet figure, would be Seigen,

---

nothing of transplanting them when they are twenty or thirty feet tall or even larger. Such trees continue to live and grow almost as if nothing had happened to them. Every tree and shrub which goes into a new Japanese garden today is the proper size and shape when it is put there—no one wishes to wait years for a tree to grow when even then it might not develop to fill out the design of mass and line being created. After transplanting, trees and shrubs are maintained in proper size and shape by vigorous pruning, this being another of the things in which Japanese horticulturists excel. To obtain fine trees, tree brokers send out scouts to locate them on windswept hillsides or old farmyards. When discovered they are purchased, and when a customer is found they are taken up and transported to the customer's estate. While trees that have been carefully trained into picturesque shape are often used, the most prized are old ones, naturally rugged, and misshapen by the years.

[3] Certain scroll paintings made in the Kamakura period show artisans at work, revealing how little changed are many of the craft processes.

the director, his clerical gown probably tucked up around his waist. Certain men would bring a great rock up to its approximate site. At a wave of Seigen's hand it would be raised or lowered, twisted or turned, with many grunts and chanteys of concerted action. A tall tripod of tree trunks with block and tackle aids this movement today, and something of the sort must always have been used. At last, when the stone seemed just right to Seigen, if the Shogun were watching, he would turn for final approval. Perhaps the stone would be shifted just a little more. Then, exactly right in its artistic relation to other stones near it and to the whole balance and rhythm of the garden, it would be fixed in place by tamping with earth and pebbles.

This business of moving rocks seems to have fascinated certain of the young warriors who, raised in the country, had probably never seen anything of the sort before. It challenged their strength and the *Azuma Kagami* tells us they tried their hands at moving stones alone. One, Hatakeyama Shigetada, succeeded in moving a stone ten feet long. We can picture this horseplay, the grinning workmen gathered round to see the fun, the tolerant Seigen, pointing where the stone was to go, the determined young brave, red-faced and sweating, tugging and heaving at the huge stone; his triumph when he succeeded, the admiring murmurs of the crowd, and the chronicler among them, noting it in his mind as worthy to put in the record.

With such intensive work the garden was completed in only three months. To celebrate the completion the Lady Masako, Yoritomo's wife, visited the temple. The garden, the chronicler exclaims, is as beautiful as Amida's paradise.

This was a stock comparison for fine pond gardens, a phrase already used in the *Azuma Kagami* to describe the beauties of Mōetsuji. The paradise referred to was the celestial garden in which those who believed in Amida, Lord of Light, might hope to be reborn after death. That form of Buddhism which made Amida its central figure instead of the Buddha Gautama became widely popular in Japan in the late Heian period. It taught that since in this sinful world man could not hope to follow the way laid down by Gautama, Amida had vowed he would not accept salvation for himself until all beings were also saved through him. Those who relied on his power would be reborn in his Pure Land (Jōdo), the paradise beyond the sunset.

Descriptions of this paradise are singularly suggestive of the Christian Heaven, except that Amida's Pure Land was not a city of gold but a celestial lake garden filled with heavenly lotus. Instead of a golden harp, those reborn in it would have a seat on a lotus blossom. Naturally this concept fired the imagination of artists, and its imagery entered largely into late Heian and Kamakura art. The large lake gardens of the time must have seemed very like this celestial land; indeed, some of them were deliberately designed to suggest it.

Such a one was the garden of Saihōji temple in Kyoto. This garden seems first to have been made at the end of the 12th century, about the same time Yoritomo was building Eifukuji in Kamakura.[4] Saihōji appears to have consisted originally of two gardens belonging to twin temples. These two expressed the Jōdo dual concept, on the one hand, of paradise, on the other, of this foul and sinful world. Eidoji, the Temple of Aloofness from the Foul World, stood on a slope with a hillside garden around it; just below, at the foot of the hill, and possessing a pond garden was Saihōji, literally the Temple of the Westward Direction, or, by implication, of Paradise. The hillside temple of Eidoji seems early to have disappeared, and the lower temple, Saihōji, to have become possessed of its garden, giving it the double aspect which characterizes it today.

Tucked away in a fold of the hills west of Kyoto, the centuries have rolled gently over this old garden, leaving it by far the best preserved of any built up to that time. Kyoto people know it today as the Moss Temple, Koke-dera, for it lies in a spot particularly favorable to the growth of mosses. Sheltered alike from cold north winds and the hot western sun, with a heavy clay soil that holds moisture, the mosses have taken such possession

---

[4] These new historical facts, completely revising all that has previously been believed, have been discovered recently by Mr. Shigemori.

of the garden they eclipse in interest the more showy plants such as trees, azaleas, and lotus.

To reach the garden we follow a narrow valley, cross its stream, and come to the white-plaster temple wall, gleaming among shadowy trees and graceful bamboo. Except for birds all is quiet. A long, flagged walk leads inward from the temple gate to the vestibule, following the wall which shuts away the garden. On either side of the flagstones mosses form a velvety lawn, a preliminary touch of what is to come. In answer to our call in the vestibule an old, black-robed priest appears, bowing on the matted floor of the little hall until his head touches the ground. We are politely invited to enter the garden through a postern gate in the wall.

The temple building, small and unpretentious, more like a residence than a temple, stands apart from the garden. The present building, although not new, has nothing in common with the original one. Beyond it lies the garden, a place of mystery, a forest deeply shadowed, with dark water gleaming in its depths. As we step in among the trees, it seems an enchanted forest, for nothing about Saihōji garden ever appears quite real; it is as if time had stood still, and we had slipped back to the beginning of folklore and the age of the gods. Eve might be sunning herself on that mossy slope, and Izanagi, her Japanese counterpart, be standing long-haired in those shadows.

Everywhere, to right and left, the mosses carpet the ground, undulating away in hummocky waves of emerald, jade, and bronzy green; often there are translucent azure highlights. They mold smooth green banks to the pool and throw a verdant shadow into rock crevices. Nineteen species are listed in a temple booklet. Some of the mosses are like finest velvet; others are coarse and large, two inches high, like tiny conifers creating a fairy forest. Patterns of varying colors and textures radiate over the ground —on mats of duller green, mysterious circles of jade like ancient instruments of necromancy; or indefinite blotched designs in overtones of grey and yellow.

Water in the pond is crystal pure and a curious emerald green in effect,

Mosses have taken possession of Saihōji's garden, wresting interest from more showy plants. They carpet the ground in hummocky waves of emerald, jade, and bronzy green, while greyish lichens on the tree trunks create a dim, mysterious haze through the shadows. (Photo by Okamoto Toyo.)

Water in Saihōji's pond is crystal pure and a curious, emerald green color, owing to the water mosses. Golden sunlight stipples the limpid surface, and the tree trunks seem twice their length in the shimmering mirror. The trees, naturally twisted, cast tenuous shadows over the moss. (Photo from Board of Tourist Industry.)

made so by the bright water mosses growing on the sandy bottom. Golden sunlight stipples the limpid surface, and the tree trunks seem twice their length in the shimmering mirror. Everywhere the trees, untrained but bent and twisted naturally, cast tenuous shadows over the carpet of moss. Their trunks are mottled with greyish lichens creating a mysterious greenish haze. Beyond them, the eye is baffled by dim parallel lines of giant bamboo stems which surround the garden. Scarlet azaleas flame in the shadows in May; in July the huge blue-green bowls of the lotus sway over the pool; in autumn the maples burn, a mellow crimson against the azure sky; in winter the mosses still hold warm promise of spring in their velvet depths.

Once there were cherry trees in this garden, splendid enough, when in bloom, to lure court nobles all the way from Kyoto. We read in a contemporary record[5] of the visit of the ex-Emperor Kōgon in the spring of 1347. The cherry trees were at their best and the party accompanying the ex-Emperor took to boats on the pond to view them. One courtier suggested music as a fitting accompaniment to this excursion, and the thin melody of flute and zithern floated up to the petaled branches. Toward evening everyone left the boats, and the ex-Emperor took his seat under one of the blooming trees while the courtiers sat around him in a circle. Ten tall lanterns threw their soft light up to where the great masses of the flowers flushed radiantly, cameo-like against the starry darkness of the sky.

The hillside garden once belonging to Eidoji, the Temple of Aloofness from the Foul World, lies on a wooded slope just above the pond garden. A gate leads through the dividing wall, and a rocky path ascends the hillside among mosses as verdant and rolling as those below. It winds through a sunny glade so perfect as to seem theatrical, a setting idealized for some play of folklore. Here in this secluded, sunny slope, peaceful and lovely with the calm of many centuries, we feel we are, indeed, far aloof from the restlessness and evils of this turbulent world.

The spirit of this hillside garden was perfectly comprehended by a young man who came here for one of the gay boating parties but remained

[5] *Entaireki.*

77

to commune with nature on the hillside. This was the Shogun Yoshimitsu who arrived on an autumn afternoon in the year 1380. He and his party had come to see the maple leaves which glowed like tapestry against the evergreens. At dusk a full moon rose and the party sat composing linked verses until a late hour. The next morning Yoshimitsu walked up to the hill garden. Its dewy freshness must have made a profound impression on him, for instead of joining once more the gay party, he settled down in the small chapel to meditate with his Zen teacher. The courtiers in the party were greatly impressed; many personages, they said, had come to Saihōji for pleasure, but none before had abandoned this to meditate.[6]

Today we cannot make out what the original layout of this hillside garden may have been, for only individual rock arrangements remain, scattered here and there about the mossy slopes. Several of these arrangements survive in nearly perfect condition, but others are now mere piles of stones whose original form cannot be guessed. Each of the surviving arrangements, however, is a masterpiece of its kind; they consist of a rocky "island," a woodland spring, and a dry cascade.

The "island" is the first arrangement we come upon as we follow the woodland path up the hill. It is a group of rather large stones, lichen-covered, laid out on the flat ground of a mossy, shadowy dell. They might be mistaken for a mere pile of rocks dumped there after some building operation, but a second glance makes us pause. Is there something familiar there? We catch a glimpse of an outline—a huge turtle swimming in the water, head back, flippers moving slowly, formed by the shape and placement of the rocks. Another look and we are not so sure—it seems, after all, only a pile of stones forming an islet, if we like to think so, in a sea of mossy waves. But suddenly, with the thrill of a fairy story come true, we realize it is *both* island and turtle—that we are looking at one of the Mystic Isles in the Eastern Ocean, isles whose rocking was stabilized by giant turtles, that it might not disturb the Immortals. The turtle is quite plain to the eye of the imagination; in the cold light of realism he disappears.

[6] *Entaireki.*

GARDENS OF THE WESTERN PARADISE

Straight out of a Chinese fairy tale, this turtle isle is one of the most delightful concepts in the world, a delicate whimsy, the product of a charming sophistication which must have had its origin in China long before. At present, I am unaware of any relic or reference to turtle islands in China, but everything points to the fact that they must have existed there. Remnants of turtle islands may be found in earlier Heian gardens but they are so obscure that the eye of an expert is needed to discern them. This one at Saihōji is the earliest graphic example but it is followed by a long line of others.

The second rock arrangement in Saihōji's hill garden is the woodland spring. Set into the mossy slope is a large flat-faced rock and below it has seeped a small, clear basin of water, shadowy and cool. The excess runs away as a tiny rill from between the flat stones which act as a curb in front. These flat stones may be used to step or kneel on when dipping up the water. On either side of the pool are large wing-stones, stabilizing and balancing the whole composition. Deep-set into the mossy hillside, the spring seems completely natural; it is the ideal concept of what a rocky, woodland spring ought to be, cool, dark, clear, and clean, irresistibly inviting one to kneel and drink. In its rhythmically balanced form it is nature as nature ought to be, but somehow never is.

Near the spring some of the scattered rocks have flat tops over which the centuries have flung furry rugs of coarse, matted moss. It has been supposed that these flat rocks were meditation seats, but the chronicles show that meditation took place in the small chapel which stood nearby. The flat-topped stones of Saihōji are, however, very characteristic of its style of rock work and have exerted a wide influence on later gardens—for Saihōji served as a model for many centuries.

Just beyond the chapel is the dry cascade. Below the fall, its pools brim with moss, the whole arrangement extending some distance back around the curve of the hillside. The spot is mysterious with the gloom of tall trees, so the large, aged rocks, blotched with lichens, jutting from the hillside, are difficult to distinguish clearly. But we can make out a rocky fall of huge stones which look as if they had been washed clear by falling water. Still, no water trickles over them now, nor has it ever; yet the feeling cannot be resisted that it must have done so for ages and may again soon. In the small pool at the foot of the rocks only moss brims and likewise in the larger pool which washes almost to our feet. The moss seems to ripple like the water of a pool disturbed by the fall of the cascade.

The pools are outlined in rocks placed with subtle artistry. We see here, carried out to perfection, the admonition of the *Sakuteiki* to follow nature as closely as possible. The stones seem to stand where they are simply because they could not be anywhere else. The thought crosses our minds "Can this after all be natural?" Then we notice how the earth has been washed away from under several rocks, leaving exposed the foundation of small stones on which they are rested, and we know that every rock in sight was placed as we see it with the greatest care. The stones in this arrangement are not remarkable for their peculiar shape or surface texture as are some of those in later gardens; they are, in fact, rather ordinary and rounded in form, yet the harmony of their rhythmic descending lines from the cascade through the inclosing borders of the pool is that of flowing water itself.

The same stone technique used in these three hillside arrangements—the cascade, the turtle island, and the spring—is used in the stonework of the lower garden, proving that both were made at the same time and by the same garden artist. In the lower garden there are several remnants of rock arrangements which cannot be identified but are believed to have been once cascades. The best surviving arrangements are true islands in the pond; one of these is a turtle island, now very difficult to identify, while beside it is a crane island.

With the introduction of the crane appears the second of the longevity creatures which served the Immortals. The association of the crane with Oriental gardens is very old, originating, it seems likely, from real cranes which alighted on islands in the lakes. It will be recalled that a crane island was mentioned in connection with the hunting park of Liu Wu of the Han period in China. Whatever the origin, by the time the tradition was established in Japan, the crane island possessed a definite form; it was made of upright, standing rocks, its general effect being perpendicular, in contrast to the turtle islands which are generally flat. Unlike the turtle, there is nothing graphic about the crane islets; no amount of imagination could see a bird depicted in one of them, although this has been attempted at times. Their function seems to be to provide the upright, perpendicular lines which serve as contrast for the level forms of the turtle.

Saihōji has also its mysterious straight line of "night-mooring" stones. Here they are very much smaller than in some of the older gardens, stretching in a double line across a small upper pond which drains into the lower lake. Realists have suggested that here they may be nothing more than the foundation stones of a building which once overhung this small pond. However, the fact that they are irregularly spaced and some are pointed, unsuiting them to support a pillar, seems to answer this point. Whatever this arrangement may have meant, as they exist here they are singularly ornamental, especially in summer when small grasses and flowers grow out of their crevices to be reflected delicately back in the shallow water.

While the Saihōji pond is large enough for boating and was often so used, it was not primarily designed for this purpose as were the large lakes of Heian mansion gardens. Since it was the garden of a Jōdo temple, the pond could have been intended only to suggest Amida's celestial lake garden. This is a concept easily understood and grasped by anyone. But times were changing. The old, unshadowed nature of the courtiers was becoming affected by adversity, and there was a turn to more thoughtful things, the beginning of a new mood of reflection and introspection. We find this mood foreshadowed here in the outward form of the garden, especially in the pond, which is winding and mysterious, rather than open, broad, and sunny as were the old boating gardens. In excavating it a large round island was left in the center so that the lake is virtually a circular channel of water, very irregular, and presenting, as one follows it, constantly changing vistas of shadowy water, rolling moss, and rocky islets. It was the beginning of transition from the old style to the new feeling of mysticism in gardening.

THE ART OF JAPANESE GARDENS

With the ascendancy of military power and the consequent overthrow of old values and old ways, had come an awakening from the idyllic dream of the courtiers. Stripped of its actual power, the court nevertheless went on its way, outwardly much as always; but its mood was one of sentimental melancholy, of looking back to past days of glory. Elsewhere men were beginning to think for themselves, and this was one of the factors which led to the marked religious activity of the Kamakura period. With the military men rough and untutored, those individuals who had no taste for military adventure sought the monasteries which were strong enough to offer them a refuge. Thus, in this period, the centers of culture shifted from the court to the temples; it is not by chance that nearly all the gardens of this period are those of temples. The creation of Saihōji at this time was strictly in keeping with the spirit of the new age.

It has long been thought that Saihōji's garden was made by the great Zen priest, Musō Kokushi, in the second quarter of the 14th century. A record of his life[7] says so, but it now appears quite certain that all he did was to rehabilitate the temple and add a number of buildings to the garden. Saihōji was a hundred and fifty years old before Musō Kokushi came to it. It had been constructed in the Kenkyū era (1190-1198) by one Fujiwara Morokazu, who was the hereditary high priest of the nearby Matsuo shrine and head of the family which had once been known as Hata.

These Hatas probably had been originally Koreans, to judge by their Chinese name. Doubtless they had been brought to Japan to teach the civilized arts and crafts. Skilled and energetic, they became possessed of extensive lands near the site of present-day Kyoto, which they developed for rice culture by building dams and irrigation systems. Although they were exceedingly wealthy and influential, they remained commoners until after the court left Nara. Then they offered some of their land for the site of the new capital and, when it was accepted, contributed heavily to the cost of building the new imperial palace, for it was greatly to their advantage to have the court so near. Some of the Hata women became wives of Fujiwaras

[7] *Musō Kokushi Nempu.*

82

and in this way, in time, the family seems to have become affiliated with the great Fujiwara clan. But they evidently maintained themselves as a separate branch, holding the family lands and fortune more or less intact. The Hatas had early built the Buddhist temple called Kōryūji and also a Shinto shrine, named Matsuo, which they dedicated to an adopted mythical Shinto ancestor. The head of the family remained the hereditary high priest of this family shrine and evidently controlled the family fortune.

It was the head of this family, the high priest of Matsuo, who, in the early Kamakura period, caused Saihōji garden to be built. A legend relates that the deity of Matsuo once manifested itself on a large rock (still pointed out to the credulous in Saihōji garden) commanding that a temple be built on the spot. A more likely reason for the construction of the temple is found in certain ancient graves on the hillside behind. There are probably the resting places of departed Hatas and the spot, doubtless, had long been sacred to them. It is probable, too, that some sort of small temple had stood on the spot before, accounting for the various legends of an early temple there. For some reason, however, in the early Kamakura period, Fujiwara Morokazu, the high priest of Matsuo, being also an ardent follower of Amida, decided to erect the twin temples of Saihōji and Eidoji on this spot. After they were completed he gave a manor for their upkeep. These facts were written on a stone monument put up in the garden by the priest Jikusen in the 13th century. He was a contemporary of Musō Kokushi and would hardly have done this if Musō Kokushi had originally made the garden.[8]

Internal evidence corroborates the age of Saihōji's gardens. Their basic theme of Amida's paradise, the foreshadowing of mysticism in their feeling, and the details of their stone technique are all characteristic of the early Kamakura period rather than of Musō Kokushi's later day. The garden was tremendously expensive to build, not only because it was very large and in a difficult location, but also because every detail was executed in the finest

---

[8] The story of the monument is found in *Saihōji Chitei Engi,* Legendary History of Saihōji, but corroboration of its existence is found in the *Heiki-zan Jitsuroku,* the diary of a visitor who went there in 1460.

and most thorough manner possible, as evidenced to this day in the way it has survived. Musō Kokushi had no resources at his command to accomplish such a work nor did he remain at Saihōji long enough. But the Hata-Fujiwara family might well have done it. Not only did they possess the wealth necessary, but they had at their command the skill and engineering resources of a family long accustomed to land development.

A century and a half after the founding, the grandson or great-grandson of Morokazu, who was then his successor as head of the family and high priest of Matsuo, conceived the idea of rehabilitating the mossy old family temple on the hillside and retaining the great Zen ecclesiastic, Musō Kokushi, for its honorary abbot. With his coming, however, a new chapter opened in the story of Saihōji.

VII. *The Transition Gardens*

IN 1337 the head of Matsuo shrine and patron, by heredity, of Saihōji temple was Fujiwara Chikahide. He was governor of a province and, evidently because he supported the military regime, seems still to have controlled the large properties of the one-time Hata family. Being as ardently interested in Zen as his grandfather had been in the faith of Amida, he decided that the old Jōdo family temple of Saihōji might, perhaps, be converted into one of the Zen sect, if the great Musō Kokushi could be induced to come and officiate, and act for awhile as its honorary abbot.

The times were troublous. During the 13th century the country had been, on the whole, quiet and well administered under the Kamakura camp government. But in the early 14th century this regime began to weaken. The real difficulties were economic, with available lands too limited to satisfy the ambitions of vassal lords who desired wealth and power. But in the court trouble had arisen over the succession to the throne. The reigning Emperor, Go-Daigo, was the center of the intrigues, and the court divided into factions for and against him. Kamakura sent an army and a general to overawe the court; but near Kyoto this general, Ashikaga Takauji, suddenly turned against his Kamakura overlords, and shortly the whole country was in upheaval. The barons took sides in the court fight, but their real hope was that they might obtain the lands of their rivals if they won. Eventually the Kamakura government was overthrown, and the rebellious general, Takauji, emerged victorious, while the Emperor Go-Daigo was forced from Kyoto. Another imperial prince was set up as Emperor in the old city while Go-Daigo, who had never abdicated, established his court at

85

Yoshino, famous for its cherry trees. For the next fifty years there existed two imperial courts in Japan, each with its adherents among the court nobles and the provincial barons.

The court in Kyoto made Takauji shogun in 1338, thus starting in his family a new dynasty of *de facto* rulers known as the Ashikaga Shoguns. Since the intrigues of the court had played such a part in this national upheaval, Takauji found it expedient to make the headquarters of his government not Kamakura, but Kyoto where he could keep an eye on things. Thus, in due course, the old capital once more became the center of all activities.

It was while these things were still going on that Chikahide invited Musō Kokushi to come to Saihōji. Chickahide was a supporter of Takauji, and Musō Kokushi was one of the new leader's confidential advisors. It was not difficult, therefore, for arrangements to be made, all the less so, doubtless, as the quiet seclusion of the temple would have its appeal in those troubled days.

The priest, Musō Kokushi, sometimes known by his other priestly name of Soseki, was one of the most astute men of his time, the recipient of high honors from the imperial court and much admired by the military men. He was also a keen lover of nature, a fact continually brought out in the records of his life. It has been customary for several hundred years to regard him as one of the foremost of the early garden designers, but it now appears this reputation was created in after ages and is based simply on his well-known love of natural beauty and his connection with a number of temples having fine gardens. His actual contribution to these gardens seems to have been, in every case, only the addition of a pavilion or summer house at some high and sightly spot where he could sit and contemplate the beauty of nature. Such a pavilion, for instance, he built in Kamakura on the hill behind Zuisenji temple, and such buildings he added to Saihōji and Tenryūji.

It is not hard to picture the effect of Saihōji garden on such a lover of nature as was Musō Kokushi. For nearly a century and a half it had been quietly collecting a patina of age until the mosses must have been as thick as they are today, and created an atmosphere as glamorous as they do now. After he settled there, Musō Kokushi changed the written characters of the temple name so that, although they were pronounced as before, they meant the Temple of Western Fragrance, a Zen allusion, rather than the Temple of the Western Direction, the old Jōdo name. The temple and garden were rehabilitated, but the garden was not fundamentally changed. A number of buildings were erected in it under Musō Kokushi's direction, all with transcendental Zen names and meanings. Chickahide, like his ancestor, the founder, was evidently very lavish with funds for this work. The new buildings were apparently all of excellent design for they met the highly exacting taste of a later generation, which made replicas of them. One of these copies survives today in the Silver Pavilion, which we shall come to in due course. But in the civil wars of the middle ages all the Saihōji buildings were burned, and we do not know otherwise what they were like.

Although Saihōji's garden was originally laid out to suggest the paradise of Amida, the way in which it foreshadowed a more subjective feeling in garden art has been mentioned. The subtleties of the circular winding pool, the path, the curious effect of the thick moss, and the long reflections in the water, all bring out this feeling strongly. The garden creates that sense of mysticism, arousing profound depths of feeling, which Oriental artists call yūgen.[1] There is no exact English equivalent for this word since it is a concept not definitely crystallized in Western thought. By one definition it might be called an atmosphere—the atmosphere of hazy unreality which brings, to a sensitive mind, the feeling of kinship with nature, the sense of one's spirit merging with the spirits of other natural things, which is the basic feeling of Oriental mysticism.

It is this mysticism which is at the bottom of Zen Buddhism. It will be recalled that in its essentials it was formulated into a philosophy in the 5th century B.C. when Taoist thinkers sought The Way to an understanding of life and man's nature and his relation to the Infinite. Many of

---

[1] A term derived from the Chinese. The "g" is hard as always in Japanese.

these philosophers retreated to mountain hermitages to free themselves from the restrictions and artificialities of society. Alone in the wilds, they could live simply with nature, feel the fundamental rhythm in all things, and sense their own harmonic relation to the universe.

The same turn of mind led somewhat later to the formulation of another school of philosophy having virtually the same objectives but taking the form of a Buddhist sect. Ostensibly derived from India, it appears as if the original Indian thought must have been so adapted that it amounted virtually to an expression of the Chinese mind similar to Taoism. However, regarded as a sect of Buddhism, it was called Ch'an. The word means meditation and in Japan came to be pronounced Zen. This sect held that, since man is one manifestation of the cosmic force, truth may be found by seeking for it within his own being. The process of intuitive introspection is called meditation and any success in its realization is termed enlightenment. The Ch'an sect originally had no other activity than this, no doctrine, no written scripture, no ritual of worship.

While the meditative branch of Buddhism had been known in Japan very early, it was not until the military era of the Kamakura regime that it assumed importance. During the 13th century there had been a good deal of travel back and forth between Japan and China, as Japanese Zen students went to the mainland to study at the fountainhead of the sect, or Ch'an priests were induced to come to Japan and teach in Kyoto or Kamakura. Simple, at first, in form, Zen came, in time, to establish many large and powerful monasteries; eventually it became almost the official religion of the country through the adherance of the powerful military men and their influence on the court.

It may appear strange, at first, to find a religion of quietude and meditation making its greatest appeal to a military society. But Zen is a highly individualistic philosophy, its meditation and enlightenment matters of direct and personal experience. It might well appeal to men of a self-reliant nature who had no taste for emotionalism, for abstruse speculation, study or ritual, and who placed a high value on self-discipline. Its quietude, moreover, offered an escape to those who lived lives of strife and uncertainty.

Zen has been one of the most profound of the influences entering into the development of Japanese culture. Superimposed on the pattern laid down by the Heian court, it reoriented almost completely most of the older cultural expressions. In place of their gaiety, brightness, and color it substituted a subtle symbolism, extreme simplicity, and naturalness. We see this transitional process taking place in Saihōji garden. While the garden was not laid out on Zen principles, it became a Zen garden through nature's influence on it, creating in its subtle harmonies and its perfect naturalism that feeling of *yūgen* which later Zen artists strove consciously to put into their work. Saihōji marks, therefore, a definite turn in the course of Japanese garden development, with the disappearance of the old, gay, Heian pleasure park and the foreshadowing of the new, subjective gardens of the next period.

A second garden which marks the transition from the old to the new with the introduction of Sung artistry—another of the profound influences in Japanese culture—is that of Tenryūji temple. It lies not far from Saihōji on the banks of the Ōi river and across from a small green peak called Mount Arashiyama. This river district, beautifully wooded, bright in spring and autumn with cherry blossoms or maple foliage, has been a popular resort since Heian days. In the 9th century the learned Emperor Saga constructed his Saga-no-in not far away, and from that time onward the court nobles often built their villas nearby. Across from Arashiyama a certain Prince Kaneaki built an estate in the 10th century which came at last into the possession of the courtly Tachibana family. This estate stood at the foot of the hill called Kameyama from which it took its later name of Kameyama-dono or Kameyama Hall.

In the middle of the Kamakura period the Emperor Saga II, or Go-Saga, who had retired young, was living in a mansion in Kyoto belonging to his wealthy father-in-law, the powerful court noble, Fujiwara no Saneuji. As Saneuji had supported the military regime, he was in much better circumstances than most of the other courtiers, so that when the mansion in which the retired Emperor was living burned, he was able to begin its reconstruction at once. He asked Tachibana Tomoshige to act as commissioner of this new building, that is, to be responsible for assembling its materials and seeing to its erection. But before the new place was completed it, too, caught fire. Tachibana, evidently feeling himself in some way responsible for this, pressed his own estate at Arashiyama upon the retired Emperor. Saneuji, therefore, turned his attention toward making this old place over into as fine a country villa as possible. When it was completed and occupied, about 1256, it became for some years the center of court life, since Go-Saga continued to exercise the powers of the throne from his retirement. Later in the century Kameyama-dono was used by his son, the Emperor Kameyama, who evidently took his name from it. But by the time Takauji was campaigning against Kamakura, and the reigning Emperor, Go-Daigo, was fleeing to Yoshino, the old estate of Kameyama-dono had lain deserted for years and was falling into ruins. Musō Kokushi, who must often have passed it on his way to Saihōji, evidently realized the possibilities it possessed for being turned into a fine temple, for not long after he caused this to take place.

The Emperor Go-Daigo, who had been forced by Takauji to flee from Kyoto and set up his Southern Court on the cherry-covered mountain of Yoshino, died there suddenly. Takauji, who seems to have had an average amount of superstition, greatly feared the vengeance of the departed spirit and sought advice from Musō Kokushi. Takauji related to the priest a dream in which he had seen a dragon rise from the Ōi river and, after circling the heavens, descend on the old estate of Kameyama-dono. Musō replied that he, too, had had a curious dream of the same place. He had seen the late Emperor Go-Daigo, robed as a priest, enter it in his imperial palanquin. Dragons being the symbol of superior beings, it was evident that the two dreams were identical and meant that Go-Daigo's spirit wished to find rest in the old estate where, perhaps, he had played as a child; that is, it should be turned into a temple with Go-Daigo's spirit as its deity.

The new institution thus established was called Tenryūji, the Temple of the Heavenly Dragon, after Takauji's dream. Musō Kokushi, who was, of course, its first abbot, set about at once reconstructing the buildings so they would be suitable for temple usage. A pagoda was the only new thing put up, but on a hill behind the garden Musō built his inevitable summer house looking out over the landscape.

The garden pond was cleaned, but there is no record of the garden's being otherwise changed and there is no evidence today that it was much changed, then or later. Today the garden of Tenryūji temple is still that built by Saneuji for the Emperor Go-Saga in the middle of the 13th century. It lies in the same quiet setting of green hills with the river winding out of its canyon nearby, now, as always, a perfect place for a retreat, sacred or secular.

The garden lies between the foot of a natural hillside and the building holding the abbot's state reception room, as once it must have lain before the main hall of the retired Emperor's villa. The garden is small compared to earlier ones, being only some two hundred feet long and a hundred and fifty feet wide. This reduced size marks one of the new trends in garden layout. The greater part of its area is taken up by the spreading pond, a bit of water as open and sunny as those of the old mansion gardens. It retains this old courtly atmosphere but could never have been used for actual boating since it is much too small. This water exists purely for ornament, to form part of the landscape picture seen from the house or to enhance the pleasure of anyone circling the path about it. In midsummer the still surface is crowded with lily pads, their small golden blossoms pushing up to open in the sunlight. In autumn, when leaves and flowers in the pool sink beneath the surface, the dark mirror reflects the gold of the fading tree foliage, while its small rocky islets rest on their own perfect reflections.

The lake is inclosed across from the buildings by a line of artificial hillocks. Tall trees growing out of them now form a high, inclosing wall of greenery which, lovely as it is, shuts out something which was once even finer. This was the view across the river to the green peak of Arashiyama which became an intrinsic part of the garden design. Musō Kokushi, who had little enough time, no doubt, to write poetry once he became abbot of Tenryūji, once jotted down a note which the temple still preserves, a note for a poem which he hoped to write when he had more leisure.

"On looking over to Arashiyama on a snowy day from the abbot's apartments," it goes.

The distant green slopes of this hill, lightly powdered in snow and seen through the whirling silvery flakes of a winter's day, would be fit subject, indeed, for poetry.

To improve the beauty of this distant hillside, Takauji caused numbers of cherry and maple trees to be planted among the perennial natural evergreens. Every spring since, the pink blossoms have misted the hills, while in autumn the maples have spread a rich russet over their slopes.

The picture created in the garden, as it appears to one sitting in the abbot's apartment, divides itself naturally into three parts, background, middle ground, and foreground. The distant peak and other natural hills form the background; the lake and its inclosing artificial hillocks are the middle ground; while the foreground is a stretch of land between the building and the near edge of the lake. This plan of Tenryūji is of particular interest since it is as nearly typical of the basic plan of an average small Japanese garden as may be found. It seems to have served as a prototype in later periods, and there is even reason to think that it was from a study of its details that all those curious rules were derived about such things as Guardian Stones, Guest Islands, and the like which encumbered gardening in the later centuries. This will be taken up again.

The general plan of this garden picture is obviously that of the old *shinden* lake gardens, but carried out on a greatly reduced scale and much better integrated. The level foreground stretching from the building to the edge of the lake is a remnant of the old forecourt before the *shinden* mansion. This foreground area gains interest in Tenryūji from a small rocky peninsula which projects out obliquely into the lake. Its shoreline is strengthened by large stones around it, while a single large rock, lying off

What does it mean, this mysterious straight line of stones across the ponds of old gardens? No one knows, but it may represent a convoy of junks moored for the night in some safe haven. This group in the upper pond of Saihōji is one of the smaller examples. (Photo by Harada Sunao.)

"Austere rocks and sublime precipices"—Mount Sumeru, a great peak rising from an illimitable ocean, was the Buddhist concept of the universe. It was often portrayed in miniature as here in Tenryūji, where the imagination is called on to lift it to transcendental heights. This rock arrangement, one of the finest in the whole range of Oriental garden art, was probably made by a Chinese rockcraftsman and represents the garden artistry of Sung China. (Photo by the author.)

the tip, forms a pointed islet. This layout is founded on sound geographical knowledge, and the emphasis and repetition of its lines are highly pleasing.

Around the shore of the lake are other peninsulas and projections, smaller than this central one, but giving, altogether, variety and interest to the picture. These projections are also emphasized by rocks, but there are smooth stretches of the lake shore between, which are quite plain, molded only with sod or moss. The lake bottom is made of clay finished on the surface with a hard pavement of small stones. It has resisted the centuries, for experts believe this same bottom has served for the whole seven hundred years the garden has been in existence.

The artificial hillock behind the lake is the "miniature mountain" so often heard about in Japanese gardens. It is a long, encircling embankment, about seventeen feet high, made of soil taken from the lake excavation. Once, it probably was rather irregular in form, with small peaks and gullies, but time has worn this down to a rounded mound. The soil is held in place today by a basketlike network of the tree roots growing in it. Here and there in this embankment are set large stones, singly or in harmonious groups, suggesting the outcropping of the stony foundation of the hills. These rocks were placed on beds of smaller stones which held them in place. In the embankment may be found places where former stones have been removed, probably to grace some other garden. The trees and shrubs growing in this embankment extend far above it and mask its actual top so that the ground seems to go much higher than in reality. Against the distant background of the actual hills, this tree-covered, artificial "mountain" forms a connecting link tying the garden into its place in the landscape with perfect naturalness.

The middle ground of the lake and inclosing embankment possesses a focal point of interest in the form of three rock arrangements, a cascade, a stone bridge, and a rocky islet. The tall, rocky cascade is set into the embankment at the head of a small inlet from the lake; the bridge crosses this inlet, while the islet near one end of the bridge balances the group. Together, they form a picture of harmonious interest as seen from the building across the water. But the details of this group may be seen much better on a stroll around the lake. The path taken on such a stroll leads around the shore and over the bridge, so that the cascade may be viewed from its foot. Looking up, it appears to tower high for it is topped by a very large boulder that forms a rocky peak. The stroll around the lake was planned by the original designer, we know, because of the size and strength of the bridge. It will hold a person comfortably and was built in the beginning with the other features of the garden. Here, the stroll around the lake took the place entirely of the boating in earlier gardens. It is another transition feature.

At one end of the lake a small, earthen island holds trees. It was once, evidently, a turtle island, but now only the stone which formed the lifted head of the creature remains to prove it. Of chief interest among the other islands in the lake is the outstanding stone group near the bridge. This is one of the finest things in the whole range of Japanese garden artistry, a masterpiece unrivaled by any other arrangement. No matter from what spot on the shore we view it, the seven stones which compose it show always a balanced harmonic form. Such an achievement in the round is supremely difficult, as anyone knows who has tried to make a flower arrangement which shall be equally beautiful from every side.

The central stone of this island group is a tall, soaring, rocky pinnacle, pointed, slightly slanting, rising some five feet above the water. About it are grouped lesser stones, some flat-topped, giving strength with their planes and pronounced angles, others pointed, in sharp contrast. Others, again, are almost level with the water, creating a feeling of strong stability in the group. A few seedling pines and other plantlets have found a root-hold on the weathered surface of these rocks and now add softening grace to their rugged outlines. But, on the whole, we see a vast mountain rising from the sea, as if we were soaring over some wild volcanic group. Its great precipices are austere and sublime—and suddenly we realize that this must be Mount Sumeru, the mythical Buddhist concept of the universe, a great peak rising from an illimitable ocean, surrounded by rocky mountains. If, in

94

China long before, the garden *shumi-sen* had followed the Buddhist picture books and been built in goblet form with seven concentric rocky rings, such a form had vanished long since. Here is only a realistic conception of a great and awe-inspiring peak rising from the ocean, lifted by our imaginations from its five feet to any height we care to make it.

Here we have a supremely artistic example of the "miniature" aspect of Japanese gardens which has been so often written about. The rocky *shumi-sen* of Tenryūji illustrates excellently the fact that always there are two phases or two scales in these "miniature" gardens, the realistic and the imaginative. In its realistic, outward aspects, the gardens remain always on the scale of the human being who is viewing it as the rocks in this group form only an islet jutting out of a garden pond. But when they are looked at with the eye of the imagination, they begin to expand and grow to any heights we care to let them.

By such a play of the imagination are some—not all—Japanese gardens made into replicas of a wide natural landscape. But the effect of an actual panoramic landscape is no more attempted literally in these gardens than it is in a landscape painting; such an attempt would only result in something akin to a topographical map. Instead, as the painter uses his brush and color, so the garden maker uses his stones, plants, and water to achieve his effects through suggestion, simplification, abridgement; sometimes by convention and symbolism. The result is an arrangement of rocks and plants which is to be taken at its face value for exactly what it is —a bit of naturalistic gardening. Or, transformed by a creative imagination, it may be much more. In other words, the larger landscape in a garden is actually not reproduced in the garden itself, but in the mind of the beholder. The onlooker must contribute almost as much as the garden maker himself. If the beholder is unable to create the larger landscape, it does not exist—for him.

This fact has been a source of wide misunderstanding on the part of foreigners who come to see the gardens not quite knowing what to expect.

THE ART OF JAPANESE GARDENS

When we first look at them, we are baffled and puzzled by the assertion that Japanese gardens reproduce great landscape pictures. We can see with our own eyes that they do nothing of the sort; that they are, in fact, only naturalistic gardens which are peculiarly successful for sufficient technical reasons. Westerners are familiar with subjectivity in music, but it is rather new to us in the plastic arts. We can, perhaps, best understand these gardens by letting them touch our imagination and speak to us directly, as music does, without words or conscious concepts.

The second stone composition in Tenryūji, the bridge, goes back entirely to realism. Crossing the small inlet which leads to the foot of the cascade, it is entirely functional, made to carry the path and nothing else. Yet it is completely harmonious with the rest of the garden. Simple, strong, and graceful in its design, it gives just the suggestion needed of man's presence in an otherwise natural picture, but it suggests man in a mood of complete harmony with nature, man adapting its forms to his use, rather than dominating and forcing them. The bridge is made entirely of natural, uncut stones, laid together without cement. Three long, thin, flat stones laid end to end serve as planks to be walked on; where the ends join, foundation pillars of natural stone rise from the water to support them. The tops of these supporting stones may be invisibly chipped so that they hold the others securely, but no hint of this appears outwardly.

The cascade behind the bridge rises directly from the lake, its main face a high, flat surface of rock some seven feet tall and four feet broad. This huge rock (which is really a thin slab) is supported on either side by large boulders which turn the little inlet into a sort of short, rocky fjord. Above the main fall, the water swirls through a rushing cascade among other large stones. One of them, several feet long, vaguely resembles a fish and is called the Carp Stone. It is meant to suggest a fish swimming up the torrent to spawn. Above this swirling cascade is the second fall, about three feet high, formed by a second flat-faced rock. At the top the cascade is crowned by a huge, pointed stone peak. In its every line the structure suggests the immense strength of rock and the tremendous dynamic movement of water. Yet there is not a drop in it, only the feeling of pouring torrents.[2]

There is a striking resemblance between the Tenryūji cascade and another, which probably was built a few years afterward by the same Saneuji who was father to Go-Saga's Empress and builder of the original Kameyama-dono. This other cascade, which we shall come to a little later, is now in the garden of the Gold Pavilion where it was originally a part of Saneuji's own villa. Both these cascades seem necessarily to be the work of the same artist, but who he was we do not know. The name of Tachibana is the only one occurring in the records of Kameyama-dono; he was the commissioner and might, of course, have been the designer as well. But probably he was not, for the style of stonework in Tenryūji leads one to think that it must have been done, not by a Japanese at all, but by some wandering Chinese rockcraftsman. Its style exemplifies the current Chinese form and feeling in landscape art, as depicted in the landscape paintings, but this style was then almost unknown in Japan.

Japanese intercourse with China had almost ceased for a long period during the latter part of the Heian epoch, and cultured Japanese had been busy creating their own distinctive art forms from the elements they had earlier assimilated. But when, in the Kamakura period, interest in Zen began to increase, travel back and forth to China was resumed once more. Those coming and going were chiefly Japanese students of Zen and Chinese teachers of its elements. It was during this time—the 12th and 13th

[2] On special occasions—for instance during the visit of the Garden Club of America in 1935—a thin flow of real water is conducted to the top of the artificial hillock and allowed to flow down through the cascade. It is lifted to the top in a bamboo conduit carried on stilts across the glade behind. This thin trickle of water is almost invisible, but this doesn't matter for its function is to sing. Across the flat face of the upper rock, which slants inward slightly, the streamlet falls into an invisible earthen pot buried at the foot. As it strikes the water, it makes a thin tinkling sound. This arrangement for water was made as a later addition to the garden; it seems quite unnecessary, for a fall of such strength as is suggested by the powerful rocks would roar rather than tinkle. But any sound of falling water is charming, and perhaps in a peaceful temple garden, this thin sound is not out of keeping with the general atmosphere.

centuries—that China was at the height of its great Sung civilization. The Mongols, to be sure, hung in the north like a dark, threatening cloud and, finally, when the storm broke, they swept down on K'ai-fêng, the northern capital, where the artist-Emperor, Hui Tsung, had built his great Ken Yu rock garden. After this loss the Sung court was reorganized at Hangchow, on West Lake. Later this city, too, was taken by the barbarians and there was no longer a Chinese empire, but only Chinese culture. This, however, was able to overthrow its conquerors at last and set up the Ming dynasty. But the years were upset ones, and many scholars and artists sought refuge in distant parts; some of them were even willing to cross the seas to Japan.

The supreme art production of the Sung period was landscape painting. These pictures were executed in black ink and watered greys on paper and silk with vigorous brush strokes or soft washes. In the hands of a master this medium was capable of conveying all the strength and vigor of vast, tumbled mountains, soaring peaks, dark valleys, and leaping cataracts. Those who painted them were attempting to represent, not a definite landscape, but the essential quality of all nature. To this end they often exaggerated the towering of great peaks or the strength of a precipice. The cascade and islet of Tenryūji hold just that vigor and power which we find in the landscapes and the same hint of exaggeration. Altogether, the likeness between them is exact; they are unmistakably works of Sung artistry.

But it must not be forgotten that this garden was made about 1256; Sung painting was then at its height in China, but very little was known about it as yet in Japan. Japanese Zen priests coming home from China may have brought back a few of the Sung paintings, but it was to take over a hundred years before the knowledge and understanding of Sung art was to show its effect in general on Japanese art.

Curiously, it was Takauji himself and Tenryūji temple which were largely instrumental in introducing Sung art to their country. At the suggestion of Musō Kokushi or some other Zen priest familiar with conditions in China, it had been decided to send a ship direct to that country to bring back the fine decorations and ecclesiastical equipment desired for the new monastery. This voyage was made in 1342 and was such a success that other institutions of the kind also sent ships. Out of their voyages grew up, in time, a renewed trade with China which was highly profitable to its Japanese sponsors and brought into Japan many fine art objects which unsettled conditions in China threw into the market. They make the Chinese collections in Japan, to this day, the finest in the world. This trade continued to be managed by Zen priests for a long time.

Tenryūji garden, however, was old long before this trade had ever begun. Because its rockwork is a masterpiece of Chinese landscape artistry and not in any way the attempt of an amateur copyist in this field, we are led to the conclusion, inevitably, that it must have been done by some Chinese garden craftsman who had wandered far from home, perhaps to escape the Mongols. No one else, it would seem, could have done it. In every line the stonework shows the hand of an experienced master in this art form. It is totally different from the Japanese stonework of this period.

This is proved to us by comparing it with its predecessor, the dry cascade in the mossy hillside garden of Saihōji temple which was made some sixty or seventy years earlier. In this earlier cascade we have, I think, a perfect example of what might be called pure Japanese stonework, the type of stone arrangement prevalent in the country before Sung artistry made itself felt, the product of independent Japanese development. When Saihōji was made, rock artistry had been developing in Japan away from any Chinese influence for a long time. It had become the cult of the Japanese garden makers to reproduce nature as exactly as possible, as we find plainly stated in the *Sakuteiki*. It is also borne out in the Saihōji cascade whose maker had obviously studied natural rock formations—Japanese of course—until he was able to reproduce them so well we are left to wonder sometimes whether, after all, they may not be natural. Nature in Japan is generally rounded, soft, and gentle, not wild and rugged as it is in parts of China. The Saihōji rockwork is likewise rounded and gentle, though by no means lacking in strength, but it is a static strength; all its stones are bluntly angled, and while many are huge, none is of peculiar or curiously distinctive shape. They have all been placed in the most stable position possible, that is, they are all "lying stones," horizontal with the ground, as time might have laid them down. The whole effect is one of repose and quiet.

Tenryūji's stonework, on the contrary, is filled with dynamic vigor. Almost every rock stands upright, its whole feeling one of powerful upward movement. In these two types of rock artistry we find contrasted the natural geographical features of the two countries; Japan, a land of mild and gentle nature, the China of the landscape painters, wild and fantastic. And out of this, no doubt, we find developed the two schools of rock artistry. Both are perfected techniques; one could not have grown out of the other in a short period. Tenryūji's rockwork must have been done by someone trained in the school of Sung rock artistry. It is interesting to realize that in this bridge, cascade, and island there exists, perhaps, the only surviving example of contemporaneously executed Sung garden art—certainly the only one known at present.

After Tenryūji, naturalism in Japan never again reached the heights it attained in Saihōji. Nature was no longer a master to be followed exactly for with the coming of Sung art, Japanese artists gave reign to their imaginations, swinging from the gentle, static quality of Japanese nature to the soaring inspiration of great cliffs and peaks. They created art first and nature afterward.

VIII. *Mansions of Muromachi*

PART I: THE GOLD PAVILION

AFTER Takauji and his vassal barons had returned and settled in Kyoto, the city presented an appearance very different from that of its old days during the Fujiwara ascendency. While the Kamakura regime lasted, life had gone on in the capital much as always. The nobles still held civilian court office and maintained much of their accustomed state. Most of them, it is true, had been getting poorer and poorer as time went on and their estates slipped into hardier hands, but, on the whole, things were not too bad. Elegance, though it had to be practiced with frugality, was still the dominant keynote of the court. Always these nobles had been the chief sight on the streets of the town, riding in their high, two-wheeled, lacquered carts drawn by slow-stepping oxen, attended by a group of outriders and retainers. The business of the other inhabitants had been to cater to their needs and fall in with their customs.

But with the coming of Takauji and the military lords from Kamakura this was changed. The new barons were now the really wealthy element in the country, their riches coming from lands fallen to them from the vanquished overlords of the Kamakura government. Takauji's generals in their gold-crested helmets and lacquered armor, laced with silken cords, were now the glittering and conspicuous figures on the streets of Kyoto. A hundred and fifty years before, the first military leaders had despised courtly effeminacy and made virtues of extreme simplicity and hardihood. But the later warriors had somewhat relaxed this code and acquired a taste for the amenities of life, learning many things from the Kyoto men who had come to Kamakura in the government service.

In Kamakura, the houses built by the military lords had been called "military-style mansions," *buke-zukuri*. They were modeled, in arrangement, upon the rambling collection of buildings that made up an aristocratic *shinden*, but they were greatly simplified as to details and decorations. The military mansions included extensive quarters for armed followers, stables for horses, and practice grounds for archery and other warlike arts. Small gardens before the main rooms may have been included, but gardening was certainly not one of the arts in which the earlier military men had been interested.

When the later barons settled in Kyoto, however, the times changed. They then set themselves to acquiring fine town houses and country estates in the manner of the court nobles. Takauji himself and his successor, who became the second Ashikaga shogun, had little leisure for such things; but their followers began to take over some of the older places, rebuilding them to suit themselves. Their activities were marked by the love of show characteristic of the newly rich everywhere. We read, for instance,[1] of Ko no Moronao, one of Takauji's most trusted lieutenants, who "made over an old mansion, building a Chinese gate and a hall with end-pavilions and tall buildings. It made a very grand sight."

Probably this "tall" building had two stories, differing from the old *shinden* halls which had but one. The mention of end-pavilions shows, however, that, in general, the old mansion style was still being followed.

We get a farther graphic glimpse of Kyoto streets as the *Taiheiki* continues with a description of Ko no Moronao's garden.

"Large stones were brought for the lake edge from the provinces of Ise, Saiga and Shima. Axles on the carts squeaked and often broke; oxen panted and lolled their tongues."

The stones from Saiga, we know from other surviving examples, were of a curious bluish color.

[1] *Taiheiki.*

Trees and plants were collected for Ko no Moronao's garden as modern
Japanese millionaires collect valuable curios. The cherries, for instance, were
brought from Yoshino, which is still the most famous cherry blossom place
in Japan. Maples and chrysanthemums came from spots made famous by
well-known poems. A "reedy hamlet" was constructed in the garden, based
on a description by the popular poet Saigyō, of a view near the seacoast at
Naniwa. All these items, expensively gathered, spread the fame of Ko no
Moronao whose haughty behavior, it is said, was what might be expected
of such a person.

The court aristocrats viewed all these goings on with the typical disdain
of the old regime for the *nouveaux riches*. With lands largely usurped and
incomes meager, these nobles yet held themselves aloof, living with whatever of slender elegance they could manage. Nevertheless, as they still controlled access to the court and its honors, they were often approached by
aspiring barons who desired social rank and court position. It is said that a
chief source of income for needy aristocrats during this period came from
their efforts in procuring such honorary court titles.

As time went on, the old Kyoto culture of the aristocrats began to
impose its restraining canons of taste on the newcomers, subduing their
exuberance. Another restraining influence was Zen with its strong association with art, which was becoming better understood, giving meaning to
much creative work. Patterned and restrained by the old courtly culture,
derived from the T'ang period, strengthened by the warrior's vigor, and
now electrified by the beauty of Sung art, inspiration and technique reached
maturity together in the next period, producing gardens which for artistry
and sheer beauty have probably never been excelled in any period or any
country.

It was the grandson of Takauji, the third Ashikaga Shogun, Yoshimitsu, who took the lead in building these gardens. Living between 1358
and 1408, he was a true product of his times, a fusion of the forces which
made it great. As an administrator, he was able to bring about a reconcili-
ation between the two imperial courts, one in Yoshino and one in Kyoto,

whose factional fights had disrupted the country for over fifty years. He also possessed a keen interest in art and esthetics and was a sincere student of Zen. It was this Shogun, who, as a young man, had astonished the gay party of courtiers on a visit to the mossy old temple of Saihōji by leaving the pleasure seekers on the lake and meditating with his Zen teacher on the quiet hillside.

The mansion which Yoshimitsu built as his palace and shogunal headquarters stood in the northeastern part of the city which, ever since that day, has been the best residential district of Kyoto. The place was called Muromachi Hall, that is, Muromachi-dono, after Muromachi, the street on which it fronted. The government headquarters centered in this place and from it has been derived the name by which historians designate the period during which the Ashikaga shoguns were greatest, that is, approximately the century between 1392 and 1490. Muromachi-dono was a splendid mansion with a great garden, occupying a large city block.[2] The garden contained such quantities of flowering trees that it was popularly called the Flowery Palace, Hana-no-gosho. The word "flowers" in Japanese poetic language always means cherry blossoms unless otherwise specified, and we know those of the Flowery Palace were the weeping cherry, for the record[3] tells how the young trees were given as an arranged gift from a court noble to the Shogun. We can picture this garden when April opened the buds, the flower-laden trees appearing like a mass of pink mist drifting around the lake or like a delicate rain of color reflected in the shimmering, dark water. To describe the scene adequately, the same record harks back to the ancient glamorous tale of the Immortals' Islands, with the words:

"A vision of the Three Isles and a ship sailing to them could not be fairer than this."

This reference to the half-forgotten Chinese tale was characteristic of the times. A tremendous new fad for things Chinese was sweeping the elite

---

[2] The present lines are written on part of its site, but no trace remains except, possibly, a large and beautiful old rock in an adjoining missionary garden.

[3] *Gukanki.*

of Japan as the result of Takauji's renewed trade with China. Every ship brought in new examples of exquisite Sung art which were eagerly appropriated and studied by the wealthy new dilettantes. Yoshimitsu took the lead in this fad as in other ways, gathering around him connoisseurs, artists, and poets. He often wore Chinese costume, it is said, and had himself carried about in a Chinese palanquin. A great revival of interest in Chinese verse also marked the times, led by Zen priests who had studied in China. Many Chinese literary allusions crept into the gardens in the naming of stones and islands.

The pace set by Yoshimitsu in building the Flowery Palace was followed by his great vassals. We read of fine estates put up in the Muromachi district by such powerful barons as the lords of Hosokawa, Yamana, and Ōuchi. Large lakes, islands, bridges, and pavilions were in all of these estates.

Yoshimitsu was on excellent terms with the court and contributed generously to its support. On one occasion, even, the Emperor resided for a time in the Flowery Palace itself, when the mansion which had been serving as his palace was burned. For a long time the sovereigns had been living in estates, such as Kameyama-dono, outside the old imperial inclosure which was nearly in ruins. One of these outside mansions, not far from the house of Ko no Moronao, belonged to a Fujiwara family whose daughters became imperial consorts. It was called Tsuchi-mikado-dono. Over a long period of years, this place was finally settled on as the permanent residence of the emperors. Of all the great estates near the Flowery Palace, therefore, only this one has survived. Its outlines exist today, approximately, in those of the Imperial Palace of Kyoto, but nothing remains of the early Tsuchi-mikado-dono. The present palace buildings are a late replica of those of early Heian, while the imperial garden dates only from the 18th century.

All the other great estates in the Muromachi district have disappeared, as houses and shops of the city have encroached on their ruins. But some of the Muromachi estates which had been built as country retreats on the edge of the town have been more fortunate. Foremost among these is the estate Yoshimitsu built for his own retirement. It is popularly called, now, the Gold Pavilion Temple, or Kinkakuji, although its correct name is Rokuonji, the Deer Park Temple. This name was given to it by the Shogun. It did not refer to real deer in the park, but was taken from the Buddhist scriptures. Rokuya-on was the place where Gautama first addressed his followers after attaining Enlightenment.

When a very young man, Yoshimitsu had once mentioned his hope [4] of some day creating a "Deer Park" where he could devote himself to leisure and the arts. He was able to do this when he was about thirty-seven, for then he ostensibly turned over his shogunal office and the Flowery Palace to his nine-year-old son. In reality, of course, he continued to govern from retirement but he was relieved from the ceremonies of his office.

As a site for the new estate, Yoshimitsu acquired a fine old villa which had belonged to that same Saneuji who had built the country estate of Kameyama-doño for his retired imperial son-in-law a century before. The estate which Yoshimitsu bought, Saneuji had inherited from his father, Fujiwara no Kintsune. This court noble had supported Yoritomo, the Minamoto leader, at the time the Kamakura government was being formed, and for this support he had been, in due course, suitably rewarded with much land and the hand of the warlord's sister, making him, probably, the richest and most powerful noble in the court. He had built for himself this country estate north of the city which was called, in consequence, the North Hill villa, or Kitayama-den. On it he constructed a temple, called Saionji, by which name the family has since been known. A generation later, when the estate came into the possession of Saneuji, opportunity apparently was taken to improve it by adding a cascade, utilizing, it would seem, the services of that same Chinese rockcraftsman who had recently been employed to make the garden at Arashiyama for the retired Emperor Go-Saga and Saneuji's daughter. This cascade still survives as part of the garden which Yoshimitsu constructed on the site of the old North Hill villa.

[4] *Kanrin Koroshū.*

This villa had stood somewhat high on a hillside, with a splendid sweeping view across to the Eastern Hills. Its large old pond, with the typical middle island of a *shinden* estate, survives to this day, although now it serves only as a reservoir for the lake of the new garden. Water flowing out of this pond and down the hillside created an opportunity for the new cascade which must have been somewhat outside the main garden of the older villa.

The main face of this cascade in the Gold Pavilion garden is a great flat surface of rock, some eight feet high and five feet wide, which rises, cliff-like, from a small pool. The rock is tilted slightly forward, so that the stream falls clear of its face. A slight irregularity at the top divides the falling water into two parallel columns which strike a large stone at the bottom and spatter in a silver shower over the whole surface of the small pool, wetting the water grasses and small ferns which grow in the crannies.

The stone which the water strikes is of curious shape, set up on one of its thin edges, twisted in form until it takes but little imagination to see it as a gigantic fish headed into the waterfall, fantastically big for the small pool. There can be little doubt that it was intended to create this suggestion, for carp swimming up a waterfall had become a Chinese symbol of virtue. In the Yellow River fish struggling over the rapids to spawn gave rise to the legend that those who succeeded became dragons, great and beneficent spirits of water and rain. From this the lesson was taught that men, also, who struggled and won over the adversities of life became dragon-spirited, or superior beings.[5]

The presence of this Chinese symbol, placed in a Japanese garden long before the fad for Chinese things had been renewed in Yoshimitsu's day, seems to provide added evidence that the master-craftsman who made it was, indeed, a Chinese of the Sung school. The very size of the stone fish,

[5] This symbolism is persistent in Japan to the present day. At the Boys' Festival, *Tango no sekku,* on May 5, huge, leaping paper fish, made on the principle of tubular flying-field flags, are hung out to leap and twist in the wind, reminding boys of the virtues of hardihood and patient endurance.

huge in that tiny pool, is one of the humorous grotesqueries which is characteristic of the Chinese but foreign to the Japanese temperament.

It may have been this cascade on the lower hillside which gave Yoshimitsu the idea of building his new retiring palace at the lower level. The mansion was put up on a broad level space which at present is carpeted with moss and shaded by old trees. The garden lake was excavated in front of the buildings. The old cascade probably became part of some small rear garden overlooked by a private apartment. The overflow from its pool may have meandered around the buildings in the *shinden* style, until at last it flowed into the lake across the forecourt.

In general, the style of the buildings seems to have followed the *shinden* type, but with considerable modification of detail. This is evident in the only one of the buildings which now survives, called the Gold Pavilion, which gives its popular name to the garden today. Originally this pavilion stood a short way in the lake and was reached by a small bridge. It seems to have been a modified form of the old end-pavilion, but new influences entered strongly into its general design.

Its name, the Gold Pavilion, prepares us for something so gorgeous that the first glimpse of it is likely to be rather disappointing. The romantic title came from the fact that the interior of the upper story was once covered with gold leaf. As we see it across the lake today, however, it is an old, unpainted wooden structure crowned by an inconspicuous bronze phoenix. Rising against its green background, it seems small, even dingy, with the centuries. We wonder why it should rank as one of the three great architectural treasures of Japan—along with the splendid old Phoenix Hall at Uji and the incredible Hōryūji monastery near Nara, 1300 years old. Yet, if we will walk around the lake, viewing the pavilion from various angles as it was meant to be seen by one floating in a boat, we begin to understand Sir George Sansom when he says:

"It is, none the less, both a technical and an artistic triumph. Its technical merits, according to specialists, lie in its successful blending of styles and in a lightness of construction obtained by what in those days must

Water in the cascade of the Gold Pavilion garden falls over the eight-foot cliff of the large rock which forms its face and spatters in a silver shower over the small pool below. This cascade apparently was made in the Kamakura period, long before Yoshimitsu's day, and seems to be an example of Sung garden artistry, like the arrangements in Tenryūji garden. (Photo by Harada Sunao.)

The Gold Pavilion, so-called from the gilded ceiling of the upper story, is one of the three architectural treasures of Japan. Its design grew out of the old end-pavilion of the shinden mansion but was strongly influenced by the current Chinese mode. Probably Yoshi-mitsu, its builder, imagined the garden and pavilion to be like those around West Lake at Hangchow in China, source of the Sung art he so much admired. (Photo by Okamoto Toyo.)

have been a daring sacrifice of the accepted margin of safety. As for its beauty, it relies upon a harmony and delicacy of proportion so just that because of its very rightness, it leaves no impression upon a careless observer."

We can appreciate this to the utmost when we see it on a winter morning with snow lying deep and untouched, the trees drooping under great loads of feathery whiteness. Against the powdered green of the hillside, the building stands out in sudden startling beauty, its slender grace and delicately curving lines etched above the coldly frozen lake. On its Japanese side, this building was undoubtedly a descendant of the old end-pavilion style as already mentioned; but in its general design and detail it reflected the new and popular Chinese mode. I think there can be no doubt but that Yoshimitsu, in building it, had in mind the romantic garden pavilions beside the lake at Hangchow, of which he must have heard much from traveled priests—pavilions like those of the Willow Pattern plate and the present day survival, at the Three Pools of the Moon's Reflection. The quiet beauty of the Gold Pavilion's setting in the lake, its Chinese lines, all point to Hangchow as its inspiration.

We can picture Yoshimitsu using this building when it was completed. The lower story was undoubtedly a miniature *shinden* hall, in which he received special guests—artists and scholarly priests. The second story was a study to which they retired for discussions of art and esthetics. From its balcony they could enjoy the most perfect view of the garden. Seated there, they handled lovingly the exquisite examples of Sung art just arrived by the latest ship, studied and ranked them as to merit. Probably in this room, too they enjoyed the incense ceremony, performed the tea ritual and here, no doubt, were planned many of the *Nō* dramas which were created under Yoshimitsu's patronage. The top story, with its gilded ceiling, gives evidence of having been a small private Zen chapel; its bell-shaped Chinese windows are like those still characteristic of Zen temple architecture.

Tea drinking, as it was practiced at the time of Yoshimitsu, was not the elaborate ritual performed for its own ends which it became at a later date. Tea had been introduced in the Kamakura period from Sung China where it was drunk in a religious ceremonial designed to induce wakefulness during meditation. Tea drinking had later developed another ceremonial form, a sort of tea-tasting competition, similar to the incense ceremony, in which the flavor of the leaves grown in different localities was to be distinguished and expressed by apt literary allusions. We do not know which of these forms was followed by Yoshimitsu in the Gold Pavilion, but tradition states that the water which he used came from two rocky springs which are now special features of the garden.

They lie at the foot of the hillside, set about with stones. The first is a squared recess in the slope, its flat roof upheld by a slab of stone which rests on the upright rocks lining the recess. Cool and inviting, the water lies in this shadowy rockbound pool and glistens as it trickles down the mossy backwall. The second spring is an open pool lying in an angle of the hillside surrounded by massive rocks. A small thatched roof keeps leaves from falling into the water; it is supported by peeled branches made into a rustic cantilever arrangement. Both pools have flat kneeling-stones in front for dipping up the water.

While the general plan of the whole estate followed the old *shinden* style, it was modified by drawing on all the elements which contributed to the times. China was there in its general similarity to Hangchow, and the influence of Sung artistry is evident in some of the rockwork. There are hints of the Elysian romance of the Immortals' Isles, and if one cared to see it that way the whole lake might be taken to represent the Western Paradise of Amida. Zen canons of taste (which have been summed up as the avoidance of the trite, the obvious, and the emphatic)[6] were influential in the careful restraint everywhere evident. And from Zen came, also, that overtone of emotional depth and the mystery of beauty called *yūgen*, which Zen artists consciously strove to create. While the garden was conceived and executed on the magnificent scale of Yoshimitsu's era, it was carried out with the freedom, freshness, and simplicity of an art in its youthful period. All

[6] Sansom.

together, these factors created a work which is probably the finest of the estate gardens Japan has known. There is a spaciousness, a regal grandeur, an artistic delicacy about it not equaled in any other garden in Japan.

There is every reason to believe that Yoshimitsu was his own designer. No mention is made of another in the records, nor is anyone else known who was capable of doing it. No doubt he sought suggestions and help from the connoisseurs with whom he consorted, but it would be directly in the tradition of great garden making in Japan if the plan were quite his own.

The pavilion was the central point for viewing the garden. Seated in it today, we can still enjoy the fine beauty of the lake and its setting. No matter what the season the outlook from the pavilion is beautiful. The lake is rimmed by fine, tremendous trees which do not, however, seem to shut it in, for above them rises a small pointed green peak, exactly the right size to fit into the landscape. It is known, from its shape, as Silk Hat Hill, that is, Kinu-gasa-yama. Rising against the sky at the foot of the garden, this little peak is definitely part of its design.[7]

The lake spreads mirror-like, holding the reflection of the green peak, the trees and islands. In spring, azaleas cast scarlet shadows into the water, and purple iris bloom in shallows along the shore. In summer, the water surface is patterned with the green polka dots of lily pads. In autumn, tall reeds rally their pointed spears around the islets, and on the distant shore maples blaze gorgeously. In winter's grey light, the white flakes whirl lazily above the silvery surface of the water, piling in silent white drifts on every rock and stone. An ineffable quietness and peace hang over the garden, not to be caught by anything tangible, but so real it is the inner essence of the scene.

It is interesting to inquire into the technique and details by which some of these effects are gained. On the outer or valley side of the garden, the

[7] The legendary extravagance of the time survives in a belief that on a hot summer day Yoshimitsu ordered this small hill covered with lengths of white silk to suggest a cooling fall of snow.

lake is supported by an embankment formed of the excavated material. Toward the right this bank rises into an artificial hillock, its broad rounded top some fifteen feet above the water. This rising ground swings round the lake and joins a spur descending from the natural hillside behind, so that the whole of the garden is embraced and protected. A path follows around the lake but it was never an important part of the garden. Boating, not walking, was the diversion provided for, a fact made clear by the placement of some of the finest rock arrangements where they can be seen only from a boat. The old records mention many boating parties floating over the mirror surface of the water, with the rocks and islands forming constantly changing pictures and the graceful form of the pavilion rising above the flood, with little Silk Hat Hill at the other end of the picture.

From the pavilion the lake appears much larger than it is in reality, an effect achieved by bold and clever handling of the vistas and perspective. Standing in the pavilion, it is not until we consider the height of the trees on the opposite shore that we realize how close to us they really are. The principal device used to obtain this effect is division of the lake into two parts, of which the inner, nearer half is filled with interesting rocks and islands to keep the eye busy, while beyond it the outer half is empty and dimly seen, suggesting vaguely illimitable distances.

The division of the lake is made by means of a peninsula and a long island. Jutting out from the right shore, the peninsula turns what would be the lake's virtually oval form into an approximate heart-outline. The long narrow island continues the line of the peninsula. A vista between them to the opposite shore is left open, and at its lower end, the lake opens into a wide sweep of clear water.

In the distance, beyond the central island, are some lesser islands and rocky islets. They are deceptively small to enhance the perspective. The far shore of the lake has almost no stones visible on it, in strong contrast to the near shore of the central island and the peninsula which hold many. This device, too, creates a feeling of enhanced distance, as if the other side of the lake were too far away for its details to be seen.

The inner half of the lake holds no less than five other islands and many rocky islets. Single rocks, jutting above the surface, are often called "floating stones" by the Japanese, for they seem to float on the quiet water. Several in this lake are of immense size, placed at a considerable distance from the pavilion where they can remain in proper proportion to the rest of the landscape. Some of these large stones were gifts to Yoshimitsu from his vassals, for a large stone of fine shape and texture was considered a princely gift. They still bear the names of the donors, great names such as Akamatsu, Hatakeyama, and Hosokawa.

Directly in front of the pavilion is a smaller pointed stone, called the "Nine Mountains and Eight Seas." Here is our old friend the *shumi-sen* wearing a descriptive subtitle. If the *shumi-sen* once possessed the characteristics of the mythical Mount Sumeru—its goblet form, and seven concentric rocky rings inclosing circular seas—they had long since disappeared. The Nine Mountain stone is here simply a limestone rock about a foot above the water, quaintly shaped like a miniature mountain with canyons worn in its flanks.

Most of the larger islands are of the turtle type, the upraised head and half-submerged flippers being easily distinguished among the other stones. In this garden the ancient concept of the isles which were stabilized by giant turtles to keep their motion from annoying the Immortals finds its most graphic and delightful expression. The stones used for the head are unmistakable, the creatures at times seem almost to look at us, while their flippers appear to move lazily through the water. Trees and grasses grow on the island so that it is not merely the crude representation of an animal. The number of these turtle islands—there is a pair passing each other at the side of the pavilion, a small one[8] in front of it, with its traditional companion, the crane, and at least two others—causes us to realize how greatly the whimsical humor of this fancy appealed to Yoshimitsu. When we have smiled with him in this, we seem to have known him across the centuries.

Other islands, especially the long narrow one which lies through the

[8] Shown in the frontispiece.

center of the lake, are bordered with stonework also. Careful artistry went into the arrangement of these stones, so that they give a feeling of strength and stability and an artistic satisfaction in their balanced forms, reflected in the water below. The most conspicuous rock arrangement is made up of three large stones in traditional balanced form, placed on the central shore of the island directly across from the pavilion. But there are other fine groupings, quite out of sight, to be discovered in a boat.

The practice of boating probably explains a group of stones in the water which seems to be the cause of considerable mystery. They are squared stones in a straight line extending out from the shore and parallel to the platform on which the pavilion stands. They are in just the right position to prevent a boat drawn up beside this platform from swinging away. There seems to be no reason for any but this perfectly practical explanation, yet some students have seen in this line of stones a development of the old *yodo-mari,* the straight line of stones which crossed some of the old *shinden* lakes. To suggest that these stones were intended to represent a line of boats stretching from the shore toward the Island of the Immortals seems quite unnecessary.

The most splendid boating party ever held on this lake was the one with which Yoshimitsu entertained the Emperor when the estate was completed in 1408. The Emperor Go-Komatsu and the greater part of the court were invited to spend several days. The invitation was accepted—the first time in history that the honor of such a visit had been bestowed on anyone not a court noble. It took place in early April when the cherry blossoms were at the peak of their perfection and it became one of the famous excursions of Japanese history.

Several chronicles[9] record the splendor of this occasion. The Emperor left his palace in great state, attended by a long procession of courtiers and nobles. Throngs of common people lined the streets between the palace gate and that of the Shogun's villa as the procession passed. Arrived at the villa, the party of guests moved up an outer avenue through a grove of

[9] *Kita-yama-den Gyokoki; Kita-yama Miyuki.*

blooming cherry trees, both single and double. The twelve days of the visit were filled with all kinds of entertainment, feasting, drinking, music, dancing, boating, and poem composition. Of special interest is the mention of an exhibition of miniature gardens only a few feet square in which were constructed Elysian islands, cascades and mountains, with pine trees, turtles, and cranes.

The first evening of the visit there was a boating and poem party on the lake. The Emperor was in one boat, Yoshimitsu in another, and still others were filled with princes and courtiers. Fragrant pine knot fires were lighted in swinging iron baskets along the shore, a form of illumination seen even today at old festivals. Probably, too, each boat had also its blazing fire basket swinging on an arched crane from the bow. Music by a group of players in a boat swept across the black water, and the glowing light was reflected from the blossoming trees to the polished dark mirror below.

Subjects for the poems were given out as the boats started; those in the Chinese language were to be on "An Imperial Progress on a Spring Day," while in Japanese they were to be about "Cranes Beside the Pond." The latter was probably chosen because of its happy suggestions of longevity, or, possibly, because a crane may have alighted in the garden during the day, a circumstance which would have been considered singularly propitious. Even yet, the wild cranes come to this old garden lake; standing sometimes on the far shore under the pines, they are as quiet as bronze images.

When the thin wavering music of flute and shō[10] stopped playing, the boats pulled into the shore, and the poems were read in the pavilion. As might have been expected, most of those whose work was acclaimed were court nobles, long practiced in this art. The poem of Fujiwara Shigemitsu has come down to us, expressing the wish for long life and happiness:

> *In the water*
> *Under the pines by the shore*
> *Stands the friendly crane.*

[10] A kind of ancient harmonica.

A thousand and eight thousand years
Will he live on.[11]

But after all Yoshimitsu did not live much longer. Two months after his grand party he was dead. The magnificent estate was turned, at his wish, into a temple, his monument and finest memorial, and, as such, has come down the five and a half centuries since.

[11] *Ike mizu no*
Migiwa no matsu no
Tomozuru wa
Chiyo ni yachi yo wo
Soete sumu ra mu.

IX. *Mansions of Muromachi*

PART II: THE SILVER PAVILION

THE son whom Yoshimitsu had left as a child shogun in the Flowery Palace grew into a youth interested only in the esthetic
pleasures his father had enjoyed in his later years. Successive
shoguns had similar interests, leaving government to their guardians and
advisors, those great barons who contended for power during the next
decades. The names of these lords appear often in garden annals, for the
building of fine estates was one of their chief expressions of prestige. But
behind this was their desire for more wealth and power through lands and
men. Among them, however, no single individual was able to make himself stronger than all the rest and so displace the weak Ashikaga shoguns.
This unstable equilibrium created a half-century of peace after Yoshimitsu's
death, during which the arts reached one of the highest points they have
ever attained in Japan.

The capital was a rich and brilliant city during this period, filled not
only with the fine estates of the court nobles and great barons, but with
hundreds of lesser residences of a high order.

"Even men who made medicine and fortune telling their professions
and petty officials like secretaries, had stately residences," says a com-
mentator.[1] "There were some two hundred such buildings constructed entirely of white pine and having four-post gates [that is, gates with flank
entrances for persons of inferior rank]. Then there were a hundred

---

[1] Quoted from an unnamed authority by Captain Brinkley in *Japan*, Volume II.

provincial nobles great and small, each of whom had a stately residence, so that there were, all together, from six thousand to seven thousand houses of a fine type in the capital."

The riches necessary to maintain the city in this state were derived, of course, from the common people, who had to be taxed almost fantastically to provide them. Japanese peasants have always been long-suffering under oppression, but during this period they were often goaded into desperate demonstrations of resistance. Riots usually followed a natural calamity, a drought or flood, which had destroyed the crops and brought on famine. In the wake of famine came epidemics when thousands of the sick and starving crowded into the brilliant capital, hoping for help. Little or nothing was done for them, and the records mention hundreds dying daily in the streets. Because of these things, the name of the Ashikagas in Japanese history is synonymous with callous indifference and maladministration. But the shoguns under whom this happened had become only figureheads of government. Even the strongest of the line, Yoshimitsu, had been unable to coerce the greater of his vassals when they cared to resist him. It is related, for instance, that he once asked Lord Ōuchi for help in building the Gold Pavilion. But that baron, being at the time disinclined, and strong enough to do so, replied with cold significance,

"My men work *only* with their bows."[2]

Indifferent to the sufferings of the poor, the wealthy and favored continued to build their fine houses and gardens. It was during this time and, doubtless due in large measure to the increase of moderate-sized houses, that architecture underwent a radical change. The old *shinden* had been simplified into the military mansion in Kamakura and now another modification created the *sho-in* style. The *sho-in* itself was a library or study, the chief room in a house or small temple occupied by a scholar. A low writing table built into a window embrasure was its distinguishing feature. Another architectural characteristic which became widespread about this time was the recess constructed against an inner wall in which was displayed a paint-

[2] *Ga-un Nikken Roku.*

118

ing or other work of art. This recess, called the *tokonoma*, has survived to the present day as the chief ornamental feature of a Japanese living room.

In the new architecture doors, which in the *shinden* had been hinged at the top and hooked to the ceiling when the room was opened, became a series of sliding panels. Inside partitions were formed of other sliding doors of light construction, faced with paper. These interior doors or screens were often decorated with paintings, one picture sometimes extending over an entire wall. Thick, cushion-like mats of straw which had been used as seats on the boarded floors of the *shinden* were now used solidly over the entire floor.

Houses were still a group of buildings but they were not symmetrically arranged as formerly. Small residences no longer had the end-pavilions, and gardens in general became smaller. Usually they were built in courtyards on which the principal room of the house opened. And more and more they were laid out merely to form a picture for this room, becoming too small even for strolling.

Diarists of the time have left us glimpses of the construction of some of the great Muromachi estates. From such accounts we realize how much more difficult it is to create a landscape with stones, trees, and water than to paint the same thing with brush, ink, and silk. Before ever a pond could be dug and the garden artist proceed with the hard-enough business of arranging his stones and trees, he had to be sure he possessed these things. Since there were, as yet, no commercial purveyors of rocks and trees, they came often from gardens already in existence. Each time a new and important garden was made, older ones were likely to suffer. Saihōji, Tenryūji, and the Gold Pavilion all show where stones have been removed from them. Rocks of large and artistic form could be found in the mountains and transported if sufficient energy were expended, but nothing could hurry the growth of a tree. Therefore, powerful personages took trees wherever they could find them. The gardens of small temples and of retainers who had received favors seem to have furnished most of the trees. The records hold plenty of evidence that these lesser folk often objected to having their gardens raided in this manner and resisted it whenever they could.[3]

An incident is related in connection with the construction of a new imperial garden made at the expense of one of the shoguns. Word had been sent out that trees should be "offered" by the temple of Daikōmyōji at Fushimi and some of its subtemples, noted for their fine blossoming trees. Three small subtemples accepted, but a fourth protested to the shogun. The decision, however, came back, "Obey the order."

A little later rumors were heard at the court of a much cherished tree, probably a juniper, which was the pride and special adornment of a small subtemple garden. Court gardeners were sent to find it; they searched everywhere, in temple grounds and even in private gardens nearby. When it was found at last, they dug it up and took it away without ceremony.

"The people," remarks the record, "were very much annoyed."

However, some of the gifts sent to these new gardens were given sincerely enough as compliments from one high personage to another. An example of this appears in the diary[4] of Prince Sadafusa, who might himself, possibly, have became emperor if the ceremonies of abdication and enthronement could have been more often afforded by the court. As it was, he was living quietly in retirement in Fushimi, enjoying the usual gentlemen's interest in the arts. In 1433 he sent a gift of pine trees and fish to the sixth shogun, Yoshinori, who was rehabilitating Yoshimitsu's old Flowery Palace. He also passed on three "sea stones" which had recently been presented to him by a certain abbot. The very night after their arrival a letter came from the Shogun saying he was delighted, as these stones were the best he had received.

The number of men at times engaged in building these gardens is astounding. Lord Akamatsu detailed eighteen hundred of his followers to bring stones from Uzumasa, a few miles away, to this same shogunal gar-

---

[3] Extensive quotations from the records including those that follow are given in Mr. Toyama's book, *Muromachi Jidai Teienshi*.

[4] *Kammon Nikki*.

den. At another time, three thousand of Lord Hosokawa's men moved rocks for another estate the Shogun was building. Serious incidents sometimes developed in the course of these operations. While transporting some plum trees presented by Lord Kuroda, a large branch of one was broken. The Shogun was very angry and imprisoned three of the gardeners. Five young Kuroda knights, who evidently were responsible for the accident, were ordered arrested. Three of them fled into exile, and two others committed suicide!

The brilliance of the Muromachi period reached its climax under the eighth Ashikaga shogun, Yoshimasa, who was a grandson of the builder of the Gold Pavilion. Born in 1435, on the death of his brother, he also became a child shogun. He was brought up in the splendid mansions of his family and nourished on the esthetic traditions which pervaded them. When only fifteen years old, we see him presiding over a company of artists and poets gathered in a recently finished hall to paint pictures for its sliding screens and write poems in its honor. Under such conditions, Yoshimasa could hardly have become other than what he was, a dilettante and man of taste. He is often compared to his contemporary in Florence, Lorenzo di Medici. Wrapped up in these artistic pursuits, he was not interested in the affairs of the country. Political history has severely censored him as an indifferent ruler, but cultural history is beginning to give him his due as the patron under whom the arts reached, in many respects, the highest point they have attained in Japan.

He gathered about him a coterie of artistic men, poets, and scholars, most of whom were also Zen priests, since the church at that time offered the best background to men of such tastes. It was an age in which talent was recognized over birth and position, aristocratic nobles from the court mingling with men of similar tastes from the military classes or even lower. The artists and connoisseurs whom Yoshimasa gathered about him in the latter part of the 15th century differed from those his grandfather had invited to the Gold Pavilion in being more conscious of what they were doing, more sure of themselves and their opinions. In Yoshimitsu's day, all thought had turned toward China, and its greatness had been without peer. Now, although there was still much trafficking and travel back and forth, the Japanese felt themselves to be possible competitors in many ways. They were, indeed, creating art which in some of its aspects was equal to that which had come out of China. The Muromachi period was the age of the great painters in Japan, men who carried on with full competence the best of the fallen Sung tradition. And out of this was growing distinctive schools of Japanese artistry, marked, as always, when the Japanese cease copying and begin to express themselves, by a turn toward nature, the soft and gentle nature of the Japanese landscape and by delicacy, refinement, and attention to detail.

Probably the most distinctive of the arts which took form under Yoshimasa's patronage was the tea ceremonial. There had been a religious tea drinking ceremony in Sung China, designed to prepare those participating for Zen meditation. This had been brought to Japan, and tea drinking had also been used there in what seems to have been virtually a guessing game of literary allusions. Out of these cultural associations, the monk, Shuko, devised the Japanese tea ceremonial. It was a secular, esthetic exercise of elegant simplicity, designed to create the proper atmosphere for group discussions of art leading to a finer appreciation and understanding. In its Muromachi form, the tea ceremonial was probably free from that formalism which marred its later development, but it seems to have followed a certain ceremonious procedure and to have been performed in a setting designed to enhance its object. A small garden building, put up by Yoshimasa and still standing, is believed to hold the first room definitely set aside for the tea ceremonial.

While all the arts were fostered under Yoshimasa, those connected with building were particularly stimulated by his delight in reconstructing houses and gardens. Among the shogunal estates which he made over was the Takakura mansion where his mother, a Fujiwara lady, resided. This he turned into a copy of Saihōji's moss garden, which at that time was regarded as one of the most beautiful places around Kyoto. Since women were not admitted to its sacred precincts, Yoshimasa conceived the idea of reproducing it for his mother. A number of other gardens were also made after Saihōji at that time.

There seems, indeed, to have been almost a cult of admiration for Saihōji led by the Shogun. It must have been particularly beautiful then, for nearly a hundred and fifty years had passed since Musō Kokushi had converted the already old gardens of Amida's Paradise and of Aloofness from the Foul World into that of the Temple of Western Fragrance. The small buildings which he had scattered through it must have mellowed, and the mosses become even greener and thicker as the years rolled over.

Yoshimasa often visited Saihōji. We read of this in a record, called the *Onryōken Jitsuroku,* kept by the priest of a small subtemple of Shōkokuji named Onryōken. This record gives us frequent glimpses into the life of the Shogun. He had first gone to the Moss Temple in 1460, when the cherry blossoms were out; he had then been entranced by its beauty. He had returned in the autumn to pay his respects on Musō Kokushi's death anniversary and a month later had come again to see the maples at their best. During the next five years he visited the garden regularly three or four times a year; in spring to enjoy the beauty of silvery rain against the pines, in summer to boat among the lush leaves of the lotus, and in autumn to gaze on the rich brocade of the changing leaves. On one of these occasions the Onryōken scribe notes that Yoshimasa exclaimed:

"The beauty of this garden never diminishes!"

By the time he was thirty, Yoshimasa had exhausted all the possibilities of existing shogunal estates and was planning an entirely new villa to which he might retire as his grandfather had retired to the Gold Pavilion. A site was found at the foot of the Eastern Hills which seemed to offer all that was wanted. The scribe of Onryōken who was sent to see and report on it wrote:

"There are undulating hills and clear water. Clouds and mist mingle together. There is a pine gate and rock garden. The place has a quiet beauty far from the dust of the town. . . . Behind it rise several hilltops, forming an outlook. On one side, water runs down and has been very usefully conducted to the small temple" (which was already on the site).

These words would fairly describe the place today, nearly five centuries after they were written. As a preliminary step, Yoshimasa provided for the removal of the two small temples already on the site and erected a retreat which he called Jishō-sho-in, after his spiritual name. This was in 1465. Plans were on foot to turn this place into a splendid estate when suddenly everything was stopped by the outbreak of civil war in the very center of the capital.

The years of uneasy peace between the great barons had at last ended and two of the strongest, Yamana and Hosokawa, were contending openly for supremacy. Their underlying aims were masked, of course, by other excuses and the Ashikaga shogunate was not threatened at the time. It was still useful in creating the fiction of legality for one side or the other as that side was able to control its edicts. As the fighting had begun in the Ōnin era, it is known as the Ōnin civil war. It was the most destructive Japan has known for it centered where there was the most to be destroyed, the very heart of the rich Muromachi district. The two factions faced each other with the old Flowery Palace and Shōkokuji temple between them. The mansions belonging to the two sides served as temporary strongholds, but as the fighting swayed back and forth, one by one they were destroyed.

The period of fighting dragged on inconclusively for months, for years, finally, for a full decade. At the end of that time Kyoto lay in ruins, not a single important building having escaped. Even isolated places like the Gold Pavilion and Saihōji temple had been looted and burned by lawless elements. With the death of the two leaders, at last, quiet came to the city, but in the provinces warfare continued spasmodically; almost any baron who felt himself strong enough turned to prey on his neighbor. The capital tried to pull itself together again, but during the years that followed, it was entered again and again by lawless armies. One hundred fifty years were to pass before, under a new regime, it regained something of its former

The woodland spring on the hillside of Yoshimasa's Silver Pavilion garden was copied, almost stone for stone, from the one made four centuries before at Saihōji. The water seeps from under the background boulder, forming a crystal pool in the circle of small rocks; excess water trickles out between the front kneeling-stones and runs away down a gravelly rill. (Photo from Board of Tourist Industry.)

Original stonework survives around this island in the pond of the Silver Pavilion garden. The foreground bridge also dates from Yoshimasa's day. The stone arrangements around the island are typical of the Muromachi period, with upright, rugged rocks, some pointed in contrast to others having flat tops. The difference between this Muromachi style and that of the later period when the garden was reconstructed may be easily noted by contrasting the island stones with those on the farther shore. (Photo by Harada Sunao.)

On moonlight nights the strange, monumental piles of white sand in the Silver Pavilion garden have their own esthetic values. Trees cast sharp shadows on the smooth sides of the cone called the "Moon Facing Height" while formalized waves on the "Silver Sand Sea" (here visible behind the cone) have a rhythmic beauty of their own. The Tōgu-dō chapel dating from Yoshimasa's time is the small building behind the cone. (Photo by Okamoto Toyo.)

A typical Zen landscape painting, attributed to Sesshū, showing the soaring Peaks of Enlightenment; the long hard path leading toward them; a pilgrim part way up it symbolizing the artist-philosopher who has climbed to this height and now looks back for a moment on the dark valley of mundane life which he has left behind and the house, evidence of man's presence, in it. Sesshū's angular brush strokes, used to suggest the quality of giant rocks and vast precipices, are very evident in this painting.

glory. And then the new period was not the equal of the old in artistic spirit.

During the Ōnin war, the Imperial residence had fallen into ruins; its rehabilitation was the most pressing construction facing Yoshimasa when, at last, it was possible to start rebuilding. Not until this had been accomplished under the extremely difficult and upset conditions of the times, could he turn his thoughts to his own long-postponed villa. In 1482, however, a full eighteen years after the estate at the foot of the Eastern Hills had been planned, its construction was once more begun.

But things could no longer be done on the spacious and elaborate scale of former days. Yoshimasa clung as closely as possible to the old elegance, and what was done was done as perfectly as possible from the artistic point of view. Accounts of the construction seem almost pathetically meager, however, compared to the grandeur of the past. Only thirty men and ten gardeners worked on the place for the first year, finally getting the roof of the main building raised. The garden had hardly been cleared and begun when Yoshimasa moved in, the second year. Twelve structures were planned for the estate and eventually completed, including a gate, a bridge, a corridor, a chapel, a study, the reception hall, and several pavilions for such purposes as the incense ceremony and Chinese football. Judging from the two of these buildings which survive, they were modest structures, very different from the gorgeous halls of former days. Yet, their size and design were not entirely a matter of economic necessity. Yoshimasa was wrapped up in Zen esthetics, which made virtually a cult of the simple and natural. He built modestly because he felt it was more thoroughly artistic.

The garden itself was never entirely completed to Yoshimasa's satisfaction. Only a few stones, a few trees, seem to have been available at a time. Many of the stones and some trees came from the ruined Flowery Palace, as men could be found to move them, but most of the trees seem to have been brought all the twenty-five miles from Nara where fire had not devastated the gardens. Occasionally some lord would make a generous gesture by detailing his men for a few days to move stones and trees. Thus in

1488 the young Lord of Hosokawa, Masamoto, allowed four thousand of his men to work at moving pine trees from the Flowery Palace. A part of this number were armored guards, a comment on the unsettled times. Other plants mentioned as going into the garden are cherries, azaleas, plums, camellias, and yews.

That Yoshimasa delighted in these flowering plants is evident from an anecdote set down in the *Onryōken* record. The scribe had been on a short journey and on his return was telling Yoshimasa what he had seen. He mentioned that the white plum blossoms had been at their best as he passed through Ōmi province.

Said Yoshimasa, smiling complacently, "White plums are at their best in my garden, too."[5]

During Yoshimasa's life the estate was known as the Higashi-yama-dono, or Eastern Hill Villa, a name parallel to the North Hill Villa of his grandfather. And also as a parallel to that older place, the new garden has come down the years under the name of the Silver Pavilion Temple, Gin-kakuji, from one of the buildings preserved in it. It is correctly called Jishōji, after Yoshimasa's spiritual name, which it received as a temple after his death and which it has held the four and a half centuries since.

For the past hundred years or so it has been thought that this garden was designed by one of the artists who frequented it, the screen painter Sōami. He came of a family of connoisseurs which had served the Shoguns since the days of the Gold Pavilion and he was undoubtedly an important artist of the time. But there is no contemporary evidence to indicate that he had anything whatever to do with the garden design. It was first attributed to him some three hundred years after Yoshimasa's death by a Tokugawa writer[6] whose statement seems to have been made from hearsay. It was copied and accepted, however, until quite recently, when search of the con-

---

[5] The Plum of Japan is *Prunus mume*. While its name, *ume,* is usually translated "plum," the tree is really a species of apricot, its flowers more scattered, waxen, and fragrant than the fruiting plum of the Occident.

[6] Ritoken Akizato.

temporary documents has disproved it. Without stating the fact in words, these records indicate plainly that Yoshimasa followed tradition by laying out the place himself. He often asked advice from scholars and artists, while he had the best garden craftsmen to carry out the work.

The chief of these rockcraftsmen was, at that time, an old man known as Kawara-mono Zenami. The prefix, Kawara-mono, means literally "river-bank person" and indicated some one belonging to the outcast class, a group something akin to *Eta*. These people, who were in some ways lower than serfs, lived in the no-man's-land along the river banks and had to do the meanest of work, including butchering: Buddhist teachings against the taking of life made the latter an abhorrent occupation. But, since they were available, the river-bank people seem to have been often employed as laborers, especially for the heavy work in gardens, until the name became, in time, almost synonymous with garden workman.

Zenami who had spent a long life working on the Muromachi estates had acquired great artistic skill in stone arrangement. He must have possessed a fine, natural artistic endowment which found expression in this medium. He was the outstanding figure in the field of stone artistry in the latter half of the 15th century, his name appearing in several temple records as the maker of their gardens. This, in itself, is evidence of the regard in which he was held. One such record[7] speaks of him as the "greatest in the world in stone placement" and remarks in the same entry that he was ninety-seven years old and "had been born in the house of a butcher."

Yoshimasa had employed Zenami now and then over a period of years. For instance, he had once ordered him to make a garden for the official scribe's own residence of Onryōken which, when completed, was described in its record with the lyrical words, "Its exquisite artistry is incomparable." Before the Ōnin war the Shogun had sent Zenami, among others, to inspect and report on the then proposed site at the foot of the Eastern Hills. When work on it finally began, nearly twenty years later, although no entry specifically mentions Zenami, it seems certain he must have been in charge.

[7] *Rokuon Nichiroku.*

His grandson, Matashiro, who had been carefully trained in stone artistry, was, doubtless, the active man on the job.

Knowing Yoshimasa's admiration for Saihōji, it is no surprise to learn that he modeled his new estate after the old garden. By that time the Temple of Western Fragrance was in ruins, but no person knew better than Yoshimasa how it had looked in the days of its perfection. The Eastern Hill Villa, therefore, had a pond garden below and a rustic rock garden on the hillside above. On this hillside, Zenami and his crew built a woodland spring which, stone for stone, is almost a duplicate of the one which had been put in the garden of Aloofness from the Foul World some four centuries before. It has the same large boulder set into the hillside to form a background, the same wing-stones inclosing the pool, and, in front, the same flat rocks on which to kneel or stand. The water lies, cool and crystal clear, in a circle of small stones, and a large flat one forms the bottom. Excess water trickles out between the front stones and flows away down a small graveled rill.

The chief difference between this spring and its protoype at Saihōji is its delicacy. Technically they are almost identical. But in Zenami's copy the rocks are less massive and rugged, more gentle and sophisticated in their grace. One would never mistake it for a natural spring as might be done at Saihōji. The two illustrate the spirit of their respective ages and the fact that, however much one age may wish to copy another, it is impossible to do so exactly, for the spirit which informs one age is different from another.

This spring and the other rocks which were a part of Yoshimasa's hillside garden were buried for a considerable period under earth washed down from the slopes above. In 1931, however, after the old documents had given a clue to the existence of the upper garden, a search was made and the spring excavated, undamaged. Moss is now beginning to creep back on its rocks and small ferns to spring up around it, restoring once more its feeling of age.

The pond garden at the foot of the hill is inclosed like Saihōji's by buildings and a wall on the north and west, by an indefinite expanse of trees and mossy ground on the south, and by the green hills behind it. The hills have been owned by the estate from the beginning and have been left undisturbed, the garden trees blending with them. The eye is led up and up over their tapestried greens to where the topmost line of trees stands silhouetted against the skyline. This line curves and dips against the sky and, in some curious way, becomes the focal point of the whole garden. A view upward, differing from the more stereotyped outlook outward or downward, is occasionally found in Oriental gardens. Here, not content with incorporating the hills, the garden plan took in the very heavens. And when the moon rises over this Eastern Hill side, the place reaches its peak of fulfillment.

In the pond garden below, the broad open lake of the older style is gone, and in its place is a smaller pond of more complicated shape. Although the present form of the pond is not what it was originally, it could never have been very large and spreading. Mention of a boathouse suggests the old tradition, but we hear of no boating parties and the probabilities are that, in the beginning as today, the chief way to enjoy the garden was by strolling through it. Following the walk around it today provides an ever changing series of views, intimate and charming. There are tiny islands at just the right points to enhance a view and bridges to concentrate a vista. Azaleas pour from among the rocks, and trees lean out to cast green shadows in the translucent depths of the water. The pond is named the Brocade Mirror, and no better words could suggest its patterned loveliness. To walk through the garden is like looking at one of the long Oriental scroll paintings of landscape, one charming scene melting into the next as the scroll is unrolled and rerolled behind.

Lotus grew in this pond, a gift from Tōji Temple. The great bluish waxen leaves and stately pink flowers were intended to suggest the Western Paradise of Amida where they served as pedestals for souls new-born to bliss. The small chapel which still overlooks one end of the pond was dedicated to Amida, Lord of Light, and housed an Amida trinity. It is one of the two original structures still standing, a simple unpainted building with roof of cypress bark and sliding doors. One of its rear rooms is that believed to have been planned for the tea ceremonial. This chapel was called the Tōgu-dō, or East Seeking Hall, referring to man's search from this world—the East—for the Western Paradise.

The second surviving building in the garden is now known as the Silver Pavilion, a name derived from a story, apparently without much foundation, that Yoshimasa intended to use silver on it as his grandfather had gilded part of the Gold Pavilion. In general form the Gold and Silver Pavilions are somewhat alike, and for long it was assumed that one was more or less copied after the other. But the *Onryōken* diary makes it clear that this was far from the case. Yoshimasa based the design of the Silver Pavilion on the Ruri-den, one of the small buildings which Musō Kokushi had put in to Saihōji's garden. It was primarily a hall for Zen meditation as is indicated by the name of the second story, Shinku-den, or Soul Emptying Hall. It also housed an image of Kwannon, the Compassionate One, and for this reason is usually mentioned in the records as the Kwannon-dō.

For the first story Yoshimasa chose the name of Choon-kaku, or Pavilion of Echoing Waves. The care and thought which went into the choice of these names and the style of writing used on name plates to go over the doorway are described at length in the *Onryōken* record. The Silver Pavilion, as a building, is not so large nor so fine a structure as the Gold Pavilion; it shows its closer relationship to the older, simpler styles of Musō Kokushi's day. Nor does it occupy any such commanding position in the garden as does the Gold Pavilion. It stands on the edge of the lake, its curved roof crowned by a bronze phoenix, blending with the trees.

From this pavilion may be obtained the best single view of the garden as it must have been in Yoshimasa's day, for it still faces the compelling skyline and the spot where the moon rises behind the hills. Perhaps it was here that Yoshimasa sat when he composed the poem which is associated with the garden in the mind of every Japanese:

My lodge is at the foot
Of the Moon-Waiting Hill—
Almost I regret, when

MANSIONS OF MUROMACHI

The shortening hill shadow
At length disappears.[8]

Highly characteristic of Zen taste and feeling is the suggestion implied that the anticipation of beauty is better than its full realization.

In 1490, barely eight years after he had begun the Eastern Hill Villa, Yoshimasa died, "that man of superlative taste." And with him ended the great days of Muromachi. Those artists who still remained in the city scattered to find protection and patronage from powerful barons in the provinces. The city lay desolate, still occasionally raided by passing troops. The faithful priest of Onryōken, who had been at Yoshimasa's bedside at the last, noted that the estate was converted that very day into a branch temple of Shōkokuji. For a few years it probably was kept up, for Yoshimasa's son, the new Shogun, came to live in it—and shortly created a scandal by bringing women to its sacred precincts. But this residence did not last for long. In 1501, a short eleven years after Yoshimasa's death, someone who visited it found it looted and going to ruin.

For the greater part of the next century, that 16th century which is the darkest in Japan's history, the garden lay disintegrating. It had never been as well made as Saihōji, its prototype, and could not resist the years as has the older garden. About 1585 an impoverished court noble, Konoe Sakihisa, took possession and apparently did a little something to rehabilitate the place. And by the time he died, times had so improved that Shōkokuji was once more able to assume control and do something for it.

At last, with peace once more restored and reconstruction going on everywhere, the rebuilding of Yoshimasa's estate-temple was undertaken. This seems to have been about 1615, and work continued for some years. It was in charge of the Lord of Tamba, Miyagi Toyomori, who had been a follower of Hideyoshi. The garden, however, had evidently gone so com-

---

[8] *Waga iho wa*
Tsukimachi-yama no
Fumoto ni te
Kata muku sora no
Kage oshizo omō.

pletely to pieces that most of it had to be entirely reconstructed. In making a lake and arranging stones around it, the original plan was not followed—it may not have been discernible. But where parts of the old rockwork remained they were left almost untouched. Fortunately, at the time of the reconstruction, garden artistry was at a high level, although not equal to the Muromachi, and the garden as it exists today is one of great charm and beauty, a combination of Muromachi and early Tokugawa styles.[9]

The greater part of the present stone work dates from the reconstruction. Of the original rock arrangements there remain the once-buried spring on the hillside, the cascade, and a small island. The cascade is in a bad state of repair, the thin stream of water which flows through it from the hillside falling now at one end instead of across the face of the great main rock. This stone is about ten feet high and four feet wide and is supported in the hillside by other large stones in the manner of those in Tenryūji and the Gold Pavilion. A large tree now grows out of its top, and behind it may be glimpsed the remains of a second fall up the slope. The water forms a small pool at the base of the rock, then runs off to join the main pond at a lower level. The cascade is called the Moon Washing Spring, Sengetsu-sen, suggesting that the moon's reflection dancing in the small pool, is being cleaned.

The small island with its original stone work lies in the pond directly in front of the Tōgū-dō chapel, where it forms the center of interest in the outlook. It is crossed by the path that leads around the garden, two bridges leading to and from it. One of these bridges is judged, on its technique, to date from Yoshimasa's day. It is very like the one at Tenryūji, composed of two natural, flat plank-stones laid end to end and supported where they join by stones rising from the water. It is massive and strong, a particularly fine piece of rock composition.

The rockwork around the island is also excellent and typical of the

[9] As this is written, plans are under way to dig in the northern part of the garden around the Tōgū-dō where is now an expanse of moss and trees. It is believed that original stone work will be found buried under soil washed down from the slope.

Muromachi technique. The stones are tall and pointed with plane sides, or they have strong, flat tops. The groupings are dominated by the old, basic three lines of an asymmetrical triangle. The general feeling is a blend of Saihōji's soft naturalism with the soaring artistry of Sung rockwork as found in Tenryūji.

Today the most arresting feature of the Silver Pavilion garden is two piles of white sand; one a tall cone, the other, a wide, flat expanse some two feet thick. These white and bulky piles appear startling in the sylvan setting of the garden and invariably provoke the inquiry, "What are they? What do they mean?"

There seems to be no answer. They have no meaning and they came there, apparently, by chance.

The cone-shaped pile is called the Moon Facing Height, Kogetsu-dai. It is flat on top, sixteen feet in diameter on the ground, six feet high, and five feet in diameter across the top. The flat pile is roughly in diamond shape, its sides beveled, its flat top kept molded into square ridges suggesting formalized ocean waves. It is called the Silver Sand Sea, or Gin-shanada.

A search through the records throws no light on how these curiosities came into existence. Documents contemporary with the original construction of the garden do not mention them, which seems good proof they were no part of the original plan—at least in their present form. Mention of the Silver Sand Sea, however, occurs in a poem written in 1576, so it existed before the garden was reconstructed. It seems possible this had its origin in Yoshimasa's day simply as a spread of white sand on the ground before the main building, as is often found in Zen temples. The cone may have been, originally, simply a pile of extra sand to be drawn on as needed in renewing the paths. Such functional ornaments may be seen in other, later Zen gardens.

A clue as to how they attained their present size may be found in a group of old books, written during the last hundred years, in which famous gardens are described and illustrated with drawings.[10] Drawings in succes-

[10] *Miyako Meishō Zue, Miyako Rinsen Meishō Zue, Gingakuji Rinsen Zue.*

133

sive books show the sand piles in the Silver Pavilion getting higher and higher as if, each time the sand was renewed, a little extra were added, the piles thus growing imperceptibly.

Today Japanese critics generally agree that these sand heaps are inharmonious with the garden; the cone is too large to be anything but intrusive in the sylvan picture, while the high expanse of the Silver Sand Sea interferes with the view of the garden from the main building. Moreover, the symbolic suggestion of water in the etched waves is incongruous beside the actual water in the pond.

Yet, by themselves these sand piles are not without certain esthetic values, particularly in moonlight. Then their clear, white forms shine in strong and pleasing contrast to the dark trees. Shadows fall across the smooth sides of the cone; from the second story of the pavilion its round top might suggest the reflection of the full moon. In moonlight, also, the Silver Sand Sea has a certain ghostly beauty, for its waves seem to move in silent rhythmic procession across the flat expanse.

X. *The Painting Gardens*

OF ALL the great estates built in the Muromachi period, only the pavilion gardens of Yoshimitsu and Yoshimasa remain today. Yet, many small temples and lodges had gardens also, like the one that was made for Onryōken. Many of these small temple gardens survive, which is fortunate, for in them gardening reached its apex as fine art and as expressionistic art. The great estates possessed beauty, charm, and artistry along with considerable feeling, but they were, after all, gardens first of all, meant to provide the environment for the mansion of a great and important personage.

The small temple gardens, on the contrary, had no such purpose. Their one and only function was to aid the mood of contemplation, leading to Enlightenment. The scholars, artists, and mystics who designed them—often all three in one person—were free to do almost exactly as they pleased. And since it was an age of artistic ferment, it often pleased them to experiment with this medium. Artists made pictures of exactly the same kind they created with their brush; scholars symbolized their philosophy; and mystics expressed their feeling of relationship with the Infinite. They created art first and gardens afterward.

Of all the art forms in which Japanese genius has flowered, the greatest, probably, is painting. As the Western world becomes familiar with the best in Oriental art, the names of Sesshū and others of the Sung-Muromachi school are being recognized as among the great painters of all time. The 15th century in Japan was the age of these painters; of Josetsu, Shūbun, and Sōtan; of Sesshū, Jasoku, and Keishoki; of Nōami, Geiami, and Sōami; of Kano Masanobu and Kano Motonobu.

In Japan these Muromachi painters carried on the tradition of art that had come over to them from the time of the Chinese Sung dynasty. There had been great painters in China even in the T'ang period, seven centuries before, when Japan was first learning from her neighbor. But under the inspiration of Buddhism at that time, the sculpturing of images appealed more strongly to the Japanese than painting. When Hangchow was capital of the Southern Sung dynasty (1127-1279 A.D.) Chinese introspective painting reached its apogee. Sung civilization, as before stated, was probably the finest China has known. It was peace-loving, mature, intellectual, and artistic. Of its expression in the paintings which were its greatest product Fitzgerald says:[1]

"Better than any detailed history or work of literature, one Sung landscape will illuminate the gracious spirit of that refined and sophisticated age, soon to be overwhelmed in the Mongol invasion, from which, in art, there has been no recovery."

But the tradition of idealistic painting was not obliterated by the Mongols; it was carried to Japan where it survived under Muromachi patronage. Works of the Sung masters had first arrived in Japan in their own day, the Kamakura period, brought by the Ch'an monks and students who went back and forth between the two countries. Later, through the trade inaugurated by Takauji and the Zen monks, pictures came in increasing quantity. Troubled times in China brought many fine pieces into the market which the Muromachi connoisseurs bought eagerly; we have glimpsed some of them delightedly poring over these treasures in the Gold and Silver Pavilions. This sophisticated Sung art, falling into the well-prepared soil of Muromachi, came to a second flowering, belated but perfect, nearly two hundred years after the Southern Sung period itself had ended in China. Although separated both in time and space, the Japanese Muromachi painters may be regarded as an integral part of the Sung school. Their work is slightly but not fundamentally different. A little later the distinctly

[1] C. P. Fitzgerald, *China, a Short Cultural History.*

136

Japanese Kano school of painting developed, but the early Muromachi masters themselves were, to all intents and purposes, Sung artists.

These pictures were executed with a special technique. They were drawn with black ink mixed with water on semiabsorbent paper or white silk. The ink color ranged from faintest grey to wet black; sometimes they were lightly tinted with other colors, green, blue, red, or yellow. The brush technique was that used in brush writing, each stroke necessarily firm, definite, and final, for there was no erasing a false line nor covering it with a second. The brushwork was greatly varied, made up of washes, lines, and strokes, fine, bold, or dashing. Simple as were these materials of black ink and white paper, in the hands of a master this technique was capable of suggesting the infinite aspects of nature—mistiness of distant mountains, the bold form of sharp rocks and crags, the dark texture of pines, and the white leap of a waterfall.

The pictures cover a wide variety of subjects, flowers, birds, animals, men, and landscapes. But the landscapes, as Fitzgerald points out, are in a class apart, "unrivalled in their own Far Eastern art and unequalled in the painting of any other land." Landscape is not portrayed realistically, but its emotional effect on the artist is put down—how it *seemed* to him. It is not surprising then to find it often appearing unreal and fantastic. But when we remember that the original inspiration for these pictures was the strange and wild scenery of certain parts of China, where the peaks are actually curiously shaped, the valleys deep and dark, it is not quite so peculiar.

The pictures are painted from the viewpoint of one who has climbed to high places and now looks back over the panorama below him and up to the heights still ahead. Vast "chimney spire" cliffs soar in the background, tremendous precipices and craggy rocks rise nearer at hand, waterfalls leap into dark valleys, while weatherbeaten pines cling to the rocks. Often a steep path can be seen winding upward, and on it, hardly distinguishable at first, one or two pilgrims. Buildings or boats are frequently present in these pictures but they never dominate the scene as they are likely to do in Western landscape.

On the effect of these landscapes, Fitzgerald continues:

"To the European of today the Sung landscapes seem 'modern' because, in spite of a different artistic tradition, they are the products of a people on the same level of artistic culture as ourselves. The 17th century would not have appreciated them. Indeed, the early European travelers to the Far East never thought of bringing home pictures, although they admired and imitated other Chinese works of art. It was not only because Chinese art followed a different convention to that of the West, but because the spirit which informed the landscape painters of China was then alien to European taste. To the modern, the Sung landscapes are a revelation."

These words, I think, would be just as true if applied to the gardens created by the Muromachi artists. Even a few decades ago, foreigners in Japan admired only the formalized Tokugawa gardens of Tokyo. Conder barely touches on the Gold and Silver pavilion gardens and does not mention at all those of Daisen-in and its kind.[2] But a growing interest in the old gardens is evident on the part of the Western world; enthusiasm for them is mounting as they are seen and, at least partly, grasped. No longer do foreigners in Japan find them merely quaint and pretty little miniatures. The average visitor, uninformed, is still aware of something deep in them that he does not understand.

The landscape pictures and the gardens derived from them were filled with symbolism, since the Zen artist was also a philosopher. Interpreted in one way, these landscapes present a picture of man's spiritual life; the dark valleys stand for his cramped physical existence from which he seeks to lift himself, the path and the pilgrims on it indicate the long hard way to the soaring peaks of Enlightenment. Boats on the river, houses and villages are signs of mundane life; a temple where dwell those who aspire to higher things often rears its stately roof on higher ground. The philosopher-artist must himself have gone a certain distance along the way in order to look back and grasp its significance. But always the peaks soar above him, chal-

[2] Josiah Conder, *Landscape Gardening in Japan.*

lenging him onward and upward. The tiny figures of men in this tremendous setting suggest the relative importance of man in the cosmos; but though man may be small, he is an integral and harmonious part of it.

But behind all this objective symbolism, which is, after all, rather simple, there lies a deeper meaning in these pictures, something which can hardly be expressed but must be felt emotionally. It is the attempt of the Zen artist who was also a mystic to reach through to the inner essence of all things. The great landscapes have about them a universal quality; they are not the representation of a specific scene but hold the essential quality of all landscapes. In drawing a mountain, a rock, or a waterfall the Zen artist did not make a portrait of an individual thing. He studied many and sought to find and depict the quality that was common to them all. As he succeeded in finding the essential quality of all rocks, all mountains, and all trees and recording it so that others might feel it also, he was successful as a philosopher and a painter.

The decade of Ōnin warfare in Kyoto drove a large part of its population into the provinces. Artists and scholars, except for the few who found refuge with the Shogun, sought shelter in outside temples or settled at the provincial seats of feudal lords who acted as their patrons. A great deal of Muromachi art was thus created outside the capital and left scattered over the nation. Among such works were paintings and gardens by the artist Sesshū.[3]

Sesshū (1420-1506) was a Zen monk who, like that earlier garden lover Musō Kokushi, spent most of his life wandering from temple to temple, in Kyoto, Kamakura, and the western provinces. But unlike Musō Kokushi, Sesshū had no interest in politics; he became a national figure purely as an artist, his fame resting on his superlative paintings. However, like the other artists of his day, he tried his hand at contemporary art forms, composing verse, performing the incense ceremony, and making gardens. He seems to have been also an expert judge of art, and along with it, some-

[3] Jon Carter Covell has kindly allowed me to use material from her unpublished book, Under the Seal of Sesshū, for much of what follows.

thing of a business man, for he is spoken of as the "purchaser-priest." The China trade was still largely in the hands of Zen monks and Sesshū seems to have acted sometimes as appraiser and buyer of art imported from China.

This connoisseurship is probably what obtained for him the opportunity to go at last to China, a trip that was the ambition, no doubt, of every Zen monk and artist. Among Sesshū's patrons was the great baron, Lord Ōuchi, who was deeply interested in art and esthetics. The Ōuchi family controlled wide provinces at the western end of Japan, their castle seat being in the town of Yamaguchi. During the Ōnin war and later, this town achieved an urbanity which had hitherto been found only in the capital. Much of the trade with China went in and out of its port. Sesshū sailed from the port of Hakata, in 1468, the year after the Ōnin war broke out in Kyoto. He was commissioned, it is believed, by Lord Ōuchi to go to China and buy rare art objects.

We can imagine Sesshu's excitement as he set sail. It was his hope, as he himself has written, to find a Chinese painting teacher who could still create masterpieces like those he had so long studied and admired and who could teach him this art. By the time he arrived in China, the Mongol hordes had been driven back to their northern steppes, and China had risen again to a great era under the Ming dynasty. But Ming genius did not blossom in painting; it found its best expression in new outlets—in drama, ceramics, and architecture, with Peking as its masterpiece. Ming landscape painting become increasingly decadent, formalized, and pedantic.

Sesshū went to Hangchow, the old Sung capital on West Lake. A painting of it (Chapter II) attributed to him shows its ancient beauties plainly, but by the time Sesshū arrived its great artists had gone. Instead of the painters he sought, he himself was hailed as a great artist and given high honors as a Zen monk.

Under the circumstances this praise was hardly an exaggeration, for Sesshū was unquestionably the supreme painter of the Muromachi period. His finest work was done, however, after he returned to Japan carrying the

The garden of Jōeiji temple at Yamaguchi, probably made by Sesshū, is a pond and island garden but with a wide, flat foreshore area over which are scattered stone groups in characteristic Muromachi style. (Photo from Board of Tourist Industry.)

The Crane Islet of the Jōeiji temple garden at Yamaguchi, probably designed by Sesshū, makes typical use of the large rocks with flat tops and strong plane surfaces, used to suggest vast crags and giant precipices of nature in its grander aspects. The similiarity of this rock technique to the angular brush strokes of the painters is self-evident. (Photo from Nihon Teien Shizukan.)

The garden of Daisen-in temple is a landscape done in the mood of the Zen painters. Accepted in its natural, man-sized scale, it is only a collection of unusual rocks, crowded into a tiny L-shaped courtyard around a small temple building. Regarded, however, as a Zen landscape painting, executed in stones instead of paint, it shows the typical soaring peaks, the leaping waterfall (back right), the giant crags and precipices of great mountains. Nearer, the river flows over a dam, its movement suggested by striated rocks. In the quiet foreground lake, an individual stone, remarkably like a Chinese junk, suggests the presence of man in this scene. (Photo by Harada Sunao.)

To the uninitiated, the temple garden of Ryōanji appears like a sanded tennis court with groups of stones projecting above its surface. It may be viewed as an impressionistic landscape, perhaps as a flowing river or the sea with rocky islands. Others find it a subtle sermon in stone. (Photo by Okamoto Toyo.)

inspiration of Chinese mountains and rivers and the knowledge that no man living was his peer.

When he came once more to the shores of Japan, the Ōnin War was still wasting Kyoto. There was no reason why he should go to the capital, so he settled in Lord Ōuchi's domains in western Japan. The remaining decades of his long life were spent in this part of the country, the years filled with painting, teaching, and visits with old friends—those other monks and artists who had left the ruined capital and wandered to the west. Sesshū's wanderlust never allowed him to stay many years in one place. He lived in various localities, in temples, or in studio-residences which he built for himself. One of these, outside Yamaguchi and within view of its castle, is described by the monk Keigo, of Tōfukuji monastery, who visited him in 1488. Sesshū called the place the Heaven-Created Painting Pavilion—Tenkai Zuga-rō. Keigo's description of it is written in the traditional Chinese phrases used by the Five Monasteries school of literature to which he belonged. He even followed conventional Chinese garden descriptions to the extent of mentioning "unusual birds and strange animals" which certainly never had a place in any Muromachi garden, although they were part of early Chinese gardens. Yet while the words suggest strongly the description of Po-Chü-i's retreat on Lu-shan, Keigo's lines do bring before us a picture of the idyllic life led in the Heaven-Created Painting Pavilion. They give us a glimpse of the atmosphere in which the Muromachi artists lived and created their paintings and gardens.

". . . From afar it appears rustic, with mysterious rocks and winding streams. A step inside transports one into a world entirely different from the city. Here [too] the artist put up a tablet inscribed, 'Heaven-Created Painting.' The house faces the castle's north window. If one opens the door, one can see the rising and setting sun, clouds or fog which appear suddenly, haze and mist, curling smoke, the sky covered with storms; wind, the darkness of rain and crystal purity of snow and moonlight. Wherever one looks, variety meets the eye. More than a thousand, ten thousand changes, varying with the instant. . . . The Wise Lord [Ōuchi] often walks here and curious scholars and groups of officials gather also. The venerable Sesshū sits on his bamboo seat and reed cushion, or busies himself with his daily work, sweeping, drawing water, or preparing the incense for burning.

"A stream murmurs over here. There, large stones rise to a precipice. Rare plants and strange flowers achieve great loveliness. Unusual birds and strange animals appear and disappear. The cry of birds is heard; highly colored fish swim about; butterflies cluster 'round. During the heat of a midsummer day, the host and his guests exchange poems over their wine. The wind and the moon come here, too. All these things are present in the Heaven-Created Painting Pavilion. . . ."[4]

No trace of it is left today, but four other gardens believed to have been built by Sesshū are scattered over the western provinces of Japan.[5] At present no documentary evidence exists to prove definitely that he did these four or any others existent, but he is known to have lived in their vicinity. If these gardens are not the work of Sesshū, but of another person, it is of little consequence, for whoever did them was very like him, a Muromachi artist, filled with the spirit of that age and possessed of its abilities. Sesshū we may think of as the archtype of such men.

The four Sesshū gardens, although varying considerably in size, are temple gardens of the pond and island type. Their pools lie inclosed by rising ground behind, while a level space in front extends from the buildings which overlook them to the near edge of the pool. The shore and islands are bordered with exceptionally fine stones remarkably well placed. In the gardens of Kiseki-bo and Jōeiji, the level foreshore area holds scat-

[4] Translation by Jon Carter Covell. Found in the *Koga-Bikō,* Vol. II., pp. 670-671.

[5] Kiseki-bō, belonging to a temple which has since disappeared, is located in the little mountain village of Hikosan in northern Kyūshū. Its isolation has saved it from change so that today it is regarded as the best preserved of the four gardens generally attributed to Sesshū. The second belongs to Jōeiji near Yamaguchi. It is the largest of the four, probably made when Sesshū was living in Yamaguchi under the patronage of Lord Ōuchi. Mampukuji and Ikōji, two small temples located in the village of Masuda-machi near the north seacoast, hold the other two Sesshū gardens. In this vicinity Sesshū spent the last years of his life.

tered groups of ornamental rock arrangements, suggestive of the flat, rock gardens which were to develop later. In all four, the stones and their arrangements have the characteristics of Muromachi rock technique.

Perhaps the most striking characteristic of these painting gardens is the consistent choice of flat-topped stones. Except for certain tall, pointed rocks used to secure the soaring "chimney spire" effects of the paintings, nearly all the rocks in the painting gardens are either actually flat-topped or otherwise possessed of simple, large, plane surfaces and decisive angles. The nubby, commonplace stone of nondescript character had no place in such gardens. The planes and angles of these selected stones link them definitely to the landscape paintings, for a peculiarity of the brush technique in these pictures is the frequent use of straight strokes angularly combined. Sesshū was supreme in this angular technique. As Fenollosa says, he "is the greatest master of straight line and angle in the whole range of the world's art. There is no landscape so soft he cannot, if he wills, translate it into terms of oaken wedges split with an ax."[6]

In the paintings, this technique manages to reproduce the quality and feeling of stones—perhaps the most difficult objects to paint in the world. By means of it, the Muromachi artists were able to suggest vast precipices, giant crags, or smaller stones, catching their very essence. In creating gardens the Muromachi artists translated this angular brush work by choosing angular rocks. That they were successful in securing the same effects as seen in the pictures may be realized by comparing, for instance, the crane islet in Sesshū's Jōeiji garden with one of the Sesshū paintings.

The best example of a whole garden modeled after a Sung landscape painting is found in Daisen-in, a small subtemple of Daitokuji monastery of Kyoto. This garden lies in an L-shaped courtyard around two sides of the main building, inclosed on the outside by walls and hedges. It is very limited in size, its width being some thirteen feet and its length on the longer side about forty-seven feet. The principal landscape picture is ar-

[6] E. F. Fenollosa, *Epochs of Chinese and Japanese Art,* Vol. II.

ranged in this longer rectangle, rocks, sand, and a few plants creating a garden quite different from any described up to this time.

Looking up its length from the lower end, we find its proportions about the same as the paintings themselves. Our viewpoint, too, from the raised arcade at the end is that of the pilgrim or painter who, from a high place, looks down upon the landscape spread below him. Precipitous cliffs rise at the back; beside them a waterfall drops into the valley. The river curves down among rocky gorges until, near our feet, it broadens out to quiet smoothness. There is no actual water in the garden, but its presence is suggested by striated rocks and white sand.

Such a representation sounds as if it came perilously near to being one of the topographical maps we first expected all Japanese gardens to be. But this one, like others of its type, is built on a double scale or double perspective. The outward, obvious and natural, scale is proportional to man; what may be called the inner or supernatural scale exists in the imagination. It is in this latter that we see the landscape painting. Instead of a topographical map, as a matter of fact, it takes a good deal of contemplation to see the larger landscape at all, for at first sight the garden seems to be a jumbled collection of large, unusually shaped stones, crowded into the L-shaped space around the building. The sanded ground between them is overgrown with coarse moss, while a few shrubs grow here and there, and a hedge incloses the space.

A little study of this jumble, however, reveals, first of all, the usual garden pattern carried out here in a highly impressionistic way. Sand represents water, the tall stones at the back are the hills. The waterfall is unmistakable, suggested by a curious stone highly graphic in its pouring lines. The "stream" is crossed by a bridge, a single, long, flat stone large enough for one to walk on in passing over to a rock group evidently meant to be the crane island. This man-sized bridge sets the scale for the normal aspect of the garden in its conventional form. The same scale carries over into the shorter arm of the garden. Here a large rock group forms a second island, the usual turtle. Close to the edge of the porch is an arrangement centering around a stone handwashing basin, probably put in some years after the rest of the garden was made. Both arms of the garden as a unit might be seen from a seat in the room which stands in their angle, were its sliding doors widely opened. Viewed thus as a total, the two arms form a unified design, with the tall stones of the waterfall in the center, the bridge in front, and the two islands on either side.

The strange shapes of the stones in this garden have inevitably caused ignorant onlookers to give them descriptive names. Thus there is the "recumbent ox stone," the "turtle stone," the "saddle stone," and the "boat stone." The latter is a curious boulder, almost exactly the shape of a medieval Chinese junk. Of all the named stones this is undoubtedly the only one in which the likeness was intentional. It was put there, plainly, as part of the landscape picture, just as boats were part of the landscape paintings. Similar boat stones may be found in other painting gardens, notably in Sesshū's Jōeiji.

The large stones in this garden probably stand today in their original places, but it seems likely that some of the smaller ones now in the garden have found their way there since it was made. At the present time there are far too many small stones scattered through the bottom without reference to the unity of the design. Most of these are odd or are suggestive of something, a turtle for instance. A collection of such fine stones as the originals may have seemed the proper place to put others.

At the present time the shrubs in the garden have been allowed to grow out of all proportion to the picture. The garden is not neglected in one sense, but these large shrubs are allowed to remain, spoiling the effect unless one is willing to look through and beyond them. The original background is known to have been a white plaster wall instead of the present hedge, and white sand covered the ground which is now patchily overgrown with moss. With the white wall and sand as background, the effect of a landscape painting on white silk must have been much more pronounced than it is at present. The Japanese, however, are very cautious nowadays about "restoring" their old treasures, so many have been spoiled in the process. They prefer to leave them alone, even though, as in this case, it only means the removal of a few commonplace shrubs.

When we contemplate the Daisen-in garden with the eye of our creative imagination the landscape painting comes vividly to the fore. All the characteristics of a Sung landscape picture are present, the soaring chimney spires, the leaping cascade, the precipices of strange and awe-inspiring form, even the evidence of man's presence in the boat on the river. And everywhere are the straight lines and sharp angles of the brush technique of these pictures.

In looking at this landscape painting, the creative imagination must not be realistic and critical, demanding exactness in all details; only the final effect matters. Thus in the painting garden we can overlook, for one thing, the plants which are so greatly out of scale. Probably, when it was first made, this garden contained no plants at all, or, possibly, only some small pine trees. The bridge-rock, which is large enough to hold a man, disappears completely as a bridge in the larger landscape; for if the tall stones behind it suggest soaring precipices, a visible bridge would be merely absurd. This bridge-stone becomes in the picture merely one of those accents which artists are allowed to make. It forms a striking cross line in the composition, balancing strongly and pleasingly the upright movement of the rocks behind it.

A second similar artistic accent repeating this cross line exists in another long, thin stone embedded in the ground halfway down the garden. In its practical aspects this stone serves to support a slightly higher level of sand behind it, suggesting a dam or low, broad cascade. At one end a flat-topped stone of equal height with deep vertical striations gives a graphic suggestion of water pouring over the dam. Artistically, this cross-rock dam is a rhythmic parallel to the bridge and serves again to balance the upright lines of the taller rocks near it.

Daisen-in garden was made about 1512. Yoshimasa had been dead twenty years, and with him had departed the glory of the Ashikaga line. Civil disturbances, which started with the Ōnin war, had never really ended but had spread over the whole nation until now there was intermittent fighting in practically every province. Any baron or vassal who saw an opportunity to extend his domains at the expense of a neighbor did not hesitate to start a little war of his own. In this way the great Ōuchi family, which had been Sesshū's patrons, were soon to be overthrown by one of their own vassals, the Mōri family. Kyoto itself again became the scene of fighting, with the shoguns who succeeded Yoshimasa as mere pawns of contending factions. Since the Ashikagas had always supported the imperial court, and were themselves now penniless and powerless, the court suffered actual poverty. When Daisen-in was built the reigning emperor had been on the throne a dozen years, but because there were no funds, the ceremonies of his enthronement had never taken place—nor were they to be held for nearly another decade.

Under the circumstances it is a wonder that even a small garden could have been newly built. That it was, is due to the force and personality of the monk Kogaku Sotan. He was one of the leading Zen ecclesiastics of his time, much honored by the imperial court. These honors of necessity could not be very substantial—hardly more than the right to wear his hat in the imperial presence and be carried in his palanquin into the palace courtyard. In a happier day he might have become a great national figure; as it was, he seems to have concentrated his ability in the perfecting of this one small temple garden.

The temple of Daisen-in seems to have been in existence as a subtemple of Daitokuji long before Sotan retired there in 1509. Probably it was in a very dilapidated condition, for he determined to rebuild it and after four years succeeded in raising the necessary funds and having the work done. Landscape paintings on the sliding paper screens that panel the reception room are believed to be by the artist Sōami. He might well have done them for he was in his prime at that time, and they look like his work. It was probably through these screens that Sōami's name came later to be associated also with the garden. It is first mentioned in this way, however, more than a hundred years after the garden was built. No known contemporary record mentions Sōami in connection with the garden.

There is, on the contrary, a brief mention in the account of Sotan's life[7] which says that after the building was finished—about 1513—he "planted rare trees and placed strange stones to make a landscape." This is as much as is known from documents about the designer of the garden; it is considered not improbable that new facts will come to light sometime. But the internal evidence of the garden points also very strongly to Sotan as the designer. It is plainly the work of a person deeply versed in Zen philosophy and imbued with Zen feeling. The same record contains a poem given to Sotan by his teacher, Daiko Zenshi, when he passed on to him the inner secrets of Zen.

This poem, which is written in Chinese characters, is too abstruse to make sense if translated. But it draws a typical Zen paradox by referring to mighty precipices and ten thousand peaks so lofty that they transcend differences. This poem may well have served as the direct inspiration for the peaks and precipices depicted in the garden. If it did not, its theme illustrates very well the turn of thought in the monasteries of the time and proves that this garden and the others of its type were deliberately and deeply esoteric in their meaning.

Assuming that Sotan planned the garden to illustrate this poem, we yet do not know who actually placed the stones nor where they came from. Whoever arranged them was someone obviously possessed of superlative skill and a deep understanding of what he was attempting to do. It was undoubtedly a stonecraftsman of the Zenami school, very likely the old man's grandson, Matashiro. It is not impossible that this unknown was the greatest garden technician in the whole history of Japanese rock art, for he not only possessed the skill, but the feeling as well.

The stones themselves obviously came from some pre-existent garden. In the lean and dangerous days of the early 16th century, the little temple

---

[7] *Ko Daitoku Shōbō Daishō Kokushi Kōgaku Dai-oshō Dōgyōki.* (Record of the way and conduct of the great priest and national teacher, Kogaku of Daitokuji.)

would hardly have been able to send out men to search for new stones, and with Kyoto full of ruined estates there was no need. We have seen how casually, in a brighter day, rocks and trees were taken up and transported from one place to another. It would have been so in this case. There is a story to the effect that the whole garden was moved to the temple from the estate of some Ashikaga retainer. Without accepting this completely, it probably holds the elements of truth, but it is more probable that the stones came from the Ashikaga estates themselves. Each of the Daisen-in stones is a rock in a thousand—in ten thousand—not to be found but by the rarest good fortune. The best of such stones found their way as gifts to the Shogun. It seems probable that in this small temple garden are the very finest of all these, turned over to Sotan as gifts from the ruined shogunal estates, gardens which could no longer be maintained. It is impossible to account for their quality and presence there in any other way.

To arrive at a just conclusion about Daisen-in is extremely difficult. Is it, indeed, as some claim, the greatest example of garden art in Japan? To base such a conclusion merely on its likeness to the Sung paintings is to realize that it would be, in this respect then, only a copy, an imitation of a painting and as such clever rather then great. But we are justified, I think, in assuming that the creator of this garden was not thinking only of reproducing a painting, but was filled with the same inspiration that animated the painters. Like them, he was trying to express a great truth, but in a different medium. By choosing stones which showed the same angular lines as the brush strokes, he conveyed, as did they, the feeling of mighty peaks and soaring precipices, the precipices of man's existence and the peaks of Enlightenment.

XI. *Sermon in Stone*

GARDENS described up to this time have all been based on nature, on hills and streams, forests, rocks, and cascades. That is, they have all been *landscape* gardens, no matter how filled with meaning. The artists who made them might idealize their subject, so suggesting and symbolizing it that its final relation to reality might not be at once apparent. But they have all had landscape as their theme and inspiration.

We come now to something different, gardens in which landscape as the pattern was discarded. Instead, the artist-mystics who made them went directly to the inherent qualities of their materials for a medium in which to express their thought and feeling. This feeling was, of course, some abstract Zen concept. The materials being rocks and sand, it was their qualities on which the pattern was formulated.

The creations which resulted should probably not be called gardens, for certainly they come within no definition of that word by Western usage and hardly, indeed, within the expanded Oriental meaning. If there were a better word, we should use it but, lacking a more exact term, we must continue to speak of them as gardens.

A number of such gardens exist in the Zen temples of Kyoto, but all, apparently, stem from one supreme original, that of Ryōanji.[1] This garden is so different from all that have preceded that it seems best to describe it briefly at once.

The garden lies on the outskirts of Kyoto on what was once the country estate of a Heian noble. Remnants of the old lake garden, called Daiju-in,

[1] Sometimes incorrectly pronounced and spelled Ryūanji.

survive in a pond with islands which we must pass to reach the temple buildings. Peaceful and lovely, the wide old lake is mossy green in the bright sun of summer, while cicadas shrill in the leafy trees which shelter our path beside it. The garden we seek lies behind the walls and buildings of the temple. We must remove our shoes in the vestibule and walk in our stocking feet to the broad, darkly polished verandah which overlooks it along one side. The garden was intended to be seen only from this verandah or from the open chapel rooms which border it. No one ever sets foot on the ground except the acolyte who keeps it raked and clean. Its purpose was simply to form an outlook and an inspiration to one sitting in meditation in the temple hall.

The area of ground making up this garden is wider and somewhat longer than a tennis court—thirty by seventy-eight feet to be exact. The wide verandah extends down nearly the full length of one side, and a small auxiliary building incloses one end. The opposite side and end are shut in by an earthen wall protected along its top by a small roof of tiles. This wall was once faced with white plaster but is now stained and weatherworn to a rusty mottled brown. Its original light color undoubtedly formed a more simple and pleasing background to the garden than does the present color.

The flat rectangle of ground is covered deeply with a coarse whitish sand kept raked into a pattern of scratched lines. Out of this rise up fifteen stones. Coarse moss grows about the base of each, but otherwise there are no plants in the garden. The fifteen stones are arranged in five groups consisting respectively of five, two, three, two, and three stones. It so happens that a small stone at either end is always hidden from any ordinary angle of vision so that only fourteen are visible at a time.

These rocks, unlike those of Daisen-in garden, are in no way remarkable for size, shape, or color, although some of them are fairly good sized boulders. Only one of the fifteen has the flat top characteristic of Muromachi stonework, and none of the others possesses those planes and angles so typical of the stones in the painting gardens. The Ryōanji stones have character and definite shape but they are not oddities nor remarkable in themselves. Their interest lies wholly in the relation of their shape and size to each other and to the areas of sand about them.

This is all there is to the garden, a rectangle of sand set about with groups of ordinary stones, a bit of moss at the base of each, a green backdrop of tall trees behind the garden wall. The average Japanese, seeing this garden for the first time, is dimly aware of something about it to which he responds; his response, of course, depending on the development of his artistic sensibilities. But foreigners shown to the place for the first time look at the sand and rocks with helpless and puzzled bewilderment. Is *this* a garden? Is it beautiful? Has it meaning? Is it art? We have explained that it is not a garden in the ordinary sense. The other questions can all be answered in the affirmative.

The beauty of this garden is subtle but powerful when we can bring ourselves to the point of perceiving it. Appreciation of something so new and strange, however, does not come at once—perhaps not until after five or six visits. We must sit down near the edge of the verandah, with no sense of time pressure, and look at the garden at length. First we must study it objectively with our minds; finally, feel, subjectively, with our intuitive perceptions, what the maker was trying to express here.

The best time to view the garden is when its rocks and sand are wet from recent rain, and the sky is still pearly grey and misty. The garden may even be thought most beautiful when it is still lightly raining, for then the depth of mystery in the stones seems to be enhanced. Wetness brings out all the subtle tones and shadowy texture of the rock surface; it darkens and softens the sand color and brightens and heightens the green of moss and tree. When this garden is dry, much of its beauty vanishes in a parched and dusty look; when the sun shines hard and bright it dispels that quality of depth and mystery the Japanese call *yūgen* and hold most precious.

It is quite possible to interpret this garden, if we try, in terms of the conventional landscape. The stretch of sand with its scratched, flowing lines may be regarded as a river and the stone groups as islets scattered in it. This accepts the scene on its actual, man-sized scale. Or, if we choose to look at it with the eye of the creative imagination building up a larger landscape, we see the scratched sand as sea waves and the rocks as bare, craggy islands. Just such views of the level sea with islands rising above it may be found at many places in the Inland Sea or along the old route to China by the Korean coast. But while such landscape interpretations are possible, they seem too simple and, almost, trite. We search for additional meaning and run across the tiger story, based on the name of the garden.

This name is the Garden of Crossing Tiger Cubs, Tora no Ko Watashi. It seems to be a very old one, given, perhaps, at the time it was built. Possibly it even antedates the construction as a sort of generic name for all such gardens. If the stones are to be taken as literally representing tigers and cubs swimming the river, this name is no more than one of those explanations for the dull witted, like the named stones of Daisen-in. Dr. Tamura,[2] however, suggests that the name was derived from China; tigers retiring to their dens across the river symbolize the Confucian teaching that the virtue of a good ruler protects the country from even the danger of ferocious animals.

The tiger story, elaborated, relates that a mother tigress with two cubs and a young leopard is attempting to cross the stream. She dares not leave a tiger cub alone with the fierce young leopard, so, after the first trip across with one cub and the leopard, she forces the leopard to return with her when she goes back to carry the second cub across. Mr. Saito thinks the back and forth movement here suggested is intended to convey a hint of the rhythmic movement in the garden stones.[3] The story is somewhat like a Zen parable, and this may be its explanation.

It seems to me, however, that the ultimate meaning of this garden can only be appreciated after a careful study of its rock arrangements. It will be noted by reference to the diagram that the five stone groups scattered about in the sand are divided in the center into left and right halves; on the left are two groups and on the right are three. Occult balance between the two

[2] *Art of the Landscape Garden in Japan.*
[3] *Nippon Teien no Shuhō.*

sides is maintained because the two are individually larger than the three.

Next, balance is maintained within each half through the size and position of the groups on the sand rectangle. The first group on the left, larger and nearer, is balanced by the smaller second group, more distant against the wall. Within the half with three parts, two small groups balance a single larger group.

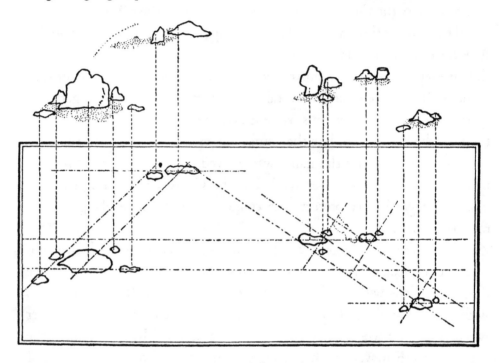

Diagram of the arrangement of Ryoanji's stones; below, their projection on the sand rectangle; above, in silhouette. (After Shigemori Mirei in Kyoto Bijutsu Taikan, Teien.)

Finally, perfect balance is maintained within each individual group. The first one on the left contains five stones, the center a large, upright rock supported by two smaller ones and by two that are almost level with the ground; the total effect is of fine stability. The second and fourth groups achieve balance through their relative forms; both contain one long, reclining stone and one short, upright stone which balance each other. The third and fifth groups are made up of three stones each; in both a larger rock is balanced by two smaller ones, but the arrangement is quite different in each.

From this analysis it is obvious that not a single stone could be moved or taken away from this composition without spoiling it. Harmonic balance has been created, not only in the relationship of each stone to those nearest it, but to every other stone in the garden.

Balance, however, is not the only quality present in this composition. In contrast to static strength, the rocks achieve movement; it hardly seems possible, indeed, that stones could convey such dynamic feeling as do these.

In general, there is a strong sense of flowing movement from left to right. If we think of the garden as a river, there is no doubt in our minds in which direction it is flowing. From the largest group on the left, the others seem to taper away; but the direction is indicated, also, by a subtle obliquity of direction in the position of the stones. Those that are upright are not exactly perpendicular but slant slightly to the right, while all the long, reclining stones seem to point in the same direction.

There is just one exception to this directional movement; the fourth group from the left is definitely reversed in direction and straight upright. It is as if it were standing out against the current. Through it, contrast and interest are created and monotony avoided.

Rhythm is obtained by the alternate upward and forward movement of every group and by contrasting movements within each group. If we start again at the left, we find the general movement of the first group is upward, of the second forward, the third again upward, the fourth again forward, while the fifth is neither but gives a sense of indefinite continuance.

The same rhythm is repeated in detail within each group. The first, although its predominating movement is upward as expressed by the large central stone, holds contrasting cross movement in its smaller stones, especially in the level cross stones lying flat in the sand. The second group moves strongly forward because of the long, reclining stone, but upward contrast appears in the short, perpendicular stone at the end. The same technique of movement and contrast can be traced in each group in continuous flowing repetition. It is obvious again that it would be impossible to move a single stone without spoiling the entire effect of the garden.

Having dissected the mechanics of balance and rhythm in this composition, we realize how completely the creator knew and followed the universal laws underlying all design. The harmony achieved is complete; harmony of color in moss, rocks, and sand; harmony of line in the shape and size of the rocks; harmony of movement in their spacing on the rectangle and relationship to each other.

After we have finished our intellectual analysis and our minds are no longer thinking about it, we give ourselves up to an emotional understanding and appreciation of the garden. We sit and just look at the composition as a whole, its utter stability soothing us, our feelings tranquillized by its perfections. Grey, green, and brown, the soft mistiness of rain, the rise and fall of the stones, flowing and continuous. . . .

Without any effort we know intuitively what the garden maker was trying to express here. It was Harmony, that Harmony which underlies the universe, the world, and man; the Harmony of force, of matter and of spirit; the Harmony that makes the morning stars to sing together, the heart of nature to beat in rhythm, and man to know himself a brother of the rocks and wind and sun. Modern science has confirmed this knowledge through intellectual research; the ancient Hebrew poet sang it in terms of his religious concepts when he said:

"*Be still,* and KNOW that I am God!"

A sermon in stone, a whole philosophy bound up between the covers of an earthen wall—undoubtedly this garden is one of the world's great masterpieces of religiously inspired art.

And with it the Muromachi garden makers reached their climax.

Wetness brings out the subtle tones and shadowy texture of the sand and stones in Ryōanji's strange garden. When the light is pearly and misty, it possesses yūgen, that quality of the depth and mystery of beauty which the Zen artist holds most precious. (Photo by Harada Sunao.)

Detail of one of the Ryōanji stone groups showing the flowing movement of lines joined to the static strength of perfect balance and proportion which is characteristic of all the groups. (Photo by Harada Sunao.)

Inevitably we are filled with an overwhelming curiosity to know who made this garden—where he received his inspiration—how such a concept took form—what lay behind it?

Unfortunately, we do not know the answers to these questions. A few facts have come to light about who made the garden but of the forces that lay behind it almost nothing. We may guess at them, however, and with a background of knowledge we probably shall not be far wrong in our surmises.

A creation as striking and unique as this garden inevitably has been the object of much speculation and comment among Japanese connoisseurs. Until very recently, however, almost no actual research was done on its background and history. Like the Silver Pavilion and Daisen-in, Ryōanji has generally been credited to the artist Sōami—crediting him with gardens became almost a habit. But, as with the others, the first mention of his name in connection with it appears a good two hundred years after it was made.[4] The 17th century tea master Kanamori Sōwa has also been given the credit for Ryōanji. Sōwa, however, may be ruled out by the fact that one of his own friends, writing in the *Kaiki* a few years after his death, repeats the statement that Sōami made it. If Sōwa had made the garden, his friend would certainly have said no such thing. Probably, the similarity of the names Sōami and Sōwa accounts for the later story.

What literary evidence exists about the origin of the garden carries us back to the days of Muromachi greatness, before the Ōnin war. In 1450, Katsumoto, the powerful Lord of Hosokawa, who later became one of the leaders in that war, acquired an estate called Daiju-in. It lay not far from the Gold Pavilion and contained one of the old lake gardens. Presumably, Katsumoto rehabilitated this place and on the hillside above the lake built a small Zen temple, which he called Ryōanji. When the Ōnin war broke out, the estates of Katsumoto were among the first to be attacked and burned by roving bands of the opposition, this one among them.

For some years afterward the priests connected with Ryōanji found

---

[4] In the *Saga Kotei*.

sanctuary outside the city. But in 1488, with Katsumoto dead and the city trying to rehabilitate itself, his son, Masamoto, caused a new temple building to be put up on the site of the old one. All evidence indicates that the present stone garden was constructed at that time. The priest in charge of the re-founding, was called Tokuhō Zengetsu; he was probably largely influential in causing the garden to take its unique form. But it was in this very year, it will be recalled, that Masamoto, the young Lord Hosokawa, allowed several thousand of his men to work for a few days moving pine trees from the old Flowery Palace to the Shogun's new Eastern Hill Villa. Obviously, he and Yoshimasa were good friends at the time and both were interested in Zen and in estate building. I think we may assume that Yoshimasa's fine taste was influential in creating this garden.

But whence came its unique form, its sweep of white sand, and curiously placed rocks? There seems to be only one possible place for the prototype—China. Almost certainly some of the Ch'an monasteries—or at least one—possessed gardens of esoteric significance made of sand and stones. A work of art such as the Ryōanji garden does not come into being all at once; it is the outcome of a long period of development when inspiration works on form and technique to perfect its expression. At present I know of no literary or vestigial evidence of any Chinese sand gardens, but I feel sure future research must disclose it. Had the Japanese developed the rock and sand concept independently, we would certainly find some traces of the preceding forms, the steps which led up to it. But, instead, suddenly there appears in the Muromachi period this perfected piece of work.

It is not alone in its sudden appearance. Almost contemporaneously several other gardens were made showing influences of the same form. For example, there is the mysterious "Silver Sand Sea" in Yoshimasa's Eastern Hill Villa. Yoshimasa was in the forefront of new artistic endeavors, the leader in establishing new esthetic concepts. What is more reasonable than to suppose this present bulky sand pile originated simply as a spread of white sand before the main building of his villa, placed there in accordance with reports from China, to mark the ecclesiastical nature of his retreat?

More definite evidence pointing to a common prototype in China is found in the garden of Jōeiji in Yamaguchi, far west of Kyoto. This garden, it will be recalled, was probably made by the painter Sesshū after he had returned from China where he had visited many monasteries. The Jōeiji garden is a naturalistic landscape with a pond, islands, and a dry cascade. But between the pond edge and the buildings is a level stretch of ground with rock groups scattered about in it; it is somewhat as if Ryōanji had been set down in front of Tenryūji's pond. This level space might once have been sanded, and its stone groups are individually very like those of Ryōanji. But in their general arrangement on the open space they lack, at least at present, the carefully balanced relationships which are the essential beauty of the Ryōanji garden. There can be no doubt, however, but that somewhere these two gardens had a common ancestor.

Evidence again of a contemporary interest in rock and sand creations is found in the small garden around the tomb of the priest Ikkyū, at Shuon-an temple. Ikkyū was born an imperial prince, son of that Emperor whom Yoshimitsu had entertained in the Gold Pavilion; but he lived to become a great Zen ecclesiastic in his own right. During the Ōnin trouble he fled from Kyoto and rehabilitated the small temple of Shuon-an, hidden in the hills halfway to Nara. Here, some years later, when he was around eighty, he built his own tomb and presumably the small rock and sand garden which surrounds it. The tomb seems to have been originally a monument, or *stupa,* but today it has been rebuilt into a small square building. The space around it is covered with sand out of which rise a number of stone groups, their style very like those of Ryōanji and Jōeiji. Low, small-leaved azaleas form a green base around these rocks, as the moss grows around the Ryōanji stones.

It remains, then, to account for the Ryōanji garden as a perfected piece of art. It can be laid, I think, to the Muromachi period itself, that era when inspiration and technique reached maturity together. The Muromachi landscape painters became, at last, the equals of their masters, the Sung painters of China. There is every reason to suppose the stone artists did likewise; or they may have become even better, inspired by the never changing love of nature in Japan which kept the ideal always before them. In the persons of old Zenami and the other men who had spent their lives making the great gardens, the Muromachi period possessed a technical ability which was equal to the inspiration of the task set them by Hosokawa Masamoto and his priest, Tokuhō Zengetsu.

Who actually made the Ryōanji garden? The answer seems to lie in two written characters roughly cut on the back of one of the garden stones. They may be deciphered to read Kotarō and Hikojirō, men's names. Painstaking search[5] through the records discloses that there actually were two garden craftsmen by these names in Kyoto at that time; men who, like Zenami, must have been outstanding in their work even to have had their names mentioned briefly.

Let us then, re-create in our imagination the scene of this garden's construction. Tokuhō Zengetsu may himself have been a priest who had been to China, bringing back directly the idea of the garden plan. Or there may have been another in Kyoto about that time who was telling the Shogun and the coterie of priests and artists about the rock and sand creations in the Ch'an monasteries. Probably sketches were available, illustrating the idea. When these were shown to Kotarō and Hikojirō, who had been called in for consultation, they became enthusiastic. Garden craftsmen at that time were beginning to think of themselves somewhat as creative artists with an understanding of what lay behind the mere execution of the work.

Stones were gathered and work begun. Day by day, Zengetsu and other priests sat on the newly finished verandah of the temple, watching its progress, directing, discussing it. Often they must have been joined by the patron, Masamoto, whose opinion would be deferred to. Physically it was no great undertaking to collect and arrange the few stones in this garden; but artistically it was a prolonged operation. There must have been much trying and rearrangement, many rejections and fine shiftings before

[5] By Mr. Shigemori, who has discovered the other historical material used here but is not accountable for the theories.

all was pronounced exactly right. I have seen a young Japanese student of esthetics sit with a tray of sand and an assortment of small stones, attempting to achieve something of the balanced artistry of Ryōanji, finally to give it up with a resigned shake of the head.

But at last all was perfected, the ground was leveled, the wall built, and white sand spread over the ground and raked into long straight lines. Then the rain fell and as its pearly, misty light filled the garden there appeared the feeling of *yūgen*—the mystery of beauty. Kotarō and Hikojirō, feeling that they had created a masterpiece, cut their names awkwardly into the back of one of the stones, as artists put a seal to their paintings. Ryōanji is probably the only signed piece of garden art in the world.

And so the garden has stood for four and a half centuries, its rocks weathering to ancient greys, moss creeping around their bases, trees springing high beyond the aging wall. Still the garden presents its puzzle to the world and still it speaks its subtle sermon to those who can understand it.

XII. *Hideyoshi's Gardens*

THE weary decades of the 16th century dragged on, marked by fighting and disorder. It was not a single, long-drawn-out campaign, but scattered, intermittent fighting, as one baron or another found opportunity to enrich himself at the expense of a weaker neighbor. The emperor lived as always in Kyoto, but eventually his palace became hardly habitable, and even food was often a problem. The city itself was shabby and shrunken, only a ghost of the former glorious capital. Nevertheless, away from it, the actual wealth of the nation seems to have increased during this period, for with the exception of the Ōnin war, which ruined Kyoto, fighting in Japan has never been highly destructive.

It was during this century (probably in 1552) that Europe first learned of Japan through shipwrecked Portuguese sailors. Shortly after the discovery, came Portuguese Jesuit missionaries and traders and not far behind them, other traders, Dutch and English. The Jesuits were to play an important part in Japanese religious history, while the Dutch and English made some contributions to general Japanese knowledge, notably of firearms. But, on the whole, these Europeans had remarkably little influence on the cultural and artistic life of the nation and none, so far as we can see, on the gardens.

The early 16th century, like the Kamakura age, was a period when a type of culture which had been developing in the capital under special conditions spread out over the nation. Muromachi esthetics, reaching its climax under Yoshimasa, had been first taken into the provinces by such men as Sesshū, and from them it radiated in widening circles. But the canons of austere simplicity which governed the Muromachi esthetic were far too severe for general or popular acceptance. They survived in modified form in the tea ceremonial and its adjuncts, the tea equipment, the tea room, and the tea garden; but with the rise of a new set of provincial conquerors in the last quarter of the 16th century a new spirit entered the nation. In the words of Sir George Sansom, "there began a time in which gold glittered, colour came back into pictures and the arts veered toward those Japanese equivalents of the rococo and baroque which distinguished the period called Momoyama after Hideyoshi's palace by that name."

Peace and power were brought once more to Japan by a succession of three great captains and administrators. The first was Oda Nobunaga, the second his lieutenant, the one-time peasant Hideyoshi, the third his ally and neighbor, Tokugawa Ieyasu. Nobunaga, a small baron of central Japan, by luck and skill was able to establish himself in the capital and there receive the imperial commission to pacify the country. Under him disappeared the last of the Ashikaga shoguns. When Nobunaga was murdered, Hideyoshi stepped into his place, and when Hideyoshi died, Ieyasu became his successor.

Nobunaga, a typical provincial military baron, is of little interest compared to his lieutenant and successor, Hideyoshi. This man is probably the most remarkable that Japan has produced. He was born in 1536 as one of the lowest of Nobunaga's retainers, son of a common footsoldier and peasant. The boy grew up, small, dark, monkey-faced and mischievous, his unprepossessing physical appearance being a handicap all his life. Yet behind his monkey face the boy possessed a sagacity which was to make him, eventually, the actual ruler of the nation. He rose from lower, to higher servant of Nobunaga, becoming advisor and finally trusted general, for the unsettled times made it possible for genius to rise to its level. Nobunaga undoubtedly owed his success to Hideyoshi's guidance.

The work of Nobunaga and Hideyoshi consisted of forcing the other feudal barons to submit to a central controlling government, either by military force or by negotiation and alliance. Nobunaga began, and Hideyoshi completed this work. When it was done, such was the expansive spirit of the new age, Hideyoshi started out to conquer China. This appears to have been largely a gesture of personal glorification on his part, added to hope of plunder, rather than a movement based on animosity toward China. However, in two successive attempts, Hideyoshi's armies could get no farther than Korea. The effort of repelling them was a final drain on the weakened Ming dynasty in China, and a short time afterward it was overthrown by the northern Manchus.

Nobunaga built the castle of Azuchi in 1576, with a great keep, walls, and moat. Although it differed greatly in outward appearance from a European castle, with its tower covered with many small-roofed gables, it has been assumed that the fundamental idea was derived from descriptions given by Europeans with whom Nobunaga was very friendly. Its living apartments were lavishly decorated with gold and colored painting, a form which set the style of gorgeous exuberance in art and decoration for the whole following period.

Other barons quickly erected new castles like Nobunaga's, but when Hideyoshi came to power, he built in Osaka, in 1583, the largest, strongest, and most gorgeous castle of them all. It was an expression of his megolamania, for everything Hideyoshi undertook had to be on the largest and most magnificent scale imaginable. Partly, no doubt, this was a reflection of the expansive spirit of the new age; but we can assume also, I think, that it was the born peasant demonstrating his ability to be the greatest and strongest in the nation. His grandiose gestures, however, were never made entirely for show; invariably they reflected cannily back on himself in some useful way, if only by impressing his enemies with his power.

To use again the words of Sir George Sansom:

"The castle of Osaka could not compare as an architectural monument with, let us say, one of the great cathedrals of the middle ages in Europe, but in sheer size, in the effort required to transport and assemble its massive materials of stone and timber, it probably rivalled any building in the

Hideyoshi's Osaka Castle has recently been re-erected in modern materials. It towers now high on its hill, impressive even compared to modern skyscrapers. The five-storied keep is built in the unique style of Japanese castle architecture, each story marked by small gables, decorated by carvings, and crowned by a golden dolphin. This building is, no doubt, characteristic of Hideyoshi's other great castle-palaces which have since disappeared. (Photo from Board of Tourist Industry.)

Kokei, the Tiger Glen garden, originally in a courtyard of Hide-yoshi's Fushimi Castle, creates the suggestion of a glen. It is on a nearly natural scale, the effect being obtained by the use of huge stones. The Sago palms growing in this garden must be covered in winter with straw wrappings which are made artistic as well as utilitarian. (Photo by Hararda Sunao.)

The elegant and opulent little garden of Sambō-in temple is a Momoyama miniature of an old shinden lake garden. Fine stones are used lavishly, constituting a form of ostentatious display which corresponds exactly to the use of golden ornaments in the buildings. (Photo from Board of Tourist Industry.)

Stone arrangements in Sambō-in are generally very well done, and the stones are individually excellent. This is not surprising, considering that they are probably the choice gleanings from a hundred other gardens. (Photo from Board of Tourist Industry.)

West. As to its beauty there is no room for comparison, for there is no exact counterpart in the West to the scheme of decoration depending upon elaborate wood-carvings, usually poly-chromatic, and the free use of pigment and gold foil on partition and folding screens, which characterizes the castles and palaces of this period." Regarding its fittings and utensils he continues: "they were all of the most costly materials and lavish to the point of absurdity. Hideyoshi liked to show them off to visitors, one of whom records that all the ceiling and pillars were plastered with pure gold, that kettles, bowls, tea-cups, medicine chests, almost every kind of vessel, in fact, were of pure gold, as were the locks, bolts, hinges and ornaments of shelves and wardrobes, doors and windows. Another writer . . . concludes, 'the very privies are decorated with gold and silver and painting in fine colours. All these precious things are used as if they were dirt. Ah! Ah!' "

Today, the tremendous stone bastions above the moats of Osaka Castle still remain, and the great keep has recently been duplicated in its original form, but in modern materials. It towers now, high on its hill above industrial Osaka, impressive even when compared to skyscrapers. The keep of five stories is built in the unique and characteristic style of Japanese castle architecture, each story marked by small gables decorated with carvings and crowned by a golden dolphin. From this building we gain a good idea of how Hideyoshi's later castle-palaces must have looked, buildings which have now entirely disappeared. In addition to the towering central fortress, there were other buildings within the moats which formed the palatial living apartments and audience chambers. No trace of any original garden now remains, but no doubt there was one, as we know there were others in the later castles.

One of Nobunaga's first steps on making Kyoto his headquarters was to order the Imperial Palace rebuilt. He started other improvements, but it was Hideyoshi who brought the city to its next great period. New streets were laid out, a moat and rampart built entirely around it, the Imperial Palace further improved, and many other buildings reconstructed.

Most impressive of all these new buildings was the great castle-palace Hideyoshi built as his own headquarters. It was called Jūraku-tei, the Mansion of Assembled Pleasures, and stood on part of what had been the original Heian palace inclosure. Evidently this site appealed to Hideyoshi's notion of grandeur. For a long time the emperors had not even been crowned in the old enthronement hall, for the last buildings there had been swept away by fire and the area was waste ground. Jūraku-tei which Hideyoshi built on it was more a palace than a castle, although the place was inclosed by a moat with iron gate, and included a barbican which, according to a contemporary record "towered like a mountain." This account goes on:[1]

"The pillars of the gate were of iron and the doors of copper, while the 'jade pavilion' was ornamented by stars. The pattern of the tiles was like jewelled tigers breathing in the wind, and like golden dragons intoning in the clouds. When it was finished [October 19, 1587] Hideyoshi moved thither from Osaka Castle. He arrived at Yodo [the head of river navigation] with several hundred vessels coated with gold and silver and with appointments of the same metals. From Yodo, with five hundred carriages and five thousand bearers, he came to the capital. The courtiers and feudal lords came to meet him, and all the way from Yodo and Toba the thoroughfare was crowded with people. From the next day to the end of the month there were rejoicings and it was as if market were being carried out in front of the gates. . . . In the garden was a dancing stage and left and right of it music rooms. All the way to the apartments of Hideyoshi's wife, the carpenters had used their utmost skill, the colourists had put forth their best endeavours. The splendour was intense. People all said they had never seen the like."

Certain buildings and gates of Jūraku-tei still survive, having been given to various temples when the palace was dismantled. One splendid gate, called the Kara-mon, is at Daitokuji temple and another building,

---

[1] *Taikōki*. This translation taken with slight changes from Ponsonby Fane's *History of Kyoto*.

poetically called the Pavilion of the Flying Cloud, or Hiun-kaku, belongs to Nishi Honganji temple. Within the immensity of the Jūraku-tei inclosure this latter building served as the private apartment of Hideyoshi himself. It is a three-storied structure, showing plainly its derivation from such older garden buildings as the Gold and Silver Pavilions. But it is considerably larger than they are and is asymmetrical in form, with the curving gables and carved eaves characteristic of Momoyama architecture. Light and graceful in its design, some critics rank it even above the Gold Pavilion in architectural merit.

The sliding screen panels which form its walls are covered with gold leaf on which are scenes painted by Kano Eitoku and Kano Sanraku, the best artists of the day. In spite of its gold and color, there is a restrained richness, a delicacy, in the decoration of this building, both inside and out, which is quite different from the overwhelming gorgeousness of the great audience halls in which Hideyoshi impressed his vassals. It suggests that his personal taste was probably not so flamboyant as other evidence would indicate. He was an earnest devotee of the tea ceremonial as we shall see, a fact which probably accounts for the tone of this building.

The Pavilion of the Flying Cloud stands at present in a portion of Nishi-Honganji garden called Tekisui-en. The setting is small and cramped, in no way worthy of the building. The pavilion is perched some feet above the water, on the rocky shore of a small pond, leaving a portico which served as a boathouse hanging pathetically useless. Under this portico boats could be brought entirely inside the building and reached by steps leading down to the water level. It is obvious that the pavilion stood originally either entirely within a lake or beside one large enough for the old pastime of boating.

Today the small pond of Tekisui-en is spanned by an immense stone bridge which leads to the pavilion. This bridge, cut from a single gigantic stone, is over twenty feet long, three and a half feet wide and nearly a foot thick. Undoubtedly it also came from one of Hideyoshi's gardens and was brought here at the time the pavilion was moved. Its massiveness and great size are typical of Momoyama garden stones.

We know little more about the garden of Jūraku-tei except that it contained a hillock, many rarely shaped trees, and large beautiful stones. These facts are gained from authorities quoted by Ponsonby Fane. They relate, for instance, that the citizens of a nearby ward in the city were called upon to provide and transport 4,763 loads of earth for the hillock. Trees and rocks were commandeered, in the traditional manner, from various temples and even from private gardens.

Hideyoshi was not the first high personage, as we know, who used his position and power to obtain desirable garden material. But he has come down in Japanese garden tradition as the archtype of stone pre-emptor. From the number of stones we find crowded into his later gardens, he must have been insatiable; doubtless he deserves his reputation. According to general belief, he took stones whenever he saw any that appealed to him, his method, apparently, being to hint they would make suitable gifts. With no place safe from his depredations, it was a matter to mention in the records when the artistry of one garden—that of Ryōanji—so appealed to him he put up a sign prohibiting the removal of any of its stones.[2] In the surviving Hideyoshi gardens we can distinguish many rocks of typical Muromachi shape, rocks with flat planes and strong angles. Doubtless these came from ruined Muromachi estates, but instead of being set up to display their once-prized form, they now are jumbled in with the many others. Were we able to identify them, we probably could find, among these, many of the stones which have disappeared from older gardens—although he may not have been the first to take them from their original setting.

Hideyoshi had planned Jūraku-tei with the express purpose of entertaining the emperor there, even as Yoshimitsu had been host to the sovereign two hundred years before in the Gold Pavilion. This earlier event now served as a basis for the study of court ceremonial, for no one then living had taken part in an imperial progress of such magnitude. The occasion was planned for early May, 1588. It is the time of year when the azaleas in Kyoto reach their peak of color and brilliance. This flower has

[2] Toyama, *Muromachi Jidai Teienshi.*

168

never been one of those with strong literary associations in the Orient, and so we do not find it mentioned in poems and other records as we do, for instance, the pine. But remembering the Momoyama love of color and brightness, I think we cannot be far wrong in assuming the azalea was planted extensively in Jūraku-tei, although there is no mention of it as far as I know. I believe the imperial visit was timed to coincide with its blooming, as the visit to the Gold Pavilion took place in the cherry blossom season.

On the great day of the visit Hideyoshi, in his official capacity of regent, carried the long train of the emperor as he walked to his ox-coach, and himself rode in a lesser coach in the procession. He would not have missed being part of the show himself, of course. The procession accompanying the emperor was longer than the mile which separated the gate of Jūraku-tei from the gate of the Imperial Palace. Great crowds lined the way, for such a sight had not been seen in the capital for many weary years of poverty. Great days had come again to the city.

At Jūraku-tei, as at the Gold Pavilion, there were banqueting, music, dancing, and poem writing. The visit had been planned for three days but was extended to five. At the poem party the subject chosen was the traditional one of "Pines," inspired, no doubt, by the fine trees which had been moved into the garden. Wrote the Emperor Go-Yōzei:

"Well doth it repay me, having waited until today to see the pine branches in unchanging prosperity, age after age."

To which Hideyoshi replied:

"It is because my Liege Lord hath deigned to visit me that the beautiful pines show themselves so green against the eaves."[3]

Hideyoshi lived in Jūraku-tei only four years, then nominally he turned it and his office of regent over to his nephew, having then no son, and retired to Osaka castle. But a few years later, a son having been born, he quarreled with the nephew who was forced to commit suicide and Jūraku-tei was entirely dismantled. Some of its buildings and, probably, most of its

[3] Poem translations by Ponsonby Fane.

garden stones were moved to the new castle-palace which Hideyoshi had begun.

The new estate was located in Fushimi, a suburb just south of Kyoto.[4] Probably, it was the most magnificent assemblage of buildings ever created in Japan. When it was dismantled, only twenty-five years after Hideyoshi's death, some of its gates and halls were given away to various temples. The best, probably, went again to Nishi Honganji where they still stand, the most splendid examples remaining of Momoyama architecture and art. Speaking of these great audience halls and the art of Momoyama in general, Sir George Sansom says:

"On the walls, mostly of bright gold, there are blue-eyed tigers prowling through groves of bamboo, or multi-coloured *shishi*—mythical beasts like lions, but amiable and curly haired—that gambol among peonies against a golden background. There are gorgeous landscapes thick with old pines and blossoming plum-trees, where bright birds perch on fantastic rocks or float amid ripples of deep blue. There are groves and banks and gardens, rich with brilliant leaves and flowers; bearded and sinuous dragons winding their complicated length through sepia clouds; gaggles of wild geese sweeping across the moon; and scenes of the Chinese court peopled with ancient worthies. As a rule these apartments display, suite after suite, such profusion of colour and detail, such a deliberate effort to overwhelm the eye with splendour, that they come perilously near to vulgarity. But from this they are generally saved by a certain bravery, a boldness of stroke and a brilliance of design. Their full mastery can only be appreciated through comparison with less competent works of the same school. Their usual effect is one of size and richness, far remote from the pensive simplicity of Ashikaga ink drawings, whose artists hinted where the Momoyama painters spoke emphatically aloud."

This same gorgeousness and brilliance are evident in Momoyama gar-

[4] A hundred years after Hideyoshi's death the district was planted with peach trees, from which it is called Peach Hill, or Momoyama, the name by which it is usually spoken of in history.

dens, a form of art as typical of the period as were the golden screens. It is especially evident in a garden believed to have been originally a part of Fushimi castle itself. When the great hall of the castle and the other buildings were moved, beam by beam, and reconstructed in the grounds of Nishi-Honganji temple, a garden was moved at the same time. From a careful study of its reconstructed stone arrangements, it is believed that this garden was rebuilt, stone by stone, as nearly as possible into its original form. Today it forms the outlook to the great audience hall just as it probably did when both hall and garden were part of Fushimi castle.

The garden is named Kokei, meaning the Tiger Glen. It is a title derived from Chinese literature, being the name of a valley on famous Mount Lu. But the name is eminently appropriate for a garden belonging to Hideyoshi. Tigers were a favorite decorative motif of his day, having become known for the first time through his campaigns into Korea where there are wild tigers. They were the most magnificent animals the Japanese had ever seen, regarded as the king of beasts, and held to be a symbol of power and glory. The anatomical details and attitudes of the tigers which prowl the golden screens of Momoyama make it plain that artists had only the skins to paint from; but they did manage, somehow, to catch the tiger's strength and glory.

Strength and glory are the dominant notes in the Tiger Glen garden, Kokei. While it occupies a courtyard only ninety-five by sixty-five feet in size, it, yet, creates the effect of a wild mountain glen in which the roar of the tiger might be heard at night. It is a dry garden, its general plan somewhat similar to the small dry garden of Daisen-in temple, but it is infinitely removed in spirit from that esoteric painting-garden. Kokei was designed to harmonize with the splendid buildings around it and to uphold their colorings and gorgeous decorations. Success in this was achieved by the use of great stones crowded together, but arranged in a strongly unified design. Its focal point is a large dry cascade, topped by huge pointed boulders. The effect of water boiling down through this rocky defile is very graphic.

As the garden stands at present, the slanting, massive tiled roofs of a large building rise behind it. It is sometimes claimed that these huge ceramic slopes are supposed to represent mountain peaks; this might be so, but the construction of the garden indicates that the eye was not intended to rise above the rocks of the cascade. Probably, in its original location there was no more of a natural outlook than there is at present, and the garden was intended to be self-inclusive, forming a framed picture to one sitting in the audience hall.

This garden picture has been made by piling earth into a ridge at the back and placing large stones in it. The slant of some of these might suggest the upward slope of the mountain. Water—by suggestion only—flows out of the cascade and around two islands, but the stones which border the islands are so large, the spread of the water is but little more than a widening of the stream. The islands are in traditional crane and turtle style, the turtle, as usual, identifiable by his head. In this case it is a stone so large and graphic that we can almost make out mouth and eyes; but the island as a whole is not so well suggested as are some of those in older gardens. It is obvious that in making crane and turtle islands a traditional outline was being followed, but the original tale of the turtles supporting the Immortals' Isles had obviously been forgotten, since this island is reached by a bridge. And no bridge, nor even a ship, it will be recalled, could reach the ancient Mystic Isles upheld by giant turtles.

There are two other stone bridges in the garden, the three together linking the islands into a chain joined to the shore at either end. This linked chain of islands becomes a characteristic of the gardens of this period. The large central bridge between the two islands is cut from a single great stone more than fourteen feet long and two and a half feet wide. It makes a massive cross-note in the composition, not unlike the similar cross line found in Daisen-in. Perhaps, once there may have been some reason for taking the short stroll down the length of the garden, crossing these islands and bridges, but now the path begins and ends nowhere, and the bridges are only part of the garden design.

An innovation among the plant materials of this garden is the exotic

The famous Fujito stone in Sambō-in garden. At one time, apparently, it was the most famous stone in Japan, seeming to have had supernatural powers attributed to it. It possesses a well-authenticated history of transfer through four gardens, illustrating how garden stones traveled from one estate to another in earlier days. (Photo from Nihon Teien Shizukan.)

A tea garden in the classical style of the seventeenth century is part of Koho-an temple in Kyoto. It illustrates the path of stepping stones leading to the tea room door (from which the picture was taken), the stone laver, and the lantern beside it. This laver, designed in the likeness of a Chinese coin, is said to be the work of Kobori Enshū. Modern "improvement" with cement has now considerably marred its setting. A winter protection of pine needles has been spread over the moss. (Photo by Okamoto Toyo.)

Cycas revoluta, usually called the Sago palm. At present, only a few ancient specimens survive, but old paintings show that the garden formerly held a great many. The *Cycas* appears, also, in some of the paintings which decorate the building, indicating that it must have appealed to Momoyama artists. This is not surprising, for its massive trunk and palm-like foliage are somehow in keeping with the Momoyama feeling of size and exuberance, while its exoticism expressed the outreaching spirit of that age. In Hideyoshi's day the *Cycas* must have been very rare and expensive, for it is no native of Japan but had been introduced not long before, from its native Java by the Portuguese. Doubtless it had been grown in the gardens of Fushimi Castle, from which some of the plants were probably transferred to the reconditioned garden along with its stones. Specimens have probably been cultivated there ever since. Being a semitropical plant, it must be protected by straw wrappings through winters as cold as those in Japan, but if this is done, it will live and grow to a grotesque old age as have those now surviving in Kokei.

In the significance of its stone work Kokei differs from earlier gardens in which a single rock sometimes represented a whole mountain. Here the landscape is not abridged and symbolic but is to be taken at virtually its face value; that is, the huge rocks are not intended to suggest anything larger than themselves, and the mountain glen they create is of practically natural size. Had a reduced landscape been attempted in this garden, it would almost certainly have lost its significance and been overwhelmed by the immense size of the buildings. The imagination is called upon not to build up a landscape from hints and suggestions, but instead to picture an invisible mountain of which this glen is but a small part. Although the mountain towers out of sight, its presence is powerfully felt as we look at the massive waterfall. No work of man, even such a work as these large buildings, could overwhelm such a mountain, and so the buildings take their proper place in relation to it and in the harmony of man and the universe.

To conceive and carry out such an original scheme indicates a high degree of creative artistry on the part of the garden maker, who, obviously, was perfectly aware of the problem he faced. His solution shows that the early Momoyama garden designers were men of originality and force with a touch of genius. Though they followed a traditional pattern, they were not dominated by the past but bent it to their needs. If their work has not the spiritual quality of the Muromachi gardens, it is the fault of the times and not of the artists. It was a period of spacious materialism, of conquest and glory, and this is expressed perfectly in the massive stones and their unified arrangement.

By the time this garden was made, garden men had achieved the status of professional artists. They were no longer the monks and scholars of the Muromachi period but followed the custom of other artists in taking professional names. We hear, for instance, of two brothers who assumed as the first part of their names the old term of *Kawara-mono,* derived, it would seem, from the great Kawara-mono Zenami. Probably, they conceived themselves as carrying on the style of rock artistry that he founded. Another gardener of this period is known as Asagiri Shimanosuke; from its poetic sound (the words mean "Morning-mist, Man of the Island") it is assumed that this name also was a pseudonym.[5] Asagiri is said to have been the designer of Kokei, but little or nothing is known about him. Professional artists were not considered sufficiently important in those days of military glory to be mentioned in the records, so we know little about them. But we, probably, may safely assume that Asagiri was the head gardener of Fushimi Castle, the first, and perhaps the greatest, of the Momoyama garden artists.

One more of Hideyoshi's gardens survives, that of Sambō-in, a subtemple of Daigoji. This temple itself is old, dating back to Heian and Kamakura times. It lies in a picturesque valley just over the Eastern Hills from Kyoto and but a short ride from Fushimi Castle. In Muromachi days

[5] It has been suggested that Asagiri might have been the name used by the tea master, Sen no Rikyū, when he turned to garden making. But Rikyū had been dead several years by the time Fushimi Castle was built; also, as the foremost tea master of the time, hence an exponent of the old Muromachi spirit in art, it seems impossible that he could have designed gardens which so perfectly expressed the Momoyama age.

the subtemple of Sambō-in had risen to wealth and importance when its abbots became friends of the Ashikaga shoguns. The weeping cherry trees that Yoshimitsu planted in the Flowery Palace garden had been presented to him by a court noble, the gift being negotiated by the abbot of Sambō-in. This abbot may well have been a cherry blossom enthusiast himself and have caused trees to be planted in the vicinity of his temple. At any rate, by Hideyoshi's day, Sambō-in had long been famous as a place for viewing cherry blossoms; as it still is. Every April the profusion of flowers forms petally clouds of pink against the blue of the spring sky, and crowds of people go out to enjoy the sight. It was through these flowering trees in the vicinity of the temple that the present garden of Sambō-in came into existence, for Hideyoshi decided to use this old temple as headquarters for a grand cherry-viewing party, remodeling the place to that end.[6]

Sambō-in had suffered in the Onin war but, apparently, came through that troubled time better than most other places, for in the spring of 1596 its old Muromachi garden was still good enough to be shown to Hideyoshi when he was in the vicinity. The abbot at that time was named Gien and in his diary[7] we find the whole story. He must have hinted that the place needed reconstruction, for a note in the diary states that Hideyoshi proposed to undertake it. Nothing came of it at that time, however, but the next spring Hideyoshi came again and this time authorized the project. But it was not until the following spring, 1598, that work really started. Evidently Hideyoshi made a sudden decision to hold one of his grand outings in the vicinity of Sambō-in and wished the temple prepared immediately as a place to stay.

There were only six weeks in which to accomplish this reconditioning.

---

[6] Inside Sambō-in garden there still stands a single ancient cherry tree of the weeping variety, said to have been planted in Hideyoshi's time; that is, it is now some three hundred and forty years old. Not far from this ancient, a young tree of the same kind has been planted to carry on the tradition when the old one shall at last be gone. The custom of renewal in this manner is very nearly universal in Japan, so that much that is frail and transient has been perpetuated.

[7] *Gien Jugo Nikki.*

The temple itself was rehabilitated and decorated with finely painted gold screens which it still possesses. The garden was refurbished, and the party took place as scheduled. Camp was made on a small hill nearby, called Flower-Viewing Hill. It was customary to string curtains for privacy around such a camp but in this case, instead of real curtains, gold screens were used, painted with red silk curtains bearing Hideyoshi's crest, shown billowing in the wind. Some of these are also still possessed by the temple.

With the party ended, the complete reconstruction of the garden was begun. Three hundred workmen arrived for the purpose, in charge of Kawara-mono Sen, one of the Fushimi gardeners. When it came time to arrange the stones, he was joined by two others, his brother Kawara-mono Yoshio and Niwa-mono Kentei. It is often said that Hideyoshi designed this garden himself, in the customary manner of owners. The diary shows that he took a great interest in it, consulting with Gien on several occasions. Together they decided on some of its features—an island here, a bridge there. But for some reason the details mentioned in the diary were not carried out—or at least they are not found in the garden today. Hideyoshi fell ill shortly after the flower viewing party and could not visit the temple to watch the progress of the work, so Gien sent him frequent reports. By summer he was able to send word that the garden was virtually completed.

It is probable that Hideyoshi never saw it so, for his illness increased, and in September he suddenly died. The following spring, when he might have held a second fine party in the temple, his great public funeral took place in Kyoto.

After his death the political world was full of intrigues to secure his power. Sambō-in garden was of no interest to anyone except Gien and the gardeners. They, however, continued to work on it lovingly, as on a masterpiece. In fact, for another twenty years it received the attention of Niwa-mono Kentei during which time many things were perfected. Perhaps it was during this period that the features planned by Hideyoshi were changed. The cascade was remodeled no less than three times until at last it was exactly right.

HIDEYOSHI'S GARDENS

When the garden at last was pronounced finished, it was generally agreed by all that it was unsurpassed anywhere. If the long period of retouching took away much of its vitality and strength, it left it, nevertheless, the most finished and debonair of the rococo gardens. Few important changes seem to have been made in it since, and apparently it has always been maintained in fair condition. We can see it today probably very much as Kentei left it.

The garden fills a rectangle one hundred eighty feet long and eighty feet wide, lying on the south side of a line of buildings. The center space is filled by a lake, its irregularities of outline enhanced by large islands. Earth has been piled into banks which inclose the other three sides, their low, actual height concealed by the trees and shrubs which grow out of them. This hillocky background is very irregular in form so that the boundaries of the garden appear indefinite and an effect of size and distance is achieved. Between the porch and the near edge of the lake is a level area, varying in width, which is mostly covered with grey pebbles, to form a wide path. Small bridges lead to the islands, and there are two cascades.

While it is possible to stroll through the garden, it was meant primarily to be seen from the verandahs in front of the buildings. From there the chief weakness becomes apparent——the basic design is not sufficiently unified and integrated to create strength and distinction. From whatever point we look, we have the feeling that it might appear a little better if we moved on a bit. This feeling is curiously witnessed by the fact that no two photographs of the garden ever seem to have been taken from the same point——as would be the case were there a central unifying motif. Nevertheless, from whatever angle the garden is viewed, it always presents a more or less pleasing picture, which in itself is a considerable accomplishment.

The feature of this garden which instantly attracts attention is the great number of stones. It is easy to believe there are the seven hundred claimed. They are used lavishly, wherever there is any excuse for them and also where there is none. Great numbers border the shore, and many others are heaped on the islands. Still others are laid out in the foreground, simply to be seen. The area between the buildings and the shore is strewn with them for no possible reason except to show them off, while the background hillocks are set with them as a merchant might set out his wares for display. Almost every stone is extraordinary, of fine shape, interesting color and texture. This is not surprising when it is recalled that this collection undoubtedly represents the choice gleanings from a hundred other gardens.

Although they are so lavishly used, great skill went into their arrangement nevertheless. Indeed, only great skill could have juggled so many into place without creating a choked or jumbled appearance, and this, distinctly, is not the feeling the garden gives. The stones are well related and grouped, except for the laid-out specimens. Many of the arrangements have both strength and character when taken by themselves and are splendid examples of stone artistry. But the whole has a rather brittle quality, of the surface rather than deep-lying, for here was no mystic expressing his soul nor artist creating a symbolic work of art. The designer was not even deeply concerned, as was the designer of Kokei, with fitting the building into the landscape.

In other words, the theme of this garden is pleasure, voluptuous and extravagant, accompanied by the display of wealth. In the phrase already quoted, there is here a deliberate effort to overwhelm the eye with splendor, the stones constituting exactly the same kind of lavish display as did the golden ornaments inside the building. But as in other good examples of Momoyama art, the final effect is saved from vulgarity by the boldness and brilliance of the concept and, curiously, by a certain restrained delicacy in its very daring, a restraint which vanishes in later gardens of the kind. Sambō-in holds only the beginning of decadence.

Of its details, the most famous is a large rock known as the *Fujito* stone. It is tall and squarish, standing upright, not unlike a roughly cut monument. Two small stones balance its height on either side. On the far side of the garden against a green background, it is the most conspicuous single stone among all the hundreds. Apparently it was the most famous stone in the nation in Hideyoshi's day and may have been thought to possess supernatural properties. It has a well-authenticated history of transfer through several gardens, appearing first in one of the Hosokawa estates. Later, Nobunaga caused it to be placed in a garden which he was making for the last of the Ashikaga puppet shoguns. Of this transfer it is recorded,[8]

"Nobunaga told the garden commissioner to have the stone wrapped in silk, decorated with flowers, and brought to the garden with music."

This is a most astonishing procedure unique in Japanese garden annals. Later Hideyoshi acquired the stone by paying a thousand *koku* of rice for it, an almost equally astonishing way for him to obtain any stone. He first had it placed in the Jūraku-tei garden and later brought to Sambō-in. It seems plain that this stone was thought to possess magic or sacred properties, but if ever this were the case, the belief has been forgotten now. The Fujito stone stands today in Sambō-in simply as the most conspicuous stone in the garden, something to be pointed out to visitors as vaguely of special interest.

There are three islands in the pond, two lying at the western end and one toward the east. All are linked to the shore by bridges, the path that follows around the garden passing over them. The two lying close together were probably intended to represent the traditional crane and turtle, but they are so overcrowded with stones it is impossible to identify one or the other. Many of the stone arrangements on these islands are excellent, but the total effect is heavy, a feeling which makes the islands seem too large for the rest of the composition. They screen out the view of the cascade from important angles and mask one end of the lake.

The plan by which the bridges link up the shore and islands is very like that followed in Kokei; and the same layout is used a third time in a small garden called Entoku-en, made a little later for Hideyoshi's widow by the Fushimi gardeners. Two bridges extend in a straight line from shore to island and from island to island; the third bridge is at right angles to their line and joins the second island to the shore again. This form is considered a characteristic feature of the work of these gardeners. Some of the bridges

[8] *Juhen Zoku Ōnin Koki.*

are of flat, natural, monolithic stones and others are of wood. The latter, of course, have been renewed. One of these wooden bridges is nondescript, others are of logs and earth, a type seen here for the first time and believed to have been devised at about the time the garden was made.

This earthen bridge is made on a foundation of four strong log legs standing in the water. The floor arching over them is made of small, round saplings, and piled on this floor is earth faced with living sod. The whole structure is necessarily large and bulky, in fact out of proportion to the elegance of the garden. In a half-light, its effect is not unlike that of some huge, prehistoric creature drinking, standing with its four legs in the water, its tail dragging on one shore, its head down by the other.

The principal cascade in this garden which, it will be remembered, was remodeled three times before it satisfied the gardener Kentei, occupies the southeastern corner. Unlike the usual waterfall, it is not large and conspicuous enough to be the focal point of interest. Since it could not be high, effect is gained by breaking it into two short broad falls with a rushing rapid between. Viewed close at hand, it is unusual and charming with these double falls of smooth water at right angles to each other. Behind them, in the distance, rises the green peak of Daigo-yama, suggesting the source of the water. A second cascade in the garden is now entirely concealed and overgrown with shrubs. It is difficult to know whether this was part of the original design or not.

There are several things about Sambō-in garden suggestive of the old *shinden* style but they are plainly Momoyama adaptations, not in any sense Heian originals. One of them is a streamlet which, like the old *yarimizu*, seems to flow out from under one of the buildings. At another point the lake pushes up an irregular arm to the very edge of the buildings, so that the porch seems almost to overhang the water in the manner of the old end-pavilions. This end-pavilion theme is repeated in a projection on the porch, its carved, gable roof converting it into a small pavilion projecting toward the water. Here one can sit in the old manner and enjoy the view of the lake. All of these details make it suddenly clear that Sambō-in was, in fact, intended to be a *shinden* garden, a Momoyama miniature, it is true, but still in essence the garden of a court noble.

This throws a revealing light on what must have been in Hideyoshi's mind as he laid out the place. It must be recalled that the ancient prestige of the Imperial court and the nobles had never vanished, even though they had passed through days of actual poverty. Hideyoshi had been astute enough to ally himself to this prestige by paying honor to the court and supporting it, becoming, in consequence, its favored general. But he had been denied the logical title of shogun, which was reserved for those of Fujiwara extraction, no matter how remote the family branch; and Hideyoshi was only a peasant. He had been named instead Kampaku or Regent. In Heian times the *kampaku* had been the most powerful subject in the nation, but later the title had become a mere ornament held by a succession of nonentities.

Still, the idea of staging himself in the ancient setting of his office evidently appealed to Hideyoshi, and he built Sambō-in as a sort of playhouse where he could pretend he was what he could never be—a Fujiwara courtier. Had he lived longer, he might have sat in the little end-pavilion beside the lake and pictured himself a great gentleman, born, by rights, to sit in a *shinden* garden, not a mere peasant upstart who had put himself at the head of the nation by sheer force of intelligence and personality.

XIII. *Tea Gardens—The Dewy Path*

I T SEEMS, at first, a rather surprising fact that the tea ceremonial, acme of sophisticated simplicity, reached its climax at exactly the same time that Momoyama art attained its most resplendent gorgeousness. The richly colored and gilded paintings and carvings of Hideyoshi's period represented the surging vitality of a country re-established in strength and order; the tea ceremonial represented the survival power of the old Muromachi esthetics. And that, in turn, represented something deep and fundamental in the Japanese character, which could be temporarily eclipsed but would invariably show forth again. In the beginning this feeling had been a simple love of nature; under Zen it had developed into a highly conscious esthetic of naturalism; now, oriented about a new form, it was to have a popular flowering which eventually touched and affected almost every phase of the national life. Its influence is still strongly visible at the present day.

Tea had been known in China since time immemorial. There is a legend which attributes its origin to the Zen patriarch, Bodhi-dharma, who came to China from India in the 6th century and established the meditative sect of Buddhism. According to the story, Bodhi-dharma was much annoyed because his eyelids kept closing in sleep when he wished to meditate. Impatient, he finally cut them off and threw them away. Where they fell, green shrubs sprang up, with beautiful, dark, glossy leaves and small, fragrant flowers like tiny, single camellias.[1] The leaves of this plant, when made into a drink, possessed the power of causing wakefulness.

In reality, of course, tea had been known in South China long before

[1] The tea plant, *Thea Sinensis,* is a member of the Camellia family.

182

the time of Bodhi-dharma. In the T'ang period, it was a common beverage and it was known concurrently in Nara. There is a record which mentions that in 729 A.D. the Emperor Shōmu served tea to a hundred monks in his palace at Nara.[2] It was customary at this period to combine the tea leaves with other fragrant things, drying them into a cake which was roasted before it was made into a beverage by boiling. This process still survives among the Tibetans and Mongols.

Later the tea leaves were powdered, hot water added, and the mixture whipped to a froth with a bamboo whisk. This method was devised in the Sung period and is the way the ceremonial tea of Japan is still made, for the Japanese ritual had its roots in Sung China. Steeped tea, the only form known in the Occident and now commonly used all over the Orient, was a later development under the Mings. The Western world knows only this form, because Europeans first came to China in the Ming period.

The drinking of powdered tea, whipped into a froth with hot water, was made into a Zen ritual in China during the Sung period. The basic purpose of the monks in drinking the tea was, of course, to avoid sleepiness during meditation. But the ritual was evidently made into a means of honoring Bodhi-dharma, founder of the sect, and miraculous creator of the tea plant from his eyelids. The drinking ceremonial took place before an image of the saint which stood in an alcove of the temple, the monks drinking in succession from a single bowl. This detail, and the solemn atmosphere of a religious ritual, as well as the method of making the tea, are still features of the tea ceremonial as it exists in Japan today.

The use of tea in Japan seems to have paralleled the growth of Zen and the appreciation of Sung art and to have been closely associated with both. In the 13th century in Kamakura, seeds of the tea plant and something of the Zen tea ritual were brought back to Japan by the monk Eisai, one of those who went to China to study Ch'an Buddhism. He is regarded in Japan as the founder of both Zen and tea. Later, as an example of its association with art, we find Yoshimitsu drinking tea in the Gold Pavilion.

[2] *Chaku Sho Setsu.*

Perhaps this was a Zen exercise, but it seems more probable that, at that time, tea was drunk when a group of friends gathered to inspect and study the paintings brought from China. However, it was when Sung-Muromachi art reached its zenith in the Silver Pavilion under Yoshimasa that one of his artistic coterie, the monk Shūko, took the old Zen tea ritual and turned it into a secular exercise in esthetics, which came to be called *cha-no-yu*.

While this new ritual had broken away from its religious association, it was still, of course, thoroughly impregnated with Zen ideals and feeling. The aim of the new ritual, in the last analysis, was virtually the same as the aim of Zen meditation, to arrive at some understanding of life and the universe. Indeed, the tea ceremony might be called a form of socialized meditation. But since it was a pleasant social diversion instead of an austere religious exercise, it was of much wider appeal than meditation. Shuko's idea apparently was to create an atmosphere through the making and serving of tea in the most simple, beautiful, and natural manner possible, an atmosphere in which a little group of people might attain serenity and harmony of spirit. In such an atmosphere, art and beauty could be discussed, and perhaps some new light be thrown on the problems over which humanity ponders.

We do not know just what forms Shūko devised for the making and serving of tea, but in an age which made a cult of simplicity and naturalness, we may be certain that every move was scrutinized to make sure it really was the most simple and graceful possible, and each utensil was studied to make sure that it held no hint of floridity.

While the form of the tea ceremonial has undergone infinite variation in its details, usually on the side of elaboration, the description of a typical ceremony of the present day will aid in understanding the influence of tea and the many things derived from it.

The host invites several friends, five at the most, for a *cha-no-yu* ceremonial on a certain day. At the proper time the group assembles at the covered waiting bench provided near the garden gate, and when a signal is given, they pass through the small garden surrounding the tea house and enter the low door of the tea room. This room may be one of the regular rooms in the house which has been especially fitted up for the purpose, but more often it is a small, separate building in a secluded corner of the garden. One wall of the tea room is occupied by the shallow recess, called the *tokonoma,* its floor a low shelf a few inches above the mats. For the occasion, a painting or an example of beautiful calligraphy expressing some appropriate ideal, has been hung on the back wall of the *tokonoma* and an arrangement of flowers or, perhaps, a fine bronze incense burner placed on the low shelf below. This recess, so altar-like in its form is a sort of altar, in fact, and is derived from those original altars in Zen monasteries which stood before an image of Bodhi-dharma with an offering of flowers or incense upon it. The original Zen tea ritual, it will be recalled, took place before these altars.

The guests enter the tea room silently, with the utmost decorum. One by one they go to the *tokonoma* to look at the art objects displayed there. The picture and flowers have always been chosen and arranged to strike some significant keynote of the occasion, perhaps hinting at the reason for the gathering or commenting on the beauty of the season as expressed in its blossoms. After noting this, the guests quietly take their places on the floor down the length of the room, facing the kettle which is singing over a charcoal firebox at one side. The guest of greatest honor is seated nearest the *tokonoma.*

Now the host enters carrying the tea equipment. He takes his place before the hearth and begins to make the first bowl of tea. All his movements are slow and measured, but simple, direct, and graceful; they are minutely prescribed, but long practice makes them seem spontaneous. He lifts a bit of green, powdered tea leaf from the caddy with a bamboo spoon and puts it into the tea bowl. This bowl is larger than a teacup and generally of some rough pottery material in keeping with the prevailingly rustic atmosphere of the tea room. Hot water—perhaps half a cupful—is lifted by a small wooden dipper from the boiling pot and poured over the tea in the bowl. Then with a small bamboo whisk, which looks not unlike a stiff shaving brush, he beats the mixture until it is frothy.

A few cakes on small plates stand before each guest. The first, or most important, guest has begun to nibble at his cake as the tea making goes forward. Now the frothy bowl, strong and bitter, is placed before him. He picks it up and drinks, his movements, like those of the host, slow, simple, and direct, but also minutely prescribed. When the bowl is empty, he takes occasion to look at it, turning it over and admiring its form and glaze; finally he returns it to the host with a bow. It is then wiped clean with a bit of silk, and a second portion of tea made for the next guest. This is repeated until all have been served.

Such is the tea ritual itself. To thousands who follow it at the present time it is merely a formula of movement, something to be memorized and followed when social usage demands it. Intrinsically, it has little more meaning than the five-finger exercise of the young musician. Its purpose is only to produce an atmosphere of mellow and tranquil relaxation in which the world and its confusions can be left behind. No sense of strain or malease accompanies the ceremony in spite of its decorum, when those performing it are thoroughly familiar with it. To a group of such people, if they really understand, it is known that the talk which follows is the really important thing about the occasion. The tea drinking itself is nothing. At the present time, however, the means seems usually to be mistaken for the end, and the occasion is often finished with the ritual.

But for a group of understanding devotees, when the tea drinking ends, a certain informality descends on the gathering. The silence is broken casually by a remark appropriate to the occasion, perhaps a compliment to the painting in the *tokonoma*, or the flower arrangement, or a request to look more closely at some article of the tea equipment—spoon, caddy, or kettle. During the conversation that follows, the quiet ease created by the preliminary ritual is never broken by the introduction of an inappropriate subject such as business or politics—nor does conversation ever become heated. In the serene atmosphere of the tea room those present may be led to a new appreciation of beauty or, perhaps, even to something more.

Shūko's tea ceremony was the vehicle which saved Muromachi esthetics during the disintegrating early years of the 16th century. Men who sought peace and beauty, instead of becoming monks as in an earlier age, now turned to the tea ceremonial and became "tea masters." They gathered into it all those distinctive canons of taste that had marked the Muromachi ideal. And, like the scholarly monks and artists of the earlier period, they became arbiters of taste and authorities on cultural matters in general. When the new Momoyama art appeared like a gorgeous sunrise over the horizon, their position was not threatened for they represented something fundamentally congenial to the Japanese temperament. And as the latter part of the 16th century swept forward in new vigor and strength, the tea ceremonial reached also its high point of development.

There were many tea masters in this period, but the great name among them is that of Sen no Rikyū. Like most geniuses in an art, he came of a family which excelled in that art, a family of connoisseurs and tea men. His grandfather had served the Ashikaga shoguns as a tea master, taking the name of Senami; it was adopted as a family name by his descendants, who today are still the leading teachers of the tea ritual in Kyoto. When troubles descended upon the capital and the Ashikagas were scattered, Senami's son, Yobei, settled in the seaport city of Sakai. A suburb of Osaka today, this town has always been an important port on the Inland Sea. With the rest of the country suffering from civil wars, Sakai was but little troubled for it was rather like a mercantile Free City. The Sakai merchants were well-to-do and not without their own culture. For a tea master the move to Sakai was an astute one, and Yobei seems to have prospered. His social status was that of a high class merchant, for he seems to have been something of a dealer in art (probably in adjuncts to the tea ceremony) as well as a teacher of the ceremony.

Yobei's son, Sōeki, known later as Sen no Rikyū, was born in Sakai, probably in 1520. He began to take lessons in the tea ceremony at the age of seven, and, his talent being soon recognized, he was taught by Shō-ō [3] then regarded as the greatest tea master since Shuko. At sixteen, Rikyū presided alone at his first ceremonial, an event equivalent to his debut in the art. Raised in an atmosphere of tea, art, and commerce, young Sen seems early to have followed his father and set up his own establishment. It was first, probably, in Sakai, but, later, when Nobunaga and Hideyoshi had restored Kyoto to importance, he moved to that city. His name became famous, and wealthy patrons flocked to him, until in middle life his reputation reached Nobunaga's ears, and he was called on to preside over the tea gatherings of that general. Later, Hideyoshi also employed him.

Nobunaga was known as a patron of the tea ceremony. But it seems hardly possible that one whose taste could so accurately have set the style of a flamboyant period, as did his in building Azuchi Castle, would have had much real appreciation of the tea ceremonial. In his hands, in fact, it became little more than another means for ostentation. It is recorded [4] that when Nobunaga invited the Sakai art dealers to bring their choicest tea treasures for his inspection, he purchased all they showed him, paying more than they asked, then sent them back for others.

He seems also to have encouraged the tea ceremonial deliberately for economic reasons. Embarrassing financial difficulties might be avoided if a leader who had no lands could, instead, reward a faithful follower with some article for his tea service. Nobunaga himself, according to the same record, rewarded the vassal who superintended the building of Azuchi Castle by presenting him with a tea bowl which had belonged to Shūko.

Under the patronage of Nobunaga and Hideyoshi, the tea ceremony grew into nothing less than a popular fad. Part of its appeal was, doubtless, genuine enough, for, like the Zen meditation of an earlier day, it provided warriors with short periods of escape from the turmoil of a military life. Probably, too, its practice gave provincial captains a pleasing sense of being cultured and refined like their superiors. The tea room, however, seems

---

[3] Sometimes spelled Jō-ō.
[4] In the *Sokenki*.

The tea house of Myōki-an temple is a small structure, a sort of lean-to projecting from the south side of the temple building. The garden around it is crossed by stepping stones. A huge old pine tree, "Hideyoshi's Sleeve Brushing Pine" stands in one corner; actually it is the successor of the tree which was in the garden in Hideyoshi's time. (Photo by the author.)

Nijō Castle garden was probably originally planned to be without water or trees; it was to be merely a massive arrangement of rocks for the castle courtyard. (Photo from Board of Tourist Industry.)

occasionally to have served more peculiar ends; its seclusion, for instance, was sometimes utilized as a place for confidential meetings, perhaps between enemies, for things spoken in it were held to be unsaid.

With the Momoyama spirit blazing away in gold and color, the tea ceremony often had a struggle to maintain its tenets of simplicity and quiet. The historic example of the clash between these two forms is the event known as the Great Kitano Tea Party. It was given by Hideyoshi shortly after he moved into Jūraku-tei, in 1587. Notices were set up in surrounding towns announcing a monster gathering of tea devotees. Anyone interested, rich or poor, was invited to come on the appointed days—a period in autumn when the leaves were red. Those who wished, it was added, might erect temporary shelters in which to hold tea gatherings and show off tea treasures. Nearly four hundred people accepted this invitation. Booths of various kinds were set up, and tea ceremonials went on day and night as devotees met their friends, entertained, and were entertained. Hideyoshi's collection of tea utensils was displayed in three pavilions, and he himself served tea to some of his highest vassals. At other times he went from place to place looking at the various articles on display.

The Great Kitano Tea Party was a perfect manifestation of the "bigger and better" spirit of Momoyama; everything about it—size, ostentation, and display—was completely at variance with the true spirit of the tea ceremonial. Nevertheless, I think it would be a mistake to assume that Hideyoshi himself had no feeling for the inner meaning of *cha-no-yu*. He was too intelligent and had too good an understanding of men and events to have missed its real significance. He must often have gone into the tea room in all sincerity and entered into the ceremony in its true spirit. It would be hard otherwise to account for his long association with Rikyū. Doubtless, the tea master had his own opinion of the Great Kitano Tea Party but unless he had felt that Hideyoshi had understanding, he would hardly have administered such lessons as we find illustrated in the well known story of the morning-glories. Hideyoshi must have respected Rikyū all the more for his courage and sincerity.

The story goes that one summer Rikyū grew morning-glories in his garden, so fine that word of their beauty reached Hideyoshi. He indicated a desire to see them, so Rikyū invited him to an early morning tea ceremonial. When Hideyoshi arrived in the garden there was not a morning-glory in sight. Angry at what seemed a deliberate affront, the Dictator stalked into the tea room, to find there a single perfect blossom perfectly displayed. Rikyū, of course, was a master of flower arrangement, which he held to be one of the essential arts for a tea master. He had removed all the bright display of the other morning-glory flowers leaving but this perfect one to hint at the whole world of beauty.

Rikyū's ideas on the form of the ceremony, the tea room, and the tea garden have come to be regarded as classic standards. He is credited, also, with being the one who made it possible for *cha-no-yu* to become popular. Under Yoshimasa it had been an expensive pastime for wealthy dilettantes, centering around their collections of art. But Rikyū's ideas on its simplicity brought it within the reach of all. One of his poems on this subject goes:[5]

> *Only one kettle*
> *Can be used for cha-no-yu:*
> *How unnecessary to yearn*
> *For many utensils.*

And another:[6]

> *Ceremonial tea:*
> *It is only to boil water*
> *Make the tea,*
> > *And drink it.*
> *That's all!*

Since the object of the tea ceremony was to build up a serene detachment from the world, every feature of the setting was designed to con-

[5] *Kama hitotsu,*
Moteba cha-no-yu wa,
Naru mono wo,
Yorozuno dōgu,
Konomu tsutana sa.

[6] *Cha-no-yu to wa,*
Tada yu wo wakashi,
Cha wo tatete,
Nomu bakari nari,
Moto wo shiru beshi.

tribute to this end. Rikyū imagined the tea room to be a sylvan retreat, a hut far off in the hills or by the seashore. This, of course, was but an echo down the centuries from the Taoist hermit-sages who had fled to the mountains of China.

One of Rikyū's poems expressing this idea is translated:[7]

In the distance
Neither flowers nor maple leaves
Are to be seen;
Only a thatched hut beside the bay
In Autumn's twilight.

Carrying out this theme, Rikyū taught that the tea room should be but a hut in reality, a light little structure, perhaps with a thatched roof, walls of mud plaster, and unpainted woodwork. But humble as such a shelter was, it should show the innate beauty of its simple materials, the exquisite grain of the wood, the warm color of the sand in the plaster. It must also possess the subtle refinement which would inevitably be impressed on such a place, were it the retreat of a cultured and artistic person. Moreover, it must be free from any of the grubbiness usually associated with rustic surroundings; perfect cleanliness is one of the basic principles of the tea art.

The garden which surrounds the tea hut is now usually spoken of as the "dewy ground," or "dewy path," that is, the *roji*. This word comes from a passage in one of the Buddhist scriptures which Dr. Harada Jirō translates: "Escaping from the fire-stricken habitation of the Three Phenomenal Worlds, they take their seats on the dewy ground." The garden is thus an escape from the world, a transition area between the solitude of the tea room and the distractions of the workaday world. Continuing Rikyū's

[7] *Miwataseba,*
Hana mo momiji mo,
Nakari keri,
Ura no tomaya no,
Aki no yugure.
    (Special translation by Yukuo Uyehara.)

191

ideas, the garden represented just such a path through the hills as one would naturally take to reach the tea hut retreat.

Tea gardens at present are not only paths in the imagination but in reality, being literally passage gardens between the gate and the tea room door. They cannot be seen by those gathered inside the tea room and so they are not laid out to form a landscape picture. Instead, since they are looked at only as one comes or goes along the path, which is itself their chief feature, they are designed to suggest only a bit of the natural mountainside, and this on virtually a natural scale.

The technique of the tea garden calls for the usual abridgement, symbolism, and suggestion to create hints from which one can build up a feeling of having gone far and left worldly cares behind. But, altogether, the tea garden is the least artificially artful of all Japanese garden forms. *Yūgen,* the quality of mystery, hinting at hidden beauty, which was sought by the older Zen masters, is brought to the tea garden if possible. Another quality sought is known as *wabi* which may be translated as rustic solitude. A third quality is *sabi,* literally rust or corrosion, but implying here the patina of age. The color of weathered stones, moss, and lichens, acquired through long years, is greatly desired to give that sense of timeless serenity which is the essence of the tea setting.

Having no firm and lasting stone arrangements, no ponds or hillocks to resist the wear of time, tea gardens have not survived the years as well as have other garden forms. Rikyū seems to have built or to have aided in the construction of many, but not a single one of these, nor of his period, remains in a form which can be regarded as original. Perhaps the one which comes nearest to it is at the little country temple of Myōki-an in the village of Yamazaki, a few miles south of Kyoto. Rikyū apparently had a country house near here, and there is evidence indicating that, probably, he planned a tea room and garden for the priest of this temple. A map[8] of the vicinity, made at the end of the 16th century, shows a tea room there at that time, its outstanding characteristic being then, as now, a tall pine tree, called the

[8] Reproduced in Volume 6 of Shigemori's *Nihon Teienshi Zukan.*

Sleeve Brushing Pine. This name, according to legend, came from the fact that the garden was so small Hideyoshi could not get past the tree to enter the tea room without brushing his sleeve against it.

Hideyoshi seems actually to have found time for a tea ceremonial in this vicinity when he was campaigning here against the murderer of Nobunaga in 1582. Perhaps he came to this temple tea room then, but it seems more probable that he returned later at a more peaceful day. The garden, at any rate, has been reconstructed since he saw it. The present Sleeve Brushing Pine is only two hundred years old; in other words, it was transplanted to its present position about a hundred years after Hideyoshi's death. But as it doubtless approximates the original one in kind and position, so the tea room and garden probably approximate the originals also.

The tea house of Myōki-an temple is a tiny structure, a sort of lean-to projecting from the south side of the temple building. It may be entered from this building, but the entrance used by tea guests is an outside door on the south side, small and typically low, hardly more than a hole. Through this all members of the party have to creep in equal humbleness as an object lesson in the democracy which prevails within the tea room. The garden extends around three sides of this tea room, being a small space of mossy ground with shrubs and trees. It is crossed by two paths of stepping stones leading to the tea room door, one from the east and one from the west. The Sleeve Brushing Pine grows in the eastern half of the garden near the building. As things are at present, the path skirts the pine with ample room for anyone to pass it. Even the huge sleeves of a court noble's costume could hardly brush against it now. In the Momoyama period the arrangement may have been quite different, the original pine perhaps leaning across the path. Or possibly the legend was founded only on the comparatively limited area of the garden as compared to the grander gardens of Hideyoshi's palaces. By later garden standards, however, this is rather spacious, a fact regarded as one of its surviving Momoyama characteristics.

At present, there stands near the tea room door a low, natural stone with a basinlike depression cut in the top. The water in this basin is taken up with a small wooden dipper and poured over the hands before entering the tea room. Small stones covering the ground in front of the basin prevent the waste water from forming a muddy spot. Just back of the basin is a stone lantern, placed where it can throw light on the basin at night. A second basin and lantern stand near the gate on the west. These lanterns and basins are not of the Momoyama period, but typical of the average tea garden of later date.

A second garden associated with Sen no Rikyū is in the city of Sakai where, as one might expect, the tea master seems to have helped with the building of many tea gardens. Originally this garden may have belonged to Rikyū's son-in-law, Soan, who was also a tea master. At present it is called Jisso-in and is part of the temple, Nanshuji. Some years ago it was moved to its present location from Engetsuji Temple. From this former site, it is said, there was a fine view of the sea.

The only real connection between the present garden and Rikyū is its water basin and a story. Rikyū, very likely, designed this water basin which is cut from a tallish stone into a simple, barrel-like form. It stands now near the door of the tea room, in a slight, stone-paved depression. The story associated with it, although not authenticated, is one of those anecdotes which might and ought to be true.

When Rikyū designed the original tea garden, the story goes, he caused a hedge to be planted which entirely screened out the wonderful view of the Inland Sea. Only when a guest bent over the stone basin to dip up the water, could a glimpse of it be obtained through a small opening arranged for the purpose. His followers, puzzled by this, asked for an explanation and Rikyū recited the short poem:[9]

> *A bit of water here,*
> *There, between the trees—*
> *The sea!*

[9] *Umi sukoshi,*
  Niwa ni isumi no,
  Konoma kana.

Here was one of those parables so beloved by the older Zen masters, a symbolism of form that sought to hint of man's relation to the Infinite. Bending over the bit of water in the basin, a questing soul might see itself reflected within its small compass and so epitomized. Then, looking up and suddenly catching a glimpse of the splendid infinitude of the ocean, he would realize, in its relationship to the bit of water in the basin, the fact that man is likewise a bit of the Infinite, the same in substance and spirit.

The Momoyama tea masters contributed three things to Japanese garden art—the stone lantern, the stepping stone, and the stone water basin. These are not found in gardens before the 16th century but appear extensively afterward.

The problem of how to make a naturalistic path both artistic and practical must have received a good deal of attention from the tea men. A path worn through moss is neither attractive nor the best thing to walk on, since, inevitably, the edges become ragged and worn, while the ground grows muddy and slippery in wet weather. Whoever thought of laying down a line of flat stones to walk on, leaving the moss to grow up around them untrampled, hit upon an idea that was both practical and artistic. We do not know who this was, and no garden can definitely be said to have the first stepping stones in it. The inventor might have been Rikyū himself who had sufficient originality to have thought of it. At any rate, stepping stones were used in tea gardens in his time, for one of his notes mentions them.[10] The idea seems to have had an almost immediate appeal, for not long afterward stepping stones began to be used extensively in the finest of estate gardens.

In time a whole art and science of stepping stones was developed until, today, Japanese garden makers know precisely how to place such stones to achieve the greatest success. Rikyū is said to have advocated laying them with greater emphasis on their practical use than on their artistic appearance, while a later tea man, Oribe, reversed this. The Japanese technique

[10] In *Kyaku no Shidai* (Procedure for Guests).

195

of stepping stones is one which Western garden makers could study to advantage.

In the Momoyama period, the tea ceremonial was frequently held at night, so that some way to light the path across the garden became a necessity. Fires burning in suspended iron baskets had been the usual mode of garden illumination, but the flaring brightness of these torches was quite out of keeping with the mellow quiet of the tea garden spirit. Again we do not know who first had the idea of moving an old stone lantern from a temple compound into the tea garden, but it was a logical thought. The flickering light of a candle shining out from the paper-lined openings in the stone light-holder is subdued and charming and surprisingly effective in lighting the way in the dark.

Stone lanterns had stood in front of Japanese Buddhist temples from earliest times. They had first been brought to Japan from Korea in pre-Nara days, when Buddhism and its adjuncts were being introduced. As Shinto became influenced by Buddhist forms, lanterns were placed as votive offerings before Shinto shrines as well as before Buddhist temples.

There is an unmistakable resemblance between these stone lanterns and certain symbolic monuments, called *go-rinto*, which are found in old Buddhist cemeteries. The lantern's square base, cylindrical pedestal, round light-holder, and roof with its pointed knob correspond very closely to the five parts of these monuments, a cube, cylinder, sphere, truncated pyramid, and pointed ball.[11] The original form doubtless came from India where it may have been a phallic symbol; pagodas are probably a modification of the same original form. Since there are no stone lanterns in China, it must have been some Korean monk who first thought of turning this five-part monument into a lantern by hollowing out the spherical portion and putting a candle in it. In creating artistic stone lanterns, a sixth part was soon added in the form of a base or shelf under the light-holder, this giving a better balance and stability to the design.

[11] These symbolize the five elements which according to Chinese philosophy make up the universe—earth, water, fire, air and ether.

TEA GARDENS—THE DEWY PATH

A few lanterns survive from the earlier periods in Japan. From them it is seen that the best designs were created in the Kamakura period when stone carving reached its peak. Good designs were also made in Muromachi, but, after that, the art seemed to decline, and later designs are not so artistic.

While the stone lantern was doubtless put into the tea garden strictly for utilitarian purposes, it must at once have become a matter of esthetics also. The tea masters at first took old lanterns from neglected temples, their mossy, weather-beaten appearance harmonizing perfectly with the tea spirit. In a short time, however, lanterns had become such popular garden adjuncts that new ones had to be made to fill the demand. Excellent old lanterns were copied, the reproductions being called by the name of the temple in which the original stood. At the same time certain tea masters took to designing their own lanterns, the styles so originated being usually known by the designers' names. Other designers also turned to this form, and such ingenuity was displayed that many lanterns finally showed no relation whatever to the original temple lantern. Such, for instance, is the popular three-legged, flat-topped style called the "snow-viewing" lantern.

It was at this time that small stone pagodas became one of the ornaments of the Japanese garden. Korea, apparently, continued to develop lanterns and pagodas in its own way, for when Hideyoshi's generals arrived there on their attempt to conquer China, they found many of unusual and appealing design. Some of these they appropriated and sent home as gifts to the Dictator or to favorite temples. The fact that these generals were attracted by such things as a stone lantern indicates a widespread interest in the subject by that time. A number of these old Korean lanterns still stand in Kyoto gardens. Many of them look more like small pagodas than like the usual Japanese temple lantern.

Perhaps it was an idea arising from such a resemblance or perhaps the success of borrowing lanterns suggested the borrowing of other things. At any rate, about this time stone *stupas*—monuments like miniature pagodas —were also moved into the garden. Later, small stone pagodas but a few feet high, shaped very like the ancient towers of China, were made expressly as garden ornaments. Today these are often placed where they rise above the shrubbery at the rear of the garden, giving a sentimental and picturesque suggestion of old temples lying in the distance.

The insistence of the tea masters on cleanliness, especially on washing the hands before entering the tea room, resulted in the invention of the stone laver, or water basin. It is supposed that, originally, a wooden bucket or a tea kettle of hot water may have been placed in a convenient spot for this purpose, with a small dipper beside it. Soon, however, a more artistic and permanent arrangement must have been sought, and the appropriate idea of a stone with a depression cut in its top to hold water was thought of. Sometimes the stone was left in its natural form; again it was sculptured into some formal shape like Rikyū's barrel-like basin at Nanshuji. The early basins were made out of a single stone of ordinary size and were seldom more than a foot or two high. To reach the water it was necessary to bend or squat before them. A flat stone was arranged in front to stand on and, sometimes, others were placed at the sides, much as in the hillside spring at Saihōji. Gravel and small stones covered the ground where the water fell, preventing a muddy spot. Soon it became customary to place a stone lantern near the basin to light it at night. The arrangement of laver and lantern with their supporting stones became, then, the chief feature of the tea garden. They are often all that has come down to us from early tea gardens.

Later, when the tea influence was spreading, stone water basins were placed where they could be reached from the verandah of the house. They were adapted to this purpose by being cut in the end of a tall, upright stone so that the water could be conveniently reached.

Other materials used in making the tea garden are natural stones and, of course, plants. Decorative stones are placed casually here and there about the garden to appear as if occurring naturally along the path. Considerable artistry, of course, goes into their placement, but there is none of that conscious display of stone technique which marks the landscape gardens.

Moss covers the ground of the tea garden, if it can be made to grow, and ferns and other small, wild plants cluster around the bases of the rocks. Only simple, ordinary trees and shrubs are planted, things such as grow wild in the hills, or, at least, look as if they did. Nothing with bright, showy blossoms is allowed, for this would attract attention and, so, distract the mind from the mood of quiet serenity. Plants selected for tea gardens have graceful forms and, usually, glossy foliage but they are modest and unassuming, as wild plants seem to be. Those which do not lose their leaves in winter are preferred, since their timelessness gives the needed feeling of serenity. Almost the only exception to this rule is the modest plum which blossoms in the spring and the small-leaved maple which turns red in the autumn.

The tea garden receives the most minute care. Every dead leaf, twig, and cobweb is removed, while the dust is washed from the leaves until they glisten, and the moss is kept emerald green. Just before guests arrive, the whole garden is usually sprinkled so that it may be fresh and gleaming. To clean the garden a small twig whisk broom is used, and even a long pair of chopsticks is useful to pick out dead leaves from the inside of a shrub. Cleaning must be done judiciously, however; this is illustrated in the story of how Rikyū taught his son to clean the garden.

The boy had gone over every shrub and tree, had swept the moss, not once but several times, but still Rikyū was dissatisfied. The lad protested that there was not a single leaf or twig left to be removed, that he had done everything possible. Rikyū then stepped to a small maple tree, bright with the colors of autumn, and shook it gently, sending down a flutter of tiny scarlet leaves. They lay on the mossy carpet like small red flowers, adding the final touch of beauty and naturalness to the garden's cleanliness.

Rikyū's story ends with a tragedy. No one knows what caused the estrangement between him and Hideyoshi. Some say it was Hideyoshi's interest in Rikyū's daughter but that seems improbable. More likely, the old tea master, then seventy, had administered some kind of lesson too severe for the Dictator's pride to accept. Enemies took advantage of the coolness between them to start slanderous tales, saying there was a plot to put poison in the tea bowl. Dictators are a suspicious lot, and Hideyoshi seems to have been true to type. Word reached the old tea master that his life was expected to end.

The final scene reminds us of Socrates' death. A last ceremonial tea gathering was arranged for a few of the closest friends. All the arrangements in the *tokonoma* spoke of the fleetingness of life and of favor. When the ceremony was over, the tea equipment was distributed among those present. They left, but one remained to assist in the final rite. The ceremony of the "honorable departure" was performed in the tea room which would always be associated with the man who was forced to take his own life within it.

XIV. *Princely Estates of Tokugawa Times*

HIDEYOSHI had hoped to establish his descendants as a line of *de facto* rulers similar to the Ashikagas. At the time of his death, however, his son, Hideyori, was only a child of six. The father organized a regency council of his chief vassals to watch over the boy and take care of the affairs of the country. But two years had not passed before the members of this council were at war. Finally one of them, Tokugawa Ieyasu, made himself dominant over the others in a decisive battle. Obtaining the title of shogun, Ieyasu became the actual ruler of the country, even though Hideyoshi's son continued to live in Osaka Castle, nominally as the heir to power. In 1615, however, with the boy approaching maturity and showing signs of his father's ability, Ieyasu deliberately manufactured a pretext, attacked Osaka Castle, and the youth died in its fall. Not Hideyoshi's descendants, therefore, but Ieyasu's ruled the nation for the next period, an era of two hundred and fifty years, called after them, the Tokugawa period.

It was a time of unbroken peace, but a peace sternly maintained under military feudalism. Ieyasu with the help of his son and grandson succeeded in suppressing notions of democracy which had begun to appear in the Momoyama period. Society was settled as nearly as possible into a static condition, every individual fixed into the place where he was born. The Emperor and court continued to live in Kyoto, as always, but actual power was held by the Shogun and under him by the various lords of provinces, his vassals, who were known as *daimyō*. The military retainers of these lords were called *samurai* and constituted the upper class of society. The lower classes were peasants, artisans, and merchants.

The spacious spirit of Momoyama was not at once suppressed, of course, but continued into the early decades of the 17th century. At that time the Japanese had wide foreign contacts, for their ships went to various parts of Asia and the East Indies, and some travelers even got as far as Europe. The broadening influence of all this showed itself in the budding of many original projects. But before any of these could take definite form, the repressive Tokugawa policy checked and choked them. This process was completed by the closing of the country in the middle of the century. Japanese rulers of that time had good reason to assume that the European missionaries and traders who had come to their country were but the fore-runners to soldiers and conquest. It was a process they saw going on in the Philippines, Java, and India. As a safeguard, they took the drastic step of forbidding all foreigners to come to them and their subjects from leaving their own shores. The only exceptions to this were the Chinese and a small group of Dutchmen who were allowed to remain at Nagasaki.

The broadening foreign impetus, therefore, finally died away, and there came a time when traditional Japanese culture moved, not forward, but round and round in well-worn grooves, becoming more refined, elab-orate, and finicky at every turn. Fortunately, at the same time there began to appear, outside and below the old traditional cultural forms, a new prole-tarian expression of art which in the end rejuvenated the country. But this falls outside the present chapter.

When Ieyasu came to power, he decided, like Yoritomo four hundred years before, to center his "camp government" away from the intrigues of Kyoto. He selected the site of Edo Castle, not far from Yoritomo's old city of Kamakura. The new town, which grew up around this castle, was rather slow to assume importance, so for several decades Kyoto continued to be the center of everything but the actual government. Ieyasu paid fre-quent calls to the court there, staying at first in Hideyoshi's Fushimi Castle, but later erecting a castle of his own, which he called Nijō. It was begun in 1602 and sufficiently finished for Ieyasu to stay there the follow-ing year.

PRINCELY ESTATES OF TOKUGAWA TIMES

This castle occupied an extensive area of land just south of the old Jūraku-tei. While Nijō was a real castle with moats, walls, and a great donjon tower, it was designed to serve, not so much as an actual fortress, as a suitable residence in Kyoto for the military ruler of the nation. Its strength was real enough, no doubt, although it was never tested, but the place was primarily for show. And show was the spirit underlying all its aspects, especially the great audience halls in which Ieyasu received his vassals. Even the garden beside these halls had showiness as its basic inspiration.

Ieyasu died in 1616 but during the next decade the castle was the setting for occasions of great pomp. His granddaughter stayed there in 1614 before entering the palace to become a consort of the young Emperor Go-Mizunoo. Several years later her father, the retired Shogun, and Iemitsu, her brother, who held the title, decided that Tokugawa prestige demanded they entertain the Emperor as the Ashikagas and Hideyoshi had done. An imperial visit to Nijō castle therefore was planned for the autumn of 1625, and great preparations were put on foot. The castle was completely renovated, and many new buildings added. Hideyoshi's Fushimi Castle was dismantled, and parts of it moved to Nijō. In addition, a whole group of special buildings was put up to accommodate the imperial party.

This visit was an even grander event than had been those earlier ones to the Gold Pavilion and Jūraku-tei. As before, days were devoted to feasting, music, dancing, and poem composition, but there was no boating, for the garden lake of Nijō Castle is a mere pond. In accordance with custom, gifts of great value were presented to the guests before they left, the total value of the gold and silver thus distributed being even more than Hideyoshi had given after their visit to Jūraku-tei and that had been thought a staggering sum.

This way of overdoing things, especially things that Hideyoshi was remembered for having done, was a definite policy of the Tokugawas. They were trying in every way possible to outshine the memory of their predecessor. Ostentation was no longer the exuberant thing it had been with

Nobunaga and Hideyoshi; it had become a coldly calculated government policy, aimed partly at eliminating the memory of Hideyoshi and partly at keeping the vassals too poor to toy with the idea of rebellion. A definite intention to be grand and impressive, joined to the superlative skill of a finished technique, marks all the official works of this period. But their grandeur was a surface show; there was no meaning behind them.

This imperial visit was the high point in Nijō Castle's history. By that time Edo had begun to assume such importance that the shoguns rarely left it, and, eventually, visits to Kyoto ceased altogether. The special buildings erected for the imperial party were later taken down and moved. Finally, in 1791 the castle's great donjon tower was struck by lightning and burned. It was over two hundred years before the shoguns returned, but in the troubled days which preceded their downfall, they came back to Nijō. It was from there, seventy years ago, that the last of the Tokugawa shoguns resigned his commission and rode away, a private subject.

Today Nijō Castle is maintained virtually as a museum, although it is actually one of the imperial estates. Its walls, moats, and gates are unchanged, and Ieyasu's great audience halls are maintained in their former splendor. They are massive Momoyama style buildings, their rooms walled with sliding golden screens painted with tigers, birds, and flowers. The four halls are arranged in an oblique line so that the southwest corner of each gives toward the spacious area that contains the garden.

The garden is about an acre in extent, much larger really than it appears, set down in the center of the wide, flat courtyard. It is an ornament for this courtyard, not an inclosing landscape as is Kokei. Beyond it stretches a wide lawn, covering the area where once stood the buildings that housed the Emperor on his visit. Across the moat, which is invisible on the west, rose the great donjon tower, moved there from Fushimi Castle, its topmost roofs crowned with gleaming golden dolphins.

Water enters the garden pond from the moat behind, through a low, rocky cascade. In this cascade there is a strong, general feeling of dry-garden technique, as there is about the pebbled pond bottom and all the rock arrangements. In fact, it is believed that originally there may have been no water at all in the garden, that it was entirely a dry composition like Kokei. There is good reason to think, also, that in the beginning few or no trees grew in it. Certainly the present trees have not been there long, and there are no stumps or large old shrubs to indicate long periods of previous growth. All this points to the probability that the garden was at first simply a massive, formal set piece of rock and stone, an impressive decoration for the castle courtyard, as statuary and fountains are used in European pleasances.

In the number and placement of its stones, Nijō garden bears a marked resemblance to Hideyoshi's Sambō-in, which, it will be recalled, was regarded at that time as the finest example of landscape art in Japan. But the stones of Nijō are even larger, more numerous, more impressively individualistic than those of Sambō-in. Obviously, even in this garden the Tokugawas were pursuing their usual policy of trying to outdo Hideyoshi.

Seen from the buildings, the stones do not appear so unduly large as they do closer at hand. In fact, were they much smaller, they might seem to lack character when looked at from the necessary distance. Their size, therefore, is to some extent justified. But the garden was obviously meant to be looked at while strolling in it, as well as from the buildings which encircle it. Walking around in it now, its stones appear out of all proportion to its size. They are noticeably rough and irregular, not smoothly molded; very different in this regard from the more elegant stones in older gardens. Also, as at Sambō-in, there is, in addition to the usual stone groups on shore and island, a collection of other rocks, each an oddity, a museum piece, gathered from far and wide simply as a curiosity of shape, color, or texture. These are scattered beside the path, looking as if they might have been set down temporarily while the garden was being made, then left behind when the workmen departed.

The lake is very irregular in shape, and the islands are large enough to add to its complexities, creating a constantly changing series of vistas as one moves about. Several large bridges lead to the islands, adding picturesque touches to these vistas. The water level is rather low, so that one has always the feeling of looking down into the garden, and there are no hillocks to lead the eye upward. Monotony of level is avoided, however, by the varying slopes of the lake shore and by the islands which rise like mounds from the water.

Individual stone arrangements in Nijō garden show a high degree of conscious artistic skill. The effect created by the famous Fujito stone of Sambō-in garden is frequently duplicated—a single very large stone standing upright, supported by smaller, lower stones of harmonizing form. Conspicuous and overwrought effects are frequent, obtained by strong contrast; high stones rise very high above the others, or low, broad, massive stones may have a short, slender upright beside them. Many of the stones have flat tops and straight sides like the old Muromachi stones; but because there is so much of everything in the garden, there is no feeling of Muromachi simplicity and organization in the stonework. Even the very deliberate and effective use of empty space between the arrangements does not create simplicity, but only adds to the feeling of sophisticated artistry. Thus, while individually the stone groups have interest, and many of the vistas are charming, when the total effect is noted from a distance, it is scattered.

There is a dominant feeling of artificiality throughout the garden. At the time it was made, only the tea masters were any longer interested in studying nature and reproducing its effects. The makers of grand gardens such as this, followed the naturalistic pattern as a base, because it was traditional; but it was merely a pattern, an outline to be filled in. The feeling in the gardens which were thus produced was as artificial as that of a geometrical flower bed. All interest centered in the creation of rock forms exemplifying the artistic laws of rhythm, balance, harmony, and emphasis. It was the baroque period in garden art, when technical skill was superlative and significance nearly gone.

In this respect it is interesting to compare Nijō Castle garden with its contemporary in time and spirit, the shrine of Ieyasu at Nikkō. The Nikkō shrine buildings were begun shortly after Nijō Castle was prepared for the imperial visit. Ieyasu seems personally to have had rather simple tastes and desired only a simple monument over his grave. But Iemitsu, who caused the buildings to be erected, evidently felt that his grandfather's memory could only be properly honored by these elaborate buildings. And besides, they cost a tremendous amount of money all of which came from the various vassal lords. Superlative technical skill went into the carving and painting which covers every inch of them, but to quote again from Sir George Sansom, while they "are gorgeous in colour and marvelous in detail, they are fiddling and æsthetically ill conceived. . . . But" he adds, "they are saved from vulgarity by a noble setting among giant trees and a certain impressive profusion."

This is exactly true of Nijō Castle garden. The size and profusion of its rocks and its spacious setting in the center of the immense courtyard give it vitality, while it has the virtue of real artistry in its rock forms. The skill shown in their arrangement is very sure and masterful, even if overdone and lacking in restraint and delicacy. This garden, in short, may be regarded as a nearly perfect expression of the crystallized military spirit which produced it, aggressive, boastful, obvious, and efficient.

Nijō Castle garden has generally been regarded as the work of Kobori Enshū, one of the outstanding personalities in the cultural world of Kyoto at that time. He was a student of Zen, a tea master and poet. No document connects him with the original design of the garden, however, while everything about it contradicts it as the work of a man with such tastes. However, he was only twenty-three when the castle was built and high in the Shogun's favor; possibly he was filled with a youthful ambition to show that he could outdo the accepted masterpiece of Sambō-in. But it is much more reasonable to assume that Nijō Castle garden was the work of gardeners following the Fushimi school. These men were skilled in stone technique, and their interest centered chiefly in it; they were, moreover, familiar and sympathetic to the atmosphere of castles. When Nijō was being reconditioned for the imperial visit, twenty years after its construction, Kobori Enshū, we know[1] was responsible for constructing the new buildings housing the imperial guests. Doubtless, the garden was renovated for the occasion, but its massive stone groupings were much too large, probably, to have been much changed about. Minor details may have been added under Kobori Enshū's supervision but probably that is all.

Like Nijō, most of the oustanding gardens made in Kyoto during the early Tokugawa years now claim Kobori Enshū as their designer. Records substantiating these claims, however, are singularly lacking, considering how prominent he was. Apparently, like Sōami's name in the Muromachi period, that of Kobori Enshū has since been tied to important contemporary gardens. It is much easier to attach a resounding name than to dig through the old records in search of the right one. There is little doubt, however, but that Kobori Enshū was an important figure in Kyoto at that time who did make gardens occasionally and who may have influenced many more than the records actually indicate.

Facts about his life are well known because he was a person of high rank and an acknowledged tea master and artist. He lived between 1579 and 1647, spending most of his life in Kyoto. His father was a Tokugawa vassal and he himself was made lord of the province of Tōtōmi, by Ieyasu, at the age of twenty-seven. The Chinese characters used to write this province may also be pronounced Enshū, so that the name Kobori Enshū, by which he is usually known, is a simplified form of his family name and title. He studied Zen philosophy, painting, calligraphy, and poetry and made himself a master of the tea arts. He was a leader of the literati, a friend of the court, and an associate of important men, so that his name appears in many diaries and records of the time. In 1615 he was given the important position of governor of Fushimi, holding it for twenty-four years. He seems to have been that rare combination, a man of artistic tastes who is also an able administrator. During his period of office and even before, he was frequently appointed to serve as special commissioner on some building project which the Tokugawas were sponsoring. He admitted toward the end of his

[1] From the *Daiyuin-den Go Jikki* (True record of Iemitsu).

life to his friend, the abbot of Konchi-in, that he was tired of supervising public buildings and longed to devote himself to his own artistic pursuits. But, as he went about these public duties during the principal years of his life, he probably was often consulted about this or that garden and probably often gave help.

Several years after he had helped prepare Nijō for the Emperor's visit, he was called on to build a retiring palace for this same sovereign. Friction had developed between Go-Mizunoo and the shogunal brother-in-law. Iemitsu did not hesitate to be annoying in ways within his power, and in 1630 the Emperor suddenly abdicated, turning the throne over to an eight-year-old daughter by the Tokugawa consort. With a niece as sovereign, Iemitsu could afford to be generous, and orders were then issued to have a suitable palace built for the retired Emperor. Some of the buildings which had been used only during the Nijō visit were moved to the site of this new palace and others added. When all was complete, orders were given to build a garden and Kobori Enshū was placed in charge.[2]

It is thought that Kobori Enshū and the ex-Emperor consulted together over the plans for this garden. Go-Mizunoo being a man of highly cultivated tastes was much interested in gardens. At a later period of his life he made his own plans for an imperial villa and he often paid formal visits to famous gardens. Among others he went to Yoshimitsu's old Gold Pavilion which was rehabilitated for the occasion.

A retired emperor's palace is known as a *sentō*; the one made for Go-Mizunoo served his successors also, until the custom of abdication was discontinued not many years ago. Although the buildings of this Sentō have burned, its garden still exists in good condition. It is very large, some nineteen acres in extent, and includes two lakes. They are inclosed by artificial hillocks and shaded by many fine old trees which must date back to the original planting scheme. On the shore of the northern lake once stood the quarters of the Tokugawa Empress, somewhat apart from the Emperor's dwelling but connected to it by a long corridor. This part today is known as

[2] *Zoku Shigushō.*

209

the Ōmiya Gosho. The Emperor's residence looked out over the southern lake. These two lakes are quite large enough for the old imperial pastime of boating, but whether the retired sovereigns every enjoyed it or not is uncertain.

Stones are sparingly arranged along the shores of the lakes and islands. They are good garden stones as to shape and texture, but not extraordinary. Successive reconstructions during the three hundred years since the garden was built have so changed their original groupings it is hard, now, to know just how they might have been in the beginning. But one thing is certain; in this garden, stones and their arrangement were never the matter of super-lative interest they were in Nijō and Sambō-in.

An outstanding feature of the Sentō garden, which probably survives from its original construction period, is the formalized reproduction of a pebbled beach. The foreshore in front of the Palace was graded to slope gently into the water and was then tightly paved with round flattish stones, each about the size of an orange. The effect is very stiff and artificial. The device was copied several times in other gardens of the period but it never became popular.

A path circles the two lakes, crossing by various bridges to the islands and winding through the sylvan hillocks which separate and inclose the lakes. It crosses also the small stream which meanders among these ferned and wooded embankments. The stream falls to the lake level over a broad high cascade, large enough to be plainly seen across the rippling pond. The path leads to rustic tea houses or the foundations where they once stood. It is frequently set with stepping stones and lighted here and there by stone lan-terns. Altogether, the Sentō garden, with its broad stretches of water re-flecting ancient trees is very peaceful and lovely. It is a garden which depends largely on such natural things for its final effect.

There is evident in this garden a feeling totally different from that which inspired the showy Nijō and Sambō-in gardens. Paths, rustic houses, lanterns, and stepping stones are all details from the tea garden, as are its serenity and quiet naturalness. All suggest the atmosphere of the tea cult.

PRINCELY ESTATES OF TOKUGAWA TIMES

This then has been superimposed on the basic form of one of the old courtly lake and island gardens. The Sentō, in other words, merges these two forms, disregarding almost entirely the showy spirit of Momoyama. It is exactly what we might expect from men with the tastes of Kobori Enshū and Go-Mizunoo, given the opportunity to create a palace garden. Neither the court nor the tea men were deeply touched by the spirit of the conquerors, but went their traditional ways. And in the end it was their ideas which triumphed and survived.

The same feeling is dominant in another garden made somewhat later but by the same retired Emperor, Go-Mizunoo. He lived to be eighty-four years old, and when he was about sixty, the shogunate presented him with a large country estate near the village of Shūgaku-in. Legend says he designed the place himself, using a clay model. Whether this detail be true or not, it is evident that his scholarly tastes and his interest in tea dominated the plan. His first recorded visit in state was made in 1655, which may be regarded as the year when the garden was finished.[3] But it is certain he had been going there quietly for a long time before.

The estate, of some seventy-three acres, lies on high ground north of Kyoto, with a rim of mountains behind it and a sweeping view in front of lesser hills. The greater part of the estate acreage was given over to rice fields and wooded hillsides, but within its confines three inclosed landscape gardens were built. Each had its special purpose: Buildings in the lower garden were used by the ex-Emperor during his visits; those in the middle garden were used by the Tokugawa Empress. One of the original buildings there still survives, beautifully decorated with painted panels and making use of the Empress's personal Tokugawa crest. Around the two groups of buildings are small gardens forming a sylvan setting with a stream, a pond, rocks, trees, and lanterns.

The real interest in the visits to Shūgaku-in, however, centered in the upper garden where a magnificent view and mountain quiet can be enjoyed in tea cottages overlooking the lake. This upper garden is one of the most

[3] *Reigan Hōō Gokō Shinki.*

211

original and distinctive gardens in Japan, unlike anything that preceded or followed it. It is conventional only in possessing a large lake, which was built where natural contours in the hillside made it practical. Two large islands were left during its excavation, which are now connected to each other and the shore by bridges, forming a large peninsula into the lake. Seen from above, these islands add interest to the contours of the shoreline; from the path which winds around the shore, they create a variety of changing views.

The unusual feature of this garden, however, is the complete absence of all ornamental stones. There are neither cascade, islets, stone bridges, nor boulders around the water's edge. The land simply slopes gently down to the water level, with sodded banks. Here is striking contrast to all other gardens of the time, especially the overwrought stone work of Nijō Castle. It is as if the designer were tired to death of stones and wanted to see what could be done without any at all.

As a matter of fact, the stones are not greatly missed. In place of the usual detailed interest in stonework close at hand suggesting rugged mountains, the upper garden of Shūgaku-in has actual mountains to look at. The distant background of these hills is the superlative point of interest in this garden, not the foreground or middle ground as is usually the case. This main view is best obtained from a small rustic building perched high on the hillside above the lake, poetically called *Rin-un-tei*, or the Cloud-Touching Cottage. From its site, the hillside slopes steeply down to the lake; this lake with its wooded island becomes only a sort of foreground to the tremendous sweep of distant valley and hills. Beyond the flat valley the hills rise, range on range, fading away to the horizon in ridges of blue and purple. This view is the most spacious, bold, and daring in all Japanese garden art. Perhaps Go-Mizunoo, who had lived for sixty years within the rigid confines of the court, gave in this garden his soul freedom to range unrestricted over the world.

Shūgaku-in has also a stroll or tea garden, a long path over the hillside and around the lakeshore leading to a series of rustic tea cottages. Looked

The garden of the retired emperor's palace, called the Sentō, contains a formalized reproduction of a pebbled shore made very stiffly and formally with cobblestones. (Photo from Board of Tourist Industry.)

The upper garden of the Shūgaku-in Imperial Villa park contains the most spreading view of any Japanese estate of the early days. The garden itself serves but as a foreground for this view, with a lake in which a large island has been left cut out of the hillside. The lack of stones, with sodded shorelines instead, and scattered trees, combine to give it greater resemblance to a Western park than any other garden made before the modern period. (Photo from Board of Tourist Industry.)

The tea houses of Katsura are more elaborate structures than the simple huts advocated by Rikyū. They are, in fact, small cottages of several rooms and, like the earlier garden-pavilions, served as retreats in which the Prince and his guests might spend time in esthetic pursuits. This, the largest one, is known as Shōkin-tei.

In Katsura garden an oblique peninsula formed by two islands
linked by bridges is sometimes called the "Bridge of the Gods"
after the beautiful natural formation by that name illustrated in
Chapter III. (Photo from Board of Tourist Industry.)

upon as a tea garden it might be thought of as being on a true or natural scale. For Rikyū's idea that the tea room is a rustic retreat far away in the hills is here carried out in reality. The path is no telescoped suggestion of a mountain trail but a real path over the hills, and the tea houses are real sylvan retreats.

In its planting—which may, however, be something that has crept in since the garden was first made—Shūgaku-in is original also. The sodded banks of the lake are covered with a low growth of natural grass. Trees and shrubs are planted scatteringly over the island and the shore, not imitating the closely wooded growth on the mountain slope behind the garden. There is also a unique planting in front of the Cloud-Touching Cottage, a close, clipped, growth of shrubs extending down the steep slope to the edge of the lake. They are sheared level, like a hedge, the whole length of the hillside. These shrubs were planted originally, no doubt, to keep the hillside from washing; when they grew so tall they began to interfere with the view, they probably were trimmed down and so they assumed their peculiar shape. They present now a surface as smooth as the hillside itself but three or four feet above it. They are maintained by gardeners who creep in beneath, then stand cautiously erect, shear what they can reach, and creep on to another place.

Clipped planting, sodded shoreline, lack of stones, graveled walks around the water, shaded by scattered trees, finally, the bold magnificence of the view, combine to give Shūgaku-in more resemblance to a Western park than is possessed by any other garden made in Japan in the early period.

The merging of the tea and palace style as seen in Go-Mizunoo's *sentō* palace garden is even better exemplified in another estate made about the same time. This new garden was the villa of Katsura, made first by Hideyoshi for a prince of the Imperial family, but later developed into the greatest garden of the early Tokugawa period and one of the greatest ever created in Japan.

The Katsura river—which is called Ōi a few miles away—was a favorite locality for the villas of court nobles even in Heian days. Although the district was flat, there was a fine sweeping view of the hills which rim it. In the *Tale of Genji,* it will be recalled, Lady Murasaki has her hero owning an estate at Katsura[4]—as did Michinaga, head of the powerful Fuijwara clan at the time she wrote.[5] Nothing links the present imperial villa of Katsura with this one of Fujiwara Michinaga, although more than likely, an old Heian lake served as the basis for later development.

About the time Hideyoshi entertained the Emperor at Jūraku-tei, he took under his special patronage Prince Tomohito, a young brother of the sovereign. This youth he endowed with a fine town mansion near the Imperial palace and also, apparently, gave him this country place near the Katsura river.[6] No record mentions when the garden was first made, though Hideyoshi must have had some sort of garden laid out for his ward. But it was not until years later that Prince Tomohito, then grown into a man of refined and scholarly tastes, began to develop the place to suit himself. At the time of his death in 1629 the general features of the garden as they exist today had been completed. In subsequent years his son, Prince Tomotada, finished the estate, adding the tea rooms, the stonework, and the lanterns.

Until recently this garden was believed to be the work of Kobori Enshū. One of the most popular stories in Japanese garden annals relates that Hideyoshi engaged Enshū to lay out the estate. Enshū consented, it goes, on three conditions; first, that there should be no limit to the cost, second, that no time should be set for its completion, and third, that there should be no visits by important personages during construction—lest suggestions be made which could not be ignored. The fact that Kobori Enshū was a boy of twelve at the time this is supposed to have taken place spoils

[4] Where the winding water banquet was held. (See chapter IV.)

[5] *Nihon Ki Ryaku.*

[6] The history of the Katsura villa as given here is based on recent researches by Mr. Toyama, reported in *Heishi Magazine,* and by Mr. Shigemori in his *Nihon Teienshi Zukan.*

this story as historical material, but it throws an entertaining light on the perennial difficulties of professional garden makers.

In checking the story of Enshū's association with Katsura, recent research has failed to disclose a single contemporary document which connects his name with it. The first mention occurs some ninety years after his death in a diary written by a guest of the seventh prince. "This garden was made by Kobori Enshū" it says. The statement has all the earmarks of popular hearsay, but there may be some truth in it after all. The garden was completed bit by bit over a considerable period, and, no doubt, many friends of the two princes made suggestions. Although no record says so, Kobori Enshū was almost certain to have been one of these friends. He is known to have belonged to the same little coterie of men interested in cultural things. His part, whatever it may have been, was, however, certainly unofficial. If the Tokugawas had financed the garden, Enshū would undoubtedly have been put in charge of the work. But Prince Tomohito had been a ward of Hideyoshi, and it is hardly likely such a person would have been singled out for such special favors as this garden. The work must have been paid for out of the income provided the Prince by Hideyoshi, and any suggestions Kobori Enshū gave were made as a friend, not an official.

A country house in rather simple style was originally built on the estate. Later, the second prince enlarged it when his uncle, the ex-Emperor Go-Mizunoo, visited him. A new wing was added for the imperial relative and another to accommodate the extra attendants. All the rooms are small and simple, but very elegant in their refinement. The sliding screens which panel the walls are decorated with paintings in the Muromachi manner, done in black and white rather than with the gold and colors of the current Nikkō style. Throughout the estate there is shown a return to the old standards of Muromachi, brought about by the influence of the tea ceremony and with it, a disdain of the flamboyant Tokugawa fashion.

The villa remained in the Katsura family until some fifty years ago. When the last princess of the line died, it became an imperial estate and is maintained as such today. Apparently, although it was kept up in more or less good order during the several centuries of its existence, later princes of the family changed it but little. It is seen today, therefore, very much as it was when Prince Tomotada completed it in the first half of the 17th century.

The rambling house looks out upon the broadest part of the lake, a picture of great beauty with its islands and inclosing trees. To view this scene as the moon rose over the treetops, a special platform was built in front of the house. It has no roof and is floored simply with round bamboo poles. On clear autumn evenings—the traditional time for moon-viewing —cushions were placed on this platform, and the host with his guests would compose appropriate verses. The moon is inevitably associated with this estate because its name, Katsura, is the word for a tree[7] which, according to legend, grows in the moon.

The moon, however, is the only thing outside the garden which does have a part in it. Unlike most of the earlier large gardens, no natural view of the hills is incorporated. A strip of bamboo forest surrounds the garden, shutting away the outside world and forming an indefinite boundary of greenery. All attention centers on the enchanting views created by the complexities of the lake, islands, hillocks, rocks, and ancient trees.

While the lake is almost two acres in extent, it is so irregular that no very large expanse of water is visible from any one point. Long arms or bays extend in various directions, forming small detached water pictures quite apart from the main body and creating far flung vistas. Boats were used on this lake, for there are three landings at various places on the shoreline in the form of level stone steps. One is before the residence, others in front of the tea rooms; it was evidently a pleasant pastime to go to the tea ceremonial by water rather than by land.

To allow boats to pass freely about the lake many of the bridges are of the high-arched, log-and-earth type found in Sambō-in. A delightful winding waterway for boats is hidden between a large high island and the shore beyond it. One of the later commentaries on this garden remarks that Prince

[7] *Cercidiphyllun japonicum.*

Tomotada, who completed these waterways, modeled them after the description of the Springtime Garden in the *Tale of Genji*.[8] Katsura shows the same narrow channel that led "straight toward a toy mountain which seemed to bar all further progress. . . . The little wood on the hill beyond the lake, the bridge that joined the two islands, the mossy banks that seemed to grow greener every hour. . . ."

The "toy mountain" of Katsura comes closer to deserving this description than anything previously created in a Japanese garden. It is higher and longer than the earlier embankments. The amount of material excavated from the lake was enormous, for in order to create a flow of water from the Katsura river, the lake bed had to be dug five or six feet below the level of the ground. These deep banks do much to take away any feeling of level monotony in the garden. The earth taken out was piled into high inclosing embankments and a hilly island was built some thirty feet high, two hundred feet long, and ninety feet wide. Regarded as a "mountain" this structure may well be called a miniature; but it is a real hill supporting a heavy growth of large old trees and shrubs. There is no feeling of reduced proportions in the mind of one following the mossy path that winds over it.

Although this garden so much resembles one of the old courtly lake and island estates, this resemblance is superficial. Like all good works of art, Katsura is a perfect expression of its own time. It shows a new mood, or rather, a return to an old one, but with the inevitable changes which accompany any new period, however much it may seem to be a cyclic return. Katsura garden marks a swing back toward the old Japanese love of nature and simplicity. The brief flare of Momoyama art, so aberrant to the main stream of Japanese culture, had nearly run its course, with Nijō Castle as its final expression in gardening. The renewed interest in reproducing nature followed forms laid down for the tea cult, which was then the current expression of the old feeling.

The cloud under which Rikyū had died had darkened the tea cult for a short period and marked its end as a popular fad, but true devotees were not

[8] Quoted in chapter IV.

deterred by the disfavor of a dictator. It was revived by those men to whom it really meant something, and by the time Katsura garden was built, the ceremonial and all it implied were more strongly intrenched than ever among intellectual and artistic people. Its influence was beginning to be felt on every phase of life including gardens in general. This is plainly shown in Katsura for, like the garden of the *sentō* palace, it is really an extensive tea garden superimposed on the old lake and island form.

The fact is apparent both in its detail and atmosphere. The mood of the garden is one of sylvan quiet, of *wabi*, solitude, and of *yūgen*, the mystery of beauty. A concrete detail derived from the tea garden is the long path of stepping stones which follows the convolutions of the lake, linking a series of tea houses. Each of these buildings has its stone water basins—there are eight in all—and there are no less than twenty-three stone lanterns in the garden.

The tea houses of Katsura are more elaborate structures than the simple huts advocated by Rikyū. They are, in fact, small cottages of several rooms, and, like the earlier garden-pavilions, they served as retreats in which the Prince and his guests might spend time in esthetic pursuits. The tea ceremony was evidently but one of the uses to which they were put. Each is placed where it overlooks a different part of the garden, and the vicinity of each is developed in a slightly different way. The variety and inventiveness displayed in these various parts and in details like the stone lanterns indicate plainly that the creative spirit in garden design was still strong at this period.

Practically all of the stone lanterns are of original design, the form of some being very far indeed from the first temple style. A number are short and low, hardly more than the light-holder and roof of the usual lantern. One of the taller Katsura lanterns may hold the only European touch found in the early gardens—a small figure cut into its base, said to be the Virgin Mary. This lantern is supposed to have been designed by Furuta Oribe, a leading tea master who had been converted to Christianity. But the figure might as well be a Buddha as the Virgin and the story seems farfetched.

The stone water basins likewise show great ingenuity and variety. One of them is not a basin at all, but the lake itself; near the tea house called Shōkin-tei is a short row of stepping stones leading out into the water. The guest walked to the last, then squatting, poured water from the lake over his hands with a dipper which rested on a second stone near the last.

Perhaps the most strikingly new thing in the Katsura garden is a touch of the geometrical. An arm of the lake which lies in front of the tea cottage named Shōi-ken is rectangular in shape, its straight sides formed by walls of cut stone. The building stands on a flat terrace, and a second terrace below it is at the lake level; formal stone steps lead from one level to another. The hedges which shut in this part of the garden are clipped into squared form. Here we find the closest thing to geometrical formality existing in any garden before the modern period.

A window at the back of Shōi-ken opens out onto the rice fields which surround the estate, the encircling bamboo forest being here left open for the purpose of seeing out. This is the first concrete expression by the upper classes of an interest in the doings of the lower classes. Another indication of it is found in the tea house called Shōka-tei which is built in the shape of a primitive farm cottage. It has an earthen floor surrounded by a raised shelf which peasants used to sleep on, and it contains a charcoal brazier to show the gentry how cooking was done by the peasantry.

This cottage, Shōka-tei, perches on top of the hilly island where it has a spreading view of the entire garden. In spring the view is called "Yoshino" after the famous cherry mountain, while in autumn it conveniently becomes "Tatsuta" noted for its maples. This seems to have been one of the first times that definite Japanese landscape views were suggested or reproduced in the garden. There had always been a sentimental harking back to China, but not until now was a similar interest shown in Japanese beauty spots. The tendency became very marked a little later.

While stone groups are found, scatteringly, all over the garden, they become suddenly of dominant interest in the vicinity of the third tea house,

219

Shōkin-tei. It is the largest building, outside the residence, and the garden around it holds complicated stone artistry in contrast to the rest of the estate which is simple. Here feeling swings back to the current fashion of pretentious elaboration. Katsura could hardly escape entirely from contemporary influences, since its owner was, after all, a prominent figure of the court and, no doubt, often had to entertain fashionable guests who did not understand the simplicity of tea. He managed, however, to confine this quality to a single corner of the estate.

An irregular arm of the lake forms the center of this showy part of the garden. An oblique peninsula is formed of two small islands which are linked by bridges to the opposite shore, dividing the lake into middle ground and background. This is called today the "Bridge of the Gods" after the noted natural formation by that name illustrated in Chapter III. Because of the peninsula, with its bridges, rocks, and lanterns, which hold attention near at hand, the distant shore of the lake seems farther away than it really is. This is the device used in the Gold Pavilion lake to suggest size, it will be recalled. All the shore hereabouts is set with stones and softened with trees and shrubs; the stones are very numerous, very fine, and lavishly used. But unlike some of the other gardens of the period, every stone has its purpose in the composition; none is laid out simply for display. Thus, beside the stone bridge linking the islands of the peninsula there are placed tall upright stones, their purpose to balance the cross-line of the bridge.

From the standpoint of artistry alone, the stonework of Katsura ranks among the best ever done in Japan. It is, of course, but a surface art, for its creators had nothing more in mind than the balance, rhythm, and harmony of form they were producing within the naturalistic pattern. But the pictures they created are still beautiful. Prince Katsura was no *nouveau riche* with need to display his wealth; it appears, on the contrary, as if he had kept a restraining hand on the gardeners who were making these rock compositions, preventing them from becoming too flamboyant, insisting that their work have suavity and elegance. Nevertheless, the stone arrangements

From the standpoint of artistry alone, the stonework of Katsura ranks among the best ever done in Japan. Prince Katsura was no nouveau riche *with need to display his wealth; on the contrary, it appears as if he kept a restraining hand on the gardeners to prevent them from becoming too flamboyant, insisting that it have suavity and elegance. (Photo from Board of Tourist Industry.)*

The garden of Shōren-in temple is the type of small landscape made for the quarters of princely abbots in the seventeenth century. (Photo by Okamoto Toyo.)

are more artistic than natural, as was inevitable with work of this period, but naturalism is not entirely lost sight of. It is, however, the naturalism of perfection, nature idealized, every stone and rock in perfect harmony, every curve of the shore exactly right, everything slightly exaggerated for the sake of art.

XV. *Impressionistic Zen Landscapes*

WHILE Kyoto aristocrats were once more revelling in the building of fine estates, Kyoto temples were also enjoying a period of reconstruction after the devastating war decades. Hideyoshi had been liberal in his gifts for this purpose, and the Tokugawas donated even more. The early 17th century, therefore, saw a great renaissance of fine temple building in the capital, with gardens a part of nearly every one.

Many of these temple gardens were of the small, landscape-viewing type, similar to those constructed in front of the *shoin* of a private residence. Since temple gardens lie before the abbot's official quarters, this similarity is understandable. The principal room of these quarters, which usually had an altar and was also the chief reception room of the institution, is called a *hōjō*. Its garden, therefore, is known as a *hōjō* garden. Those belonging to small temples are usually modest and unassuming little courtyard landscapes with a few rocks, trees, shrubs, and, perhaps, a flat stone to span a suggested streamlet and so create a landscape picture. But the garden of a great and powerful institution, such as the head of some popular sect, was often very large and fine. The abbot of these institutions used frequently to be an imperial prince who lived in much the same style after taking holy orders that he had before. His residence, therefore, was like a small palace, and its garden was appropriately fine.

Outstanding among the gardens of this class is that of Chion-in temple, head of the Jōdo sect. Its present buildings were put up in the 17th century under Tokugawa patronage with Kobori Enshū in charge. Its halls are huge, ornate structures of the Momoyama type, and its *hōjō* rooms are lined with golden screens which are equal to those of Nijō Castle. The garden forms a landscape picture centering around a pond which lies at the foot of a natural hillside. It is probable that Kobori Enshū had a good deal to do with this garden because of his connection with the buildings.

A smaller temple garden of the landscape type is Joju-in belonging to the abbot of Kiyomizu temple. It forms a delightful little picture, with a pond, islands, lanterns, and old trees. Others are found in the temples of Koho-an, Rengeiji, Ninnaji, Chishaku-in, Shōren-in, Myōhō-in, Kōdaiji, and others. But all of these are the small landscape garden which has been fitted into the limited space of a temple courtyard.

While these conventional gardens were being built by some temples, an entirely new and different kind was being developed by the Zen temples of Kyoto. These Zen gardens were also landscapes of a sort, but, far from being naturalistic, they were executed in an impressionistic, abridged, and symbolic manner. Made of sand and stone with a few plants, they showed in their materials and general feeling a direct descent from Muromachi gardens like Ryōanji and Daisen-in. But, actually, they were quite different both in form and feeling from those older creations.

The splendid mysticism of Ryōanji and the esoteric symbolism of the painting gardens had come to their maturity in an atmosphere far too rarefied for the later, more material garden makers to maintain. Likewise, the sheer artistry of the older period was beyond the later one. Yet, that the meaning of the older gardens was not without some comprehension in the Zen monasteries seems clear; the new gardens made by these temples was the attempt of a later, less spiritual generation to express this feeling.

The older esoteric gardens had undoubtedly been based on Chinese prototypes, as we have noticed. But the later creations were, I think, probably without a parallel in China. They seem to have been entirely a Japanese expression, a development in garden art similar to the other arts of the period. At the very peak of the Muromachi years, Japan had begun to turn, in the way she always has, from the use of a foreign form to self-expression based on those forms. During the 16th century, therefore, the country had been in another of those nationally creative periods, well illustrated in the painting of the time.

In the Muromachi period, Kano Masanobu had taken the first steps toward forming a new school of painting, a step which had been completed by his gifted son, Kano Motonobu. Artists of this Kano school were the ones who produced the paintings on the golden screens of Momoyama castles. Another individual Japanese expression was, of course, the tea ceremony, as devised by Shūko and perfected by Sen no Rikyū. And the massive dry landscapes of Momoyama castles were an original form of garden art. But more distinctive than they were the expressionistic Zen landscapes in the temple gardens.

The beginning of this transition movement may be seen in small gardens belonging to the subtemples of the large Myōshinji monastery on the outskirts of Kyoto. During the early war years, some of these subtemples managed to survive and serve as retreats in which culture remained and even progressed. In the small subtemple of Reiun-in the artist, Kano Motonobu, lived for some time, apparently in the 1520's; there he must have done a good deal of the work which gave definite direction to the new Kano school of painting and there, no doubt, the feeling of this transition period had a center.

In the neighboring small temple of Taizō-in is a garden which tradition attributes to Motonobu himself. It is a painting garden of the Muromachi type, very small, as the exigencies of that unhappy period made necessary, but an excellent little piece of art. A pond is suggested by rocks which form islands and a bridge, while others at the back represent hills. In this garden the Muromachi feeling is still dominantly shown in the form of the stones and in the definite outlines of a landscape.

But in Reiun-in temple itself where Motonobu lived, is another garden, quite different in its technique from Taizō-in. Reiun-in had been founded by the Abbot Daikyō. He came to be greatly admired by the Emperor Go-Nara who reigned between 1526 and 1557. This Emperor made a visit to the temple to talk Zen philosophy with the Abbot. Although this was the most poverty-stricken period in the whole history of the court, the coming of the Emperor was still a great occasion, and in preparing for it the temple managed to rebuild its reception room. It is a very small building, as is the garden which lies before it and which probably was made at the same time.

The garden is a mere strip of land lying between the verandah and an inclosing wall. In this space, however, were gathered and arranged a few choice stones probably picked up from ruined estates nearby; among the stones were planted some shrubs and trees. The stones are arranged with the largest and heaviest on the left side from which they taper in size to the right, giving the immemorial direction of Oriental garden scenes. While the arrangement is pleasing, there is no easily discernible landscape picture nor is there any such expression of pure harmony as is found in the Ryōanji garden. Yet, if the imagination plays over the stone groups, it can, perhaps, see in the tallest ones at the back, a rugged cliff and from it a stream coursing down through the garden. But only the vaguest suggestion is here; impressionism was just beginning to take form.

Gardens of this type seem to have developed but slowly, doubtless because so few gardens of any kind were made. One of the most interesting of the earlier forms is that of Shukō-in[1] a subtemple of Daitokuji. In this later garden the flat rectangle of sand is considerably larger than in the small gardens of the poverty-stricken period. The space is inclosed by a hedge, shaded by a few pine trees, and holds a large assemblage of small rocks, their number causing the garden to be popularly known as the Garden of a Hundred Stones. The rocks are arranged in an extended group along the back of the sanded area, apparently as a chain of islands. This suggestion is enhanced by a stone bridge between two of them. In their fine form and their feeling, these stones retain still a strong suggestion of Muromachi artistry, making this one of the most esthetically satisfying of all the impressionistic gardens. At present the stones are largely covered with vines, while heavy moss has crept over the sand. But the effect of this

[1] Sometimes spelled Jukō-in.

greenery is to enhance the quietness and serenity of the garden and the smooth flow of the rock forms.

Impressionistic gardens came to a full development when peace was once more established over the nation and temple reconstruction was going forward on a large scale. One of the best and earliest of the true impressionistic gardens is that of Konchi-in of Nanzenji monastery.

Before the Ōnin war, Nanzenji had been one of the largest and most flourishing of the great Zen foundations in Kyoto, with no less than sixty-two subtemples grouped around it. All of these were burned during that war, and for a century afterward the temple organization seems to have done little more than exist. But early in the 1600's it was restored to importance through the Abbot Sūden.

In his youth this man had been a knight-follower of the Tokugawas but, turning monk, had become Ieyasu's advisor and secretary in the field. When the latter came to power, he placed Sūden in charge of the relations between his "camp government" at Edo and the temples of the country, making him thus the most politically important ecclesiastic in the nation. Sūden chose to administer his duties from Konchi-in, a small subtemple of Nanzenji that had been reconstructed for him. He had been given for its main building one of the halls from Hideyoshi's Fushimi Castle which was then being partly dismantled. After this very beautiful building had been moved and set up on its new site—about 1611—the garden which now lies beside it probably was made.

This garden is a rather large, sanded rectangle, inclosed by the hall on one side, a small building dedicated to Sūden's spirit at the end, and, opposite, instead of the usual wall, a wooded bank. Its trees and shrubs shut in the garden completely. At the foot of this bank stand two massive arrangements of stones, one tall and upright, the other lower and more horizontal. Lying between them is a flat connecting stone like a bridge. The two rock compositions are now so overgrown by shrubs it is difficult to make much out of them, but experts identify them as probably crane and turtle islands in traditional style. Here then, in this conventional form, islands rising from a sanded sea, is the standard garden pattern merely executed in the impressionistic manner.

It is believed that Kobori Enshū had a hand in the design of this garden, although no literary evidence supports the belief. He and Sūden, of course, were acquainted, since both were important Tokugawa officials in Kyoto. It is known, moreover, that both were also members of the little set of artists, tea and literary men in the city at that time. It is assumed that when Sūden built the small tea room which still stands near his temple he consulted Enshū about its design, and likewise, probably, with the garden. Strong supporting evidence of Enshū's part in this garden is found in another very like it, the garden of Raikyūji temple near Matsuyama on the island of Shikoku. Enshū had been made the Lord of Matsuyama by the Tokugawas and is known to have been a patron of this temple. The similarity of their designs points to him as the obvious creator of both.

One of the largest and finest and perhaps the most noted of all the impressionistic gardens is that in front of the *hōjō* of Daitokuji monastery. This temple has long been one of the most popular of the great Zen foundations in Kyoto. Its *hōjō* was rebuilt in 1636, and the garden probably was made as soon as it was finished. It is a very spacious garden, its sanded rectangle being 120 feet long and 42 feet wide. It is inclosed by a wall and hedge, and several immense trees grow beyond, their gigantic branches against the sky making splendid pictures, even though now these trees rather dwarf the suggested landscape which lies below them.

In this garden the proportion of space covered by raked sand is very large—more than sixty per cent. This is in accord with a tendency these gardens showed for the sanded area to become larger and larger, and for the stone arrangements to occupy less and less of the space. Eventually, indeed, certain gardens had no stones at all but were merely an expanse of white sand. In the Daitokuji garden are two small sand piles near the verandah edge, which appear as if they had been left there by the acolyte who last spread sand on the garden. But, actually, they have long been permanent features. Similar heaps of sand may be found in other gardens of this type;

it was, evidently, either a common practice to leave them so, or there was some forgotten significance attached to the heaps. It seems probable, as already mentioned, that from some such original pile developed the now overgrown sand structures in Yoshimasa's Silver Pavilion garden.

A foreigner looking at the Daitokuji *hōjō* garden might find it, at first, as puzzling as the garden of Ryōanji. But not for long. Here is no mystical sermon in stone as at Ryōanji. Daitokuji is simply and unmistakably a landscape picture, although it is one drawn with only suggested strokes and in peculiar media. The sand, of course, represents water—a stream or river flowing in the traditional left to right direction. Its feeling of a current sweeping scross the garden is achieved by the form, position, and diminishing size of low stones and some small clipped shrubs which lie about the foot of a suggested cascade in the left hand corner.

The cascade itself is one of the most peculiar and unusual creations in Japanese landscape art. It is made up of three tall, upstanding stones, their flat surfaces suggesting falling water. They stand embedded in the face of a large mound of green shrubbery which, clipped into rolling mounds, represents in abridged fashion the mountainside in which the cascade is located. Its contours repeat those of the distant Eastern Hills which may be seen clearly behind the shrubbery "hills" and were undoubtedly intended to be a part of the garden picture.

A final unifying touch to this garden composition is given by two low, flat rocks which rise above the sand near the edge of the verandah. It is as if the river current, sweeping down from the cascade left them as islands. Their presence at this point balances the weight of the distant cascade and the stones at its foot, creating a very satisfying harmony.

A second garden belonging to the Daitokuji abbot lies just around the corner from the cascade, on the east of the building. It is really a continuation of the cascade garden, being separated from it only by a sunken stone gutter, but these two are always regarded as separate and are thought to have been made at different times and by different people. This is because their purposes and styles are quite different, though both make use of sand,

The garden of Taizō-in temple is a small painting garden of the Muromachi type, which tradition attributes to Kano Motonobu. (Photo by Okamoto Toyo.)

The flat garden of Shukō-in is one of the earlier of the impression-istic Zen gardens. Its stones show Muromachi technique in their form and arrangement, so that it is one of the most esthetically satisfying of these gardens. They are now overgrown with vines and shrubs which add to the atmosphere of quiet serenity. (Photo by Okamoto Toyo.)

The hōjō garden of Daitokuji monastery is a wide expanse of white sand representing a river with an impressionistic cascade at one end. This is formed of tall stones embedded in a mound of green shrubbery which stands for hills. Two small heaps of white sand in the foreground are permanent features of the garden, while two stones near at hand balance the whole composition. (Photo by Okamoto Toyo.)

The abbot's garden of Nanzenji temple lies in front of a building which formerly was one of the Imperial Palace group. The trend which the impressionistic gardens took toward naturalism at the end of the seventeenth century appears strongly in this garden, its huge rocks being arranged naturally, like boulders along a stream. (Photo by Okamoto Toyo.)

stones, and shrubs. But while the cascade garden is a unified landscape picture in itself, with the distant view of the natural hills only incidental, the small garden at the eastern end was constructed to be first and only a frame for this view. Today the houses and telephone poles of the encroaching town have spoiled the outlook, but formerly there was a fine sweeping view to the Eastern Hills rising to the green peak of Mount Hiei on the left, while the wooded banks of the Kamo river wound picturesquely through the center of the valley.

Gardens like this in which the view is equally or more important than the foreground are sometimes called "borrowed scenery" gardens. Daitokuji's is only a narrow strip of land at the end of the porch, bounded by a double hedge, of which the outside half is higher than the inside. In front of the hedge is a row of ornamental stones around which grow small-leaved azaleas, clipped to a low form. This arrangement is extremely simple but very successful in blending the naturalism of the view with the formality of the building.

It has been suggested that the more or less straight-line arrangement of stones in this garden may have been derived from the line of "night-mooring" stones which sometimes stretched across a Heian lake garden. But this explanation seems unnecessarily pedantic; all indications are that the "night-mooring" stones had long since been forgotten. Rather, it appears that the straight line was used here simply because, under the circumstances, it was the most artistic and best suited to the narrow space and to frame the view, thus connecting the building with the natural outlook.

Other temple gardens built about this time made use of the straight-line form also. Such is the garden of Shinju-an temple, which lies but a few feet from the Daitokuji "borrowed scenery" garden but is separated from it by high walls. Shinju-an subtemple itself dates back to Muromachi days, but its garden was made in Tokugawa times. Its stones are arranged in three groups made up of seven, five, and three stones each. These groupings have artistic variation, the first being a close group, the second somewhat drawn out, the third close together again. The formula "seven-five-three" was probably thought to possess geomantic potency, but if so, underlying both the belief and the persistent popularity of the form was probably the fact that these are simple, odd numbers, not to be divided evenly and hence appealing to the Japanese love of occult balance.

As time went on, the age-old impulse to re-create in natural forms asserted itself, affecting even the impressionistic gardens. Toward the end of the 17th century, therefore, we find some of these gardens hardly symbolic at all but merely abridged as to detail. The best example of this, perhaps, is the Nanzenji *hōjō* garden.

From his subtemple of Konchi-in, the Abbot Sūden had exerted himself on behalf of the main Nanzenji monastery and had succeeded in obtaining to serve as its *hōjō* the gift of a fine large hall which had formerly been the dwelling of an imperial consort. The Tokugawas were rebuilding the imperial palace at that time and this building was no longer needed. The garden which now lies in front of this *hōjō*, however, was apparently not made at the time it was moved but considerably later, perhaps almost at the end of the 17th century. It took Nanzenji a long time to collect all the buildings necessary for a complete monastic institution and to finish its plans. The garden seems to have been made during one of the later periods of rebuilding.

Its late construction is evident from its large size and its general atmosphere of showiness, characteristic of the late 17th century, and from the fact that a full seventy per cent of the space is sanded. Moreover, the rocks are no longer grouped into arrangements but placed singly, hence, more naturally. The sand, as usual, represents water, but realism appears on its surface in long, waving raked lines, unmistakably ripples. The opposite side of the space is turned into a mossy bank shaded by trees. The shoreline between this bank and the sand stream is set with stones placed as they might occur naturally along a stream edge.

These stones are few but massive, expressing even in a temple garden the atmosphere of gorgeousness everywhere prevalent at that period. The heaviest one stands at the left corner, a huge boulder forming a promontory into the water. It is on virtually a normal scale, lifting the garden again back to naturalism. Lying off its tip is a small rounded islet made of a single stone. The other stones are strung along the shore, tapering in size to create the usual feeling of directional flow. All these stones lie horizontally in a natural static position very different from the erect stones used in the suggestive artistry of Daitokuji's cascade and the painting gardens. Once more, therefore, we find the old influence of nature creeping into the garden when other less powerful influences have waned.

XVI. *Literal Landscapes*

THE scene now shifts from the old city of Kyoto, which had been the center of national life for over eight hundred years, to the new town growing up in the western end of the country around Edo Castle, the Shogun's headquarters. The site of Edo possessed no such scenic beauty as that of Kyoto, for the castle had been built on the spot in earlier days merely for strategic reasons. It stood at the head of a long bay, with swampy margins forming a rear defense, while before it were wide, barren stretches of ground. The site possessed, however, one beauty—Mount Fuji, visible on bright autumn days, small, clear, pointed, and snow-capped in the distance, as a million pictures were to show it in the next centuries.

In the early years of their power, the Tokugawas put all their efforts into strengthening Edo Castle itself. It became a stronghold even more powerful than Hideyoshi's Osaka Castle and surpassed his mansions in heavy magnificence. The town grew up around the tidewater moats which ran in angular lines around it. The inner ramparts of the castle were vast walls of stone rising from these moats; their corners curved outward and down into the water with the curiously graceful lines peculiar to this type of Japanese masonry. Along the top of the ramparts, pine trees were planted and ingeniously trained to droop out and downward over the walls, as plantlets hang against lesser embankments.

Today, these broad rippling moats, with their archaic inner walls and lacy old pine trees form the medieval hub around which modern Tokyo revolves. Edo Castle became the political center of the country after 1600 when Ieyasu made it his headquarters; it did not become the capital in name, however, for more than two hundred and fifty years. But in 1868, with the beginning of the modern era, it was rechristened Tokyo, or Eastern Capital.

After the Tokugawas settled in Edo Castle, the reedy swamps around it were reclaimed, and the city began to grow. Each lord—or *daimyo*—was required to establish a residence in it and spend half his time in attendance on the Shogun. When he left it to return to his province, his family had to remain in the city as a sort of hostage. Thus the Tokugawas thwarted rebellion. With the wealth of the nation flowing into Edo, it soon became a busy, active town, filled with hundreds of *samurai*—the military retainers of the lords—and with the servants, merchants, craftsmen, and all manner of other folk who supplied their needs.

One of the first and largest of the estates to be laid out in the new city was called Kōraku-en. It was built by Ieyasu's youngest son, Yorifusa, who had been made the Lord of Mito province and given a very large income. He happened to be exactly the same age as the ruling Shogun, his nephew, Iemitsu, son of his eldest brother. The two men were friends and shared many tastes in common, in particular a taste for the tea ceremony.

It was with the idea of providing Yorifusa with a suitable place in which to hold such ceremonials that Iemitsu secured one of the most desirable tracts of land near the new city and turned it over to Yorifusa. The estate, over sixty acres in extent, was partly on rising ground and was covered with trees—two things not frequently found around Edo. Even rarer was the possibility of bringing fresh water from the river for a cascade in the Kyoto manner. The land was obtained in 1629, and work began at once on its development into a garden in the grand style. Enough of it was completed before the end of the first year to make it possible for Yorifusa to hold a tea ceremonial to which the Shogun was invited.

In the beginning, at least, it would appear that Iemitsu took almost as much interest in the new place as did its owner, Yorifusa. The Shogun named commissioners to see that the work was carried out, and secured the services of Tokudaiji Sayoe as garden designer.[1] Little seems to be known about this Sayoe except that he came of one of the noble families of the court, that same family which had originally had an estate on the site of Ryōanji temple. Certain of these families had been known for their special interest or hereditary excellence in various lines and the Tokudaiji family was, in this way, traditionally associated with gardens, although the names of its members do not appear in any of the important garden annals. His part in designing Kōraku-en seems to have been the planning of the lake, islands, hillocks, and the path which wound among them, for Kōraku-en looked back to Kyoto for its inspiration and, like its contemporaries there, Katsura and the Sentō palace, was in the pond and stroll style.

As the years went on, however, the garden became Yorifusa's hobby, and new details were added from time to time during his life. After his death, his son also put in a number of new features so that it became truly an Edo garden in the end. It is the personalities of these two owners, therefore, rather than that of the original planner which dominates the garden. A large part of their work survives today and in much of its original form. The estate is now maintained by the city of Tokyo as a unique park-museum.

In laying out the garden, the natural features of its site were taken into consideration. A low swamp was deepened to hold the lake, and the natural knolls behind were developed into a background. The excavated material was piled into a large island in the water and into embankments on the lower side of the lake, creating small valleys through which the path meanders. Part of the excavated material was also used to build a small, double hillock, its peak some thirty feet above the lake level. Steep-sided, pointed, and free from trees, this peak stands up conspicuously and unmistakably as a miniature artificial mountain.

It was the first of these artificial mounds to be left conspicuously as such and not covered with trees and shrubbery to make it look as natural as possible. Later, such obviously artificial peaks were extensively used in

[1] *Kōraku-en Kiji.*

provincial gardens, most of them, apparently, being known as Mount Fuji. Outstanding among such today is that of Seishu-en garden in the city of Kumamoto. These peaks stand up starkly, even absurdly, in the garden picture, more suggestive of the overgrown topographical map that most Westerners expect to find in Japanese gardens than anything else in the whole realm of the art.

In Kōraku-en, however, this peak is not so conspicuous against its background of trees as are some in other gardens. But that this peak dominated the garden in earlier days seems evident from the words of Hayashi Razan, a famous Confucian scholar, who wrote a description of it in 1640 in which he called the garden the "Miniature Lu-shan."[2]

In one way, however, Kōraku-en departed radically from all its predecessors. It was not built as a setting for the mansion nor could it even be seen from the house. The dwelling stood entirely outside with a small pond garden of its own for an outlook. This little residence-lake-garden now lies just outside the elaborate old Chinese gateway which leads into the main garden. The latter was a landscape park, detached in the fashion then current in China, for a new wave of Chinese influence was once more affecting garden art.

Although the mansion stood outside the garden, the latter contained many small buildings; tea rooms, chapels, and the like. The most important of these was the tea room called Kantoku-tei which stood on a wide space facing the lake, the place where, by old rules, the mansion would have been. This building was destroyed in the earthquake of 1923. A number of the other small buildings have also disappeared, only their foundations now remaining, but others are still standing, among them a chapel of Confucius.

Although designed for scholarly pursuits and the enjoyment of the tea ceremony, Tokugawa ideas of size and grandeur were not to be avoided in an estate of this kind. Everything was carried out in the most spacious

[2] Lu-shan, or Mount Lu, it will be recalled, is the sacred mountain in China, near which Po Chü-i had his hermitage.

and impressive manner possible. Even today, though considerably reduced from its original size, the garden covers nearly seventeen acres. An old map, made before 1710,[3] shows that the lake had one long winding arm which has now been filled in. At present the full size of the lake is apparent at a glance. Its broad stretches are apt to be rather monotonous as one encircles it, but there is charm in the smooth mirror surface of the water, when high clouds float across it and tall green trees lie reflected in its clear depths.

The view across the lake is varied by a large island overgrown with trees. Interest in this direction centers in a huge rock arrangement standing in the water, facing the widest part of the lake. The center of this stone group is an immense upright rock, squarish in form, its place in the composition supported by lesser stones arranged as islets. The large stone was meant, apparently, to serve as a tortoise head, converting the whole island into one of the conventional turtle islands. But the scale of everything is so large the effect of this is lost.

Since there were almost no natural rocks near the city itself, these large stones, as well as all the many others in the garden, were brought to Edo by barge from miles away. Under such circumstances their great number is impressive, especially when it is realized that originally there were many more than at present. Following the Kyoto style, they were used liberally as ornaments and as islets, as steps and as stepping stones to make the cascade and its setting, and to reinforce the hillsides. Portions of the lake shore are also bordered with stones in the Kyoto manner, but long stretches of the waterline are now finished simply with a retaining wall of small logs driven into the ground. Edo gardens which were made later than this one could not be so extravagant in the number of stones used, and so rocks were usually reserved as choice ornaments for a few special places. Wide, stoneless stretches became a characteristic of gardens in this period, even in provincial gardens where there was no lack of fine rocks near at hand.

Kōraku-en's contribution to general landscape art was the perfection

[3] Reproduced in Dr. Tamura's *Kōraku-enshi*.

Pine trees were trained to hang over the great walls which rose above the moats of Edo Castle as ferns grow over the stones of lesser embankments. The castle became the modern Imperial Palace, and these trees still grace the inner moats around the outer edge of which whirls the traffic of present-day Tokyo. (Photo from Board of Tourist Industry.)

Obviously artificial mountains like this "Mount Fuji" of Seishu-in of Kumamoto did not enter Japanese garden art until late in its history, when garden makers had become literal-minded and the art was decadent. Pine trees, trained to shapes of extreme age but at the same time kept dwarfed in size to be proportionate to the landscape, were also a development of this period. (Photo from Board of Tourist Industry.)

Kōraku-en garden in Tokyo holds a number of reproductions of noted beauty spots. One of the most graphic of these suggests the Ōi river near Kyoto. Its "portrait" in the Tokyo garden is formed by a streamlet meandering around a knoll, just as the real river flows out of a canyon, past a pebbled beach, and around large boulders. A low foot bridge represents a famous old bridge over the original river. (Photo from Board of Tourist Industry.)

*Arched bridges of the Chinese type returned to Japanese gardens
in the Edo period when the third wave of Chinese influence was
strong. This one in Kōraku-en is similar in style to the marble
bridges frequently seen around Peking. Made here in a soft grey
stone with small ferns finding a roothold in the crevices, it has
acquired the rustic effect inevitable to Japanese gardens. (Photo
from Board of Tourist Industry.)*

of the circuit or serial style of garden in which a series of interesting details are strung along the path like beads on a cord. The stroll through the garden, which first assumed importance as the "Dewy Path" of the tea masters, was carried to a high peak of development here, with almost every step of the way offering some feature of interest.

Passing through the Chinese gateway into the garden, the path winds first along a little valley below embankments, bowered in green shade. It emerges beside the lake, offering a view of the huge rock across the water at the end of the island and of its mirrored reflections. Crossing the level spot where the tea house, Kantoku-tei, once stood, the path goes over a small footbridge and skirts a stream-bed dotted with waterworn old boulders. It then ascends a small knoll where chapels and tea houses were hidden in sylvan solitudes or placed to command the leafy outlook over tiny valleys. Descending once more, the walk borders the miniature "Lu-shan" and passes by means of stepping stones across an inlet to the very foot of the cascade. The water falls like fine white skeins of silken threads. Curving, the path comes suddenly upon a high-arched Chinese stone bridge, its reflection in the water completing a perfect circle. Climbing a second knoll it leads to more summer houses, and then the descent is made by way of a flight of long, straight stone steps. Past a small rice field, swampy iris gardens, a wisteria trellis, the path comes at last to an open pine grove on the lake shore and so, at last, back to the Chinese gateway.

Varied as are all these views in themselves, they become a hundred times more interesting when their names are known and the associations they call to mind are visualized. Traversing then the path, we wander in imagination over most of the Japanese world of that day, to a dozen famous beauty spots, and even to China.

The greater part of these famous places were near Kyoto. This continuous harking back to the old capital makes clear the sentimental nostalgia for its beauties and amenities which evidently was the fashionable attitude of the day. The new town of Edo was populated by men of action, like Iemitsu and Yorifusa, who, in reality, would have fitted but poorly into the leisurely life of the old capital. But Edo's lack of such natural beauty spots as everywhere existed around Kyoto must often have turned thoughts longingly toward their old remembered charms. Given the chance, therefore, these beauties were reproduced in gardens. Thus, in Kōraku-en the little chapel overhanging its leafy valley is named Kiyomizu after the noted temple which clings to a steep hillside of Kyoto; a bridge across a maple-filled gully becomes the "Bridge of Heaven" belonging to Tōfukuji; a green knoll is Atago-yama, the mountain west of the city, while the boulder-filled stream bed was named the "Ōi River" after the one which flows near Tenryūji temple.

This scene of the Ōi River is, perhaps, the most graphic of these reproduced bits of scenery. It was intended to suggest the charming old resort on the Ōi River where Kyoto people have delighted to greet the spring and autumn since early Heian times. The river winds out of a narrow, green gorge to spread in wide, quiet shallows below the softly wooded slopes of Arashi-yama. A long, wooden bridge across the river is always crowded, even today, at favored seasons with people enjoying the beauties of the scene.

The reproduction of this spot in Kōraku-en garden makes use of a small stream which meanders around a knoll, the water then spreading out broadly to flow in gentle ripples around scattered, waterworn boulders in its bed. A mere footpath of a log bridge, covered with sod, crosses this stream; it is very close to the water so as not to be out of proportion to the picture of the Ōi River and its bridge which is being re-created in the mind. To one familiar with the original—and perhaps in a benevolent frame of mind—the miniature reproduction seems not bad. Probably, when it was made, the likeness was even better than it is now, for at the real Arashi-yama all the boulders have been removed from the river bed to make it suitable for boating. Doubtless, three hundred years ago they were there as we still see them in the garden portrait.

It is interesting to compare this realistic reproduction of landscape with the subjective gardens—the symbolic landscape pictures made in the painting gardens and the impressionistic landscapes made by Zen temples. The comparison brings to us once more how inevitably and unerringly men reveal themselves in their handiwork. The subjective gardens were made by artists and mystics seeking to express their feelings. But Yorifusa and Iemitsu were hardheaded men of affairs who thought in terms of concrete accomplishment. When they built a garden they might put into it bits of natural beauty, but these took a literal form which they could grasp and understand.

After the death of Yorifusa in 1661 his son, Mitsukuni, maintained the garden for a time as his father had left it. This second Lord of Mito was greatly interested in scholarly research and became one of the greatest patrons of learning that Japan has fostered. It was through his interest and support that the *Dai-Nihonshi*, Great History of Japan, a work in many volumes, requiring years to complete, was undertaken and carried through. Mitsukuni has also come down in popular tradition as a champion of the common people. He is said to have wandered over the country in disguise, studying the condition of the common folk and reproving the extravagance of the daimyos. To this day ballads are sung telling of his adventures on these occasions. It was through his interest in scholarship that Kōraku-en acquired many of its Chinese touches.

For, by that time, Japan was experiencing its third wave of Chinese influence. The first, it will be recalled, had come in the earliest period, bringing T'ang civilization and Buddhism; the second, in the Muromachi period, had brought Zen philosophy and Sung art. This third, in the Tokugawa period, although much less strong than the others, took the shape of a great revival of interest in Confucianism or, to be more exact, in the writings of the Chinese philosopher, Chu Hsi, who, in the Sung period, had reinterpreted Confucius. Confucianism fitted well with Tokugawa ideas and was greatly encouraged; its emphasis on proper conduct could be taken to mean conformation to the existing state of society—with the Tokugawas in authority—and its stress on the duties of relationship—a child to its parents, a follower to his lord—were in line with

Tokugawa concepts of an ideal society. Later, these studies into social philosophy led to questions being raised over the legality of the Tokugawa dictatorship and in the end their regime was largely overthrown by the knowledge brought to light. But such a conclusion was not foreseen in the 17th century.

This interest in Chinese studies did not result, however, as it had on previous occasions, in much increased travel and trafficking back and forth with China. In the latter half of the 17th century the Japanese seclusion policy was in full effect, and Japanese subjects were forbidden to leave their own shores on pain of death if they ever attempted to return. The door, however, was not barred to the Chinese and a few scholars, who were refugees mostly from the disturbances attending the Ming downfall, found their way to Japan and were received as honored teachers of the Confucian doctrine. One of these, Chu Shun Shui, was taken under the patronage of Mitsukuni; it is to his influence, it is believed, that are due many of the Chinese details of Kōraku-en.

Probably the name itself was one taken at his suggestion. It is based on a widely known Chinese poem, by Wan Wen-cheng, which sets forth that the superior man—or official—takes his ease only when the country is prosperous and contented. The words *kō raku* mean literally "afterward—ease," (*en* means garden), but the name has been freely and rather well translated as "The Garden of the Philosopher's Pleasure." Mitsukuni apparently accepted this delicate compliment to himself and the condition of the country and let the name stand. But later, through his interest in the common people, he allowed the garden to fall into neglect. A writer[4] who visited the place in 1678, some years after Mitsukuni had become absorbed in his studies, was profoundly impressed by the way he had literally lived up to the implications of the name. Having discovered that the people were *not* prosperous and contented, Mitsukuni, it seemed, could not be at ease on this extravagant estate.

Other Chinese touches in Kōraku-en include the Confucian chapel, a

[4] Yoshikawa Keikan, author of *Kōraku-en okeru no ki.*

Chinese bridge, and the reproduction of Po Chü-i's causeway across West Lake. Just below the "Ōi River" area, the spreading stream is divided for a short distance by a narrow dyke made of cut stones; it is broken at one point by a small stone arch, not more than a couple of feet long, representing the bridge. Not even the most kindly disposed imagination could find in this latter anything to suggest the beautiful, old, willow-fringed finger of land with its arched bridges, which stretches across the lovely lake before Hangchow. It is quite safe to assume that no 17th century Edoite had ever seen the original, and this lifeless form apparently satisfied the imagination. Some such representation of West Lake became, indeed, a popular feature in other gardens of the time.

A half-moon stone bridge found in another part of Kōraku-en is, however, a very good replica of those Ming style bridges so frequently seen around Peking. The Peking bridges are usually made of white marble, but this one is of some grey stone which has begun to crumble a little. Ferns grow out of the cracks between its stones, giving it that inevitable feeling of rusticity characteristic of everything Japanese. Before the reintroduction of bridges in this style, the arched bridge had not been seen in Japanese gardens for centuries. These later arched bridges are mostly too large and too heavy for their setting but they were an effective and popular means of achieving showiness.

Thus, in many ways, Kōraku-en set the fashion and became the model for all the lordly gardens which were built after it, both in the city of Edo and the provinces. Some of the other large city gardens, however, developed original features based on necessity. Since few of the sites of Edo possessed the fresh, flowing water of Kōraku-en, lesser daimyos, looking for a place to build a garden, turned to the only water available, the sea. Along the shores of the bay and the tidal river they laid out extensive estates. The land was flat and marshy, very easy to excavate, so when lakes were dug they could be very large. At high tide these lakes filled with salt water and at low tide their level was maintained by water gates. There are still a number of these old, tidal lake-gardens in Tokyo; one of the best is that of the former Shiba Palace, now another of the city's unusual parks.

A second feature developed in Edo gardens was the use of shrubs clipped into square and rounded forms to suggest and take the place of rocks. Since real stones did not exist in nature near Edo, and their transportation was too expensive for the average lord to indulge in to any extent, the invention of this device was clever. But, on the whole, it was not very successful. The groups of angular shrubs piled together to simulate a mass of rocks did, it is true, give a certain weight and mass to the garden composition; across the lake such an effect might be very good. But closer at hand it was extremely artificial, no one was deceived, and it took away from the natural grace of the plants. Clipped shrubs like this are nowadays seldom seen except in certain old gardens in out of the way places where old customs linger and old plants survive. Such gardens may be seen in some of the monasteries on Mount Kōya and at Yoshino, the cherry mountain.

Clipping and training was practiced on trees in this period as well as shrubs. In the literal landscapes of the miniature Mount Fuji type it was necessary to keep down the size of the trees in order to maintain the scale. Pines, in particular, were often trained to grow to mature shapes though not allowed to reach their full size. These reduced garden trees must not be confused with the miniatures, a few inches high, grown in pots, which are used as house ornaments. The garden trees might be as much as twenty feet high, although they were often less, but they were always large enough to be regarded as actual trees in the landscape picture. Their limbs were painstakingly trained to follow drooping, graceful lines, often rather charming in themselves, but stilted and quite different from the natural habit of the tree. Other trees and shrubs were clipped and trained also, the art, in the end, running away with itself, so that near the close of the period effects that were fantastic and even grotesque were common. Old photographs, like those in Conder's books, show these; but such fantastic forms are not to be found nowadays for they are no longer admired and constant care was needed to maintain them.

LITERAL LANDSCAPES

The Tokugawa period was an era when the upper classes and their retainers traveled extensively, since each daimyo was forced to spend at least half the year near the Shogun and usually chose to spend the other half at his castle seat. Thus large retinues of retainers accompanying the lord were constantly going back and forth across the country. Scenery became, quite naturally, a matter of widespread interest. The fashion set by Kōraku-en in reproducing famous sights found a popular response in other gardens, so that in most of them grandiose names of rivers and mountains were given to streams and hillocks even in those gardens which did not possess anything so elaborate as a miniature Mount Fuji.

This was the period of the "Eight Views," a concept originally derived from China, for the Chinese have always delighted in the numerical listing of things. Copying this, eight famous poetic views had been listed of Lake Biwa, the large body of water near Kyoto, and it became the fashion to find these eight views, or others, in the garden. It was considered a delicate compliment for a garden owner to ask some scholar to select and name the views in his place. One garden, that of Hikone Castle, is popularly known as the Eight View Garden, Hakkei-en, although it has also a scholarly name of Confucian significance.

The general style and atmosphere of Edo gardens was transferred, as would be natural, to gardens made in the provinces. Thus there is a general feeling of flatness and spreading size, of wide lakes and low knolls in these gardens. Even in localities where hills and rocks were available, but few stones were used. Curiously, for all their extensive size, the gardens of this period bring to mind the word "miniature" as the older Kyoto landscapes never do. The latter are not obvious; they call on the imagination of the beholder if he has one, and if he has not, leaves him to take the garden at its face value, a naturalistic area of rocks and trees. But the Edo gardens attempted to be literal at all times; when a mountain was to be created, the gardener piled soil into a cone as high as possible. The Kyoto garden artists used a jagged rock and let it go at that. Moreover, the very size of the Edo

243

lakes was so great that only hills of natural height could balance them properly, and the miniature hills were made more absurd by contrast. Thus, the Edo estate gardens in the city and outside represent the end of an epoch, that final period when great emotional inspiration has departed and only its traditions and old forms remain.

XVII. *Miniature Gardens and Tokugawa Conventions*

URING the middle and final decades of the Tokugawa period a fundamental reorganization took place in Japan. Wealth, which had been formerly concentrated in the hands of the feudal lords and their higher retainers, gradually came into the possession of a rising class of merchants living in Edo and Osaka. The lords and their *samurai* retainers, although compelled to keep up a certain state and an outward appearance of affluence, were often in serious financial difficulties. The shogunal government attempted to improve this situation by a series of edicts and by stringent sumptuary laws directed toward pushing the rising commoners back into their places. But the trouble was too fundamental to be cured by such means. The principal effect of these laws was to prevent middle class wealth from being too conspicuous. Merchants, for instance, who were forbidden to wear silk and bright colors, went about apparently clad in sober cottons; but underneath they often had on the gayest of silken fabrics. It is plain, therefore, why almost no great estates were constructed during the latter part of the Tokugawa period. A large garden is a very obvious expression of wealth, and its existence is not to be concealed by high walls.

Buddhism, which had been the great and vital force in earlier eras, had now come upon hard days also, since Confucianism occupied the attention of scholars and received the patronage of the wealthy and powerful. Buddhism no longer offered a new and exciting field for study as it had in early days when Zen was finding a response in the national temperament. Thus, while a few new Buddhist subtemples and their gardens were built in the 18th and 19th centuries, no large and wealthy Buddhist institutions came into being during that time. But it is in the surviving gardens of the little sub-temples then built that are found the best gardens of this period in the classical style. Among them all, however, not one is of outstanding importance.

This lack of inspiration and vitality in art was largely the result of the seclusion policy. History shows again and again that its great periods result from a fusion of men and ideas from many sources; that cultures, like organisms, tend to run out and become sterile when they fail to receive new blood. This was happening in Japan in the 18th century when the impetus generated by the international contacts of Hideyoshi's day had largely come to an end. A thin infiltration of Western knowledge trickled through the door kept open by the Dutch at Nagasaki but it had little visible effect on the nation as a whole. It was, however, one of the things which contributed to the great reorganization of the mid-19th century.

With the country settled in a deep and lasting peace, there was infinite leisure to complete the most finicky and painstaking of undertakings. At this time were developed those minute and long-drawn-out accomplishments which have seemed to the Western world the special characteristics of the Japanese culture—such things, for instance, as the growing in pots of aged, dwarf trees but a few inches high. Enough has been said in these pages, I hope, to make it clear that such things are not the chief characteristic of this culture. But this aspect of late feudalism remains sufficiently in evidence in Japan to this day to be a noticeable feature of the national scene. The Tokugawa period, after all, came to an end within the memory of many still living.

Traditional Japanese culture suffered stultification in the latter part of the Tokugawa period. It must be emphasized that it was the traditional art forms which were affected, those which had always been patronized by the upper classes. In those years, the only way for such arts to move was round and round. Eventually, they wore for themselves highly polished grooves of formalism and acquired precocity. At the same time, new and vivid arts were arising from the proletariat, notably those of the woodblock print and the theater; but these were scorned by the classicists. Nevertheless, except as the older arts touched the vitality of the common people as did painting, for instance, in the decorative work of Kōrin, they suffered stagnation. Gardening was one of the forms to which this happened; it became stilted and banal and lost most of its meaning and artistry, although it never lost a certain outward charm.

The wealthy mercantile townsman had to live under conditions as externally sober as his cotton robes. His residence, as a rule, was the rear portion of his place of business, and this usually stood in the most crowded part of the town. His garden could occupy only a small bit of land and was, therefore, heavily shaded by the surrounding buildings. Often, indeed the only space available was the tiny area between buildings which served as a lightwell. These small, open spaces were converted into tiny courtyard gardens, the "pocket handkerchief gardens" which foreign travelers, who have seen them in old style shops, have so often exclaimed over. Their words, I fear, have frequently befogged rather than clarified an understanding of Japanese gardens, because, for one thing, much misunderstanding exists as to the actual size of these small areas. While a few may be but five or six feet square, the average has at least the dimensions of an average room and a few are considerably larger. Distinctly they are not, literally, of pocket handkerchief size.

The real pocket handkerchief gardens of Japan and China are the miniature landscapes made of stones and small plants placed in wide, tray-like containers of bronze, stone, or porcelain. Such miniature landscapes seem to have had a very ancient origin, for they probably existed in T'ang China and possibly before. We see them pictured in Japanese paintings of the Heian period, for instance in the *Nenjūgyoji* scroll which shows one placed on a low table just off the verandah of a *shinden* mansion. Sung paintings show them in Chinese courtyards and we know by the *Kita-yama Gyōkō-ki* that Yoshimitsu provided an exhibition of such miniature gardens as part of his entertainment for the imperial visit to the Gold Pavilion.

The oldest tray gardens were made up of rocks of curious and irregular shape, their convolutions able to suggest tiny, jagged mountains and towering cliffs. Such rocks, smoothed on one end for a base, were placed upright in trays usually filled with water so the rocks seemed to form miniature mountainous islands; doubtless, they were often thought of as the Isles of the Immortals. A few plants, perhaps a seedling pine or tufts of coarse moss, grew out of their crevices, suggesting a forest; but sometimes the stone alone was considered sufficiently interesting. These curious rock forms were so greatly prized they were handed down in families as precious heirlooms. One such, said to date back to Heian times, now stands in the garden of Reiun-in of Tōfukuji in Kyoto. This stone, it is said, was given by the Hosokawa family to a faithful retainer who retired here. The rock stands in a stone tray on a pedestal, and this has been placed on a small, rocky foundation. There is nothing else in the garden except moss and some shade trees.

The small interior courtyard gardens of Japanese houses had their forerunners in those little gardens in the open spaces between buildings of the *shinden* mansion which were overlooked by the apartments of the ladies. These earliest ones were developed in the Chinese manner with flowering trees and pots of blooming shrubs and smaller flowers. Later, architecture was modified, but a Japanese house of any size has always remained a group of buildings more or less loosely joined. Down the centuries the bits of ground left between them have been made into gardens of which the *shoin* garden in front of the study and the *hōjō* garden of the temple were special forms. When city folk built a garden, it was, quite naturally, in such an area.

These small, interior gardens were not reproductions of landscape scenes, nor did they possess any subtle secondary dimension. They were simply home decorations, built for the pleasure of simple folk, their only purpose to bring some bit of the outdoors into crowded city areas, to be charming, friendly, fresh, and green. Yet, they were naturalistic gardens for they followed the immemorial theme of reproducing nature. When the culture of the upper classes began to filter down into the proletariat, the age-old idea of re-creating a bit of the natural outdoors in the garden found just as ready acceptance by the common man as it had a thousand years before, when the naturalistic gardens of China were first becoming known to the aristocrats.

Most of these courtyard gardens suggest in some way a corner of the outdoors. Being so closely associated with buildings, they must take on a certain architectural formality or they lack harmony with their setting. The shrubs used in them are usually glossy-leaved evergreens, rather stately in form, like the hollies, or they are hardy palms or bamboos which will grow under the trying conditions of the shaded court. Such plants give that permanent quality required by a garden which is looked at so continually. Deciduous and blossoming plants are mostly ruled out by the difficult growing conditions and also by the fact that they have their unattractive seasons. Occasionally, however, flowers may be introduced into the court with a pot of chrysanthemums placed on a rock. But, for the most part, flowers have no more place in these gardens than in the larger ones. The shrubs in the courtyard gardens are placed with a well-spaced dignity, leaving plenty of bare ground which is covered with moss or coarse sand. Everything is kept carefully trimmed, and dead leaves and cobwebs are removed every day, while the whole space is frequently watered to make it cool, glistening, and mossy.

Within the limits of their formality, these little gardens represent just such a small corner of the outdoors as might be discovered in a space of the same size in some mountain glen. They follow the principle that was worked out on such a magnificent scale in Hideyoshi's castle garden of Kokei—the Tiger Glen. That is, instead of their component parts, the rocks and trees, being reduced in size, all are on a normal scale, creating the illusion that they are part of a larger environment. We feel that beyond the small corner which we can see, there must be more trees, more rocks, more moss.

THE ART OF JAPANESE GARDENS

Hundreds of these little interior gardens may be found in the old business districts of Kyoto where they have survived more numerously than in modernized Tokyo. A good idea of their number and variety may be gained on the night of July 16th, when the festival of Gion shrine is celebrated. As part of this festival, parishioners of the shrine open their houses to display their treasures and receive their friends. These parishioners, who are mostly of the old merchant class, still live and do business on the same site and in much the same manner as their forebears. On ordinary days their places of business present a dull, blank face to the street, but for this festive occasion all signs of business are miraculously whisked away. It is an Oriental equivalent to the preparations for the Fezziwigs' Christmas ball. The sliding partitions which usually divide the spreading building into many rooms are pushed back leaving it a single deep room. The side walls are concealed by painted, folding screens which are the cherished treasures of each family; usually they are kept in the fireproof storehouse but on this night are brought out to convert the dull place of business into a palace.

Crowds of people drift up and down the street, calling on their friends who are keeping open house. In the wide sweep of the houses from front to rear, the only break in the yellow matted floor is the dark square of the little garden. Its shrubs and stone lanterns project curiously above the flat expanse of matting, the only things in the house that cannot be moved.

Just how many of these gardens actually date back to older days would be difficult to determine for they are always, of course, being changed and replanted. But even the ones recently constructed are directly in the main tradition. Such, for instance, are those in the residence-shop of my friend, Mr. S. Nomura, the silk merchant of Shinmonzen street, Kyoto, who has acquaintances all over the world. His house contains two charming and typical little court gardens.

The first is a small, open space separating the shop from the residence portion of the building. Since this garden can be seen from all four sides, particular skill was necessary to make it as attractive as possible. This was done by causing it to appear as a real little courtyard with stepping stones crossing it from one side of the house to the other. Actually, an extension of the house floor forms an unrailed verandah all around it, so no foot need ever be set in the garden itself. But the feeling of its usefulness is there just the same. The ground is covered with clean, white pebbles; in one corner stands a tall stone lantern which is lighted at night. Planted about irregularly are clumps of the dark green bamboo palm, *Rhapis flabelliformis*, which, in the Kyoto climate, will survive the winters outdoors if wrapped in straw. This wrapping is done in a way which adds ornament to the garden. The bamboo framework erected over the plant, with its straw thatching reproduces a tiny cottage like a bird house on tall foundation poles. Snow on the roofs of these little cottages pleasantly marks the differing seasons.

The second garden in the Nomura establishment is more private than the first, opening off the rear of the family living room at the very back of the house. The garden provides light and a mural decoration as well as a feeling of extended space. Yet this second garden is even smaller than the first, a mere pocket of land a few feet wide and surrounded on three sides by the blank walls of buildings. These walls have been covered up for some distance by strips of bark, the feeling created being that the garden may be a glade inclosed by the trunks of large trees. As in the front garden, but one kind of plant is used, such simplicity adding a sense of spaciousness. However, the use of a single plant is not an invariable rule in these small gardens. The plant used in this rear garden is a dwarf bamboo, *Phyllostachys puberola*, which thrives in deep shade. It grows in scattered clumps, forming a thin fringe of green around the wall. The angular grace of the tender leaves creates a delicate tracery against the warm brown of the bark background. A small stone lantern stands in the edge of the bamboo thicket, its form half concealed by the foliage.

The ground is covered with coarse, lightish sand, and in it are placed large stepping stones. There are only four of them, and they end, of course, under the bamboo against the wall. But we have the feeling that perhaps this path disappearing into the thicket may, after all, lead somewhere beyond it.

Water is present in this little garden by suggestion. A drip basin is inclosed by several large stones in one corner, its bottom lined with pebbles. A bamboo pipe stands over the basin, and although no water drips from it, the effect is as if the spring which overflows into this pipe were low for the moment but would begin to run again after the next rain.

Very closely connected with the small interior court gardens are the little passage gardens which were—and are—built between the front gate and the doorway of old-style residences and of inns and restaurants which are modeled after these residences. Very little space can be spared for these entrances, the garden often occupying no more than a vestibule of land. Frequently, when the entrance is at the side or rear of the building, the passage garden is only a narrow alley leading down between high walls. Even such an unpromising area, however, is lined with carefully pruned shrubs and converted into an inviting little path.

In the vestibule gardens, the path curves a bit whenever possible; shrubs and rocks are placed in the curve to screen the door and give a suggestion of privacy and seclusion. The walkway itself is usually of raked gravel or of cobble stones sunk to an even pavement. Stepping stones or flagstones are used only if they are quite broad and fit well together, for the walk is expected to accommodate more than one person at once.

Other rocks are put in the garden purely as ornaments. They are well chosen stones, sunk into the ground besides the walk until they give the effect of projecting there naturally. Small plants such as ferns grow around them, and shrubs may be placed behind. The stones themselves are kept so well watered they are often green with moss. Shrubs used in these passage gardens are the same broadleaved evergreens of formal habit that appear in the court gardens. When guests are expected, the whole entrance is watered down so that it may be fresh and gleaming and convey a sense of preparatory welcome.

Dwarf trees, trained during many years to exhibit all the characteristics of gnarled and picturesque old age, are not a part of true Japanese landscape art but are pot plants used as house decorations. (Photo from Bureau of Tourist Industry.)

Hiroshige, the woodblock artist, gives a graphic glimpse over the
thatched roof tops into one of the small interior courtyard gardens
of the Tokugawa period in this view of an inn; one of his series
entitled "Fifty-three Posting Stations on the Tokaidō Highway."
Life centered intimately about these little gardens, as this picture
reveals. This inn was evidently noted for its ancient Cycas in the
court garden. The art of Hiroshige was representative of the rising
tide of artistic vitality in the common people at this time.

MINIATURE GARDENS

It was in the middle and final periods of the Tokugawa regime that there came into being those curious rules and conventions of which the Western world has heard more, perhaps, than of any other phase of Japanese gardening. Inspiration was dead and even understanding of what the great garden makers had been trying to say had departed. But the traditions lingered, and gardens were still regarded as works of fine art. The best that could be done toward understanding them, however, was to try and discover the rules by which the masterpieces had been made. For that they must have been made by rule seemed inevitable to that generation; the notion of free and inspired creation was quite beyond the average comprehension. We have a very good insight into the psychology of the period in a comment found in the *Kaiki*, published in 1729. The writer was Yamashina Dōan, a priest; he records a conversation he had with a well known tea man, Konoe Iehira, on the Ryōanji and Daisen-in gardens. Says Konoe:

"The garden of Ryōanji is beyond my understanding. I do not know whether it is good or not, but there does seem to be something superior about it." And, referring to Daisen-in, he goes on, "There are some things about it I cannot understand, but certain rules seem to have been followed. I wonder what they were."

Rules were the order of the day, those about garden making being written down in a number of books on landscape practice which appeared in the late 18th and early 19th centuries.[1] Collectively these are known as the "Secret Books and Oral Transmissions," for the facts in them had long been regarded as trade secrets, kept to themselves by members of the gardening fraternity and handed down from father to son. While rules of technique had existed, of course, in Japan ever since they were introduced by Michikō, the Korean in the 7th century, no attempt had been made to codify them. To do such a thing was a turn of thought only characteristic of the later centuries. Undoubtedly, these practices had been passed from one genera-

---

[1] *Saga Ryū Niwa Kohō Hiden-no-sho; Sansui Hiden-sho; Teizō Hisho; Tsukiyama Sansui-den; Tsukiyama Teizō-den; Ishigumi Sono Yayegaki-den.*

tion to the next, but technique changes as the times change and as art develops and a differing spirit fills the artist. Thus, while the Tokugawa gardeners probably believed quite sincerely that they had inherited the secrets of the ages, particularly those of the great Muromachi period, they did not realize how considerable were the variations which time had brought about, changing the whole style and feeling of gardens. Most of the Secret Books actually set down only the elaborations and conventions current at the time they were written and never regarded as hard and fast even then. The hastiest comparison of the rules in the books with the actual Muromachi gardens makes this amply clear.

It is especially clear when the actual gardens are compared to the diagram of a theoretically ideal garden found in the Secret Books. This diagram is virtually the same in all of them, indicating either that they all gave expression to the same body of knowledge or, more likely, that one book was more or less copied from another. The remarkable thing about this diagram is that one may compare it with all the gardens in Japan and never find one that even approximates it in detail—with one notable exception. This is the garden of Tenryūji temple. The almost exact way in which this garden fits the diagram is striking, although it has only recently been noticed, I think, for the first time by Mr. Samuel Newsom. The Tenyrūji garden, it will be recalled, was built by the wealthy father-in-law of the young, retired Emperor Go-Saga in the middle of the Kamakura period and was later reconditioned by Musō Kokushi for his Temple of the Heavenly Dragon. From the close similarity between the garden and the diagram, it is obvious that there must have been some connection between them; either the garden was made after the diagram, or the diagram was inspired by the garden.

Since Mr. Shigemori has traced the story of the garden, proving that it is one of the oldest in the country, and holds as his expert opinion that it has not been basically changed in its six hundred years' existence, we can only conclude that the garden must have inspired the diagram. We get a clue as to how this probably came about and some insight into the formulation of the Secret Books when we learn that the first of these books to be published was probably that of the Saga school of gardeners. The village of Saga, which is still the center of the nursery garden business near Kyoto, gets its name from the old estate of Saga-no-in nearby and this, in turn, is but a mile or so from Tenryūji temple. Doubtless the Saga gardeners were raised on the Tenryūji garden plan, until it became a fundamental part of their consciousness and the inevitable base plan in all their calculations. With its rather small pond and picturesque landscape features such as the rocky Islet of the Immortals, the stone bridge, and the cascade, it fitted quite perfectly into the needs of the time. In putting down an ideal garden plan for the first of the Secret Books, therefore, the author was probably hardly aware to what an extent he was reproducing that of Tenryūji.

It would be unnecessary to do more than mention the Secret Books in passing, for they obviously had little direct influence on the actual making of Japanese gardens, were it not that almost every thing the West has known about such gardens (until the recent works of Harada, Tatsui, and Tamura) has been derived from them. This came about through the books of Josiah Conder, which have been regarded as the standard work on the subject for the past forty years. Dr. Conder was a young Englishman who came to Japan in the late 1870's to teach Western architecture in the Imperial University of Tokyo. He developed a keen interest in Japanese methods of arranging flowers and in Japanese gardens, an interest which led him to make detailed studies on these subjects. His writings, as a result, contained the first authentic information on them to reach Europe and America. In 1893 he published his large work, *Landscape Architecture in Japan* in two volumes with many illustrations. Its quaint and delightful reproductions of pictures from the Secret Books, the curiously poetic names of rocks and trees found in them, and the astounding conventions said to rule the garden craft of Japan, aroused the interest of the whole world. It has led to these gardens' being regarded as almost fabled creations and to the construction of the curious things called Japanese gardens occasionally found in other countries.

Today, we must recognize that Conder's knowledge of his subject was extremely limited in scope, for it was confined almost entirely to the Secret Books and to a study of the daimyo gardens of Tokyo, facts which his bibliography and a statement in the preface makes clear. In quoting this statement I italicize certain phrases for emphasis.

"The present work is an exposition of the *rules and theories* of the art of landscape gardening in Japan from *ancient to modern times,* so far as they can be *gathered from a thorough study of native authorities* added to personal observation of the *best remaining examples.*"

At the time Conder was making his studies the only "native authorities" in existence were the Secret Books and a few articles published in the eighties and nineties. Japanese scholars had not then begun to turn their attention to this subject. When a critical study and appraisal of the gardens was begun later, it became plain that the daimyo gardens of Tokyo, which were nearly all that Conder knew about, were far indeed from being, as he thought them, the "best surviving examples." Conder had heard about some of the Kyoto gardens, but there was no reason for him to think them of much importance; no one did at that time. He was able to give, therefore, but a distorted picture of the subject "from ancient to modern times" although a better digest of the material which came to his knowledge might be difficult to prepare. His book will remain the standard work in a foreign language on Tokugawa conventions, but it must be recognized that these are but a small and comparatively unimportant part of the whole story.

Conder made his greatest mistake in giving a mandatory flavor to the rules and conventions which he set down. Since many of them were connected in some way with necromancy, it is likely that they would be written in the imperative tense, but Japanese gardeners never took this very seriously. Indeed, a statement in one of the Secret Books itself makes this amply clear. Ritoken Akizato, writing in Part II of *Tsukiyama Teizō-den,* says,

"Though these are called rules, they are simply intended to show the general principles to which people should adhere. These laws are not fixed and immutable. A stone by such and such a name need not be placed here and another there unless desired. They are only suggestions to be developed appropriately. People fettered by formal ideas should realize this and strive to improve their art."

Because of Conder's writings, every foreigner who has made even the slightest study of Japanese gardens has heard about the "Guardian Stone," the "Worshipping Stone," the "Host Island," and the like. But particularly the Guardian Stone; no garden, it was emphasized, may be without it. Well-read visitors, on seeing their first Japanese garden, always look for the Guardian Stone and are puzzled at not being able to identify it at once. When they ask to have it pointed out, some stone may occasionally be made to fit into this classification, but usually no such thing exists, even in the gardens made in late Tokugawa times.

Another convention coming from the Secret Books needs clarification here. This is the classification of their styles into *shin*, *gyō*, and *sō*, which may be translated as "elaborately complete," "partly simplified," and "greatly simplified." The words come from the Muromachi period when they were used to describe various ways for writing Chinese characters. Those made with great elaboration, comparable in a way to Old English lettering were called *shin*; those partly simplified as in modern printing were *gyō*; and those abbreviated to a short script were called *sō*. The classification came to be applied to many other things and eventually to gardens. By the definitions in the Secret Books an appalling number of rocks, trees, and mountains was necessary to create a *shin* garden; fewer and fewer for the other two styles. In a certain backward-looking fashion the terms are now used as a standard of analysis; thus, the elaborate rockwork of Katsura garden is called *shin*, the suggested landscape of Daisen-in is *gyō*, and the extreme simplicity of Ryōanji is *sō*. Dr. Tatsui, however, in his *Gardens of Japan* sums up and dismisses the whole thing with these words:

"It was, so to say, only a fashion of the time, without any particular meaning. There exists in every Japanese garden a special expression and a superiority of its own, but never a definite style as *shin*, *gyō* and *sō*."

One thing of value found in the Secret Books is a simplified analysis of the art of stone arrangement. This is so good it is worthy of being studied by anyone wishing to increase his appreciation of this art or of acquiring some skill in it on a larger scale. Akizato, the most competent of those contributing to the Secret Books, must have had a fine, analytical mind, for in his *Ishigumi sono Yayegaki-den* he worked out a system of simplified stone arrangement which may be compared to five-finger exercises on the piano. It must be recognized that it is no more than this, that the great garden masterpieces were not created by any such technique. Yet, as a step toward understanding and appreciating stone art this analysis is excellent.

It is best to follow Akizato's demonstrations by reproducing them with actual stones; for just as one may learn more about painting by handling a brush than from all the treatises, so one may learn most rapidly about stones by actually handling them. This, fortunately, is possible to anyone, since stones are shaped very much alike whether they be boulders or pebbles, and what would require a derrick to do in a garden may be done just as well on a table with cobbles. Recourse to another Japanese table art will be of assistance in doing this, the art of tray-gardening, referred to already in this chapter. Modern miniature gardens are made in a flat tray-like container by using small rocks, plants, moss, and white gravel. Taking the hint from this, a deep tray or shallow box filled with sand should be used and a collection of stones about the size of one's fist. With these one may follow Akizato easily.

For purposes of classification, he assumed that all stones could be divided into five basic forms. These are illustrated here, much as he outlined them in his book. They are called the "tall vertical" or "statue" stone; the "low vertical"; the "flat" stone; the "arching" stone; and the "twisted" or "recumbent ox" stone. It is not necessary to remark that very few stones actually occur in these shapes, while a thousand other forms which might be just as good are to be found on any stone heap. Yet, it may be true that most stones, or at least most interesting stones, could be made to fit into one of these classifications of form. And as basic units in creating a design, these five shapes are very useful. In following Akizato, the first step, there-

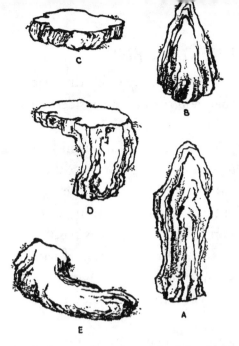

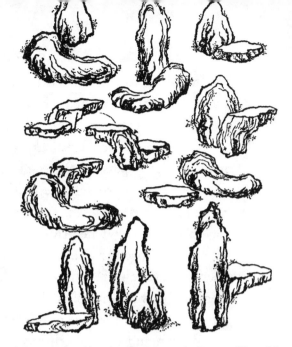

The five basic stone forms as set forth in the Secret Books. A is the tall vertical or statue stone; B the low vertical; C is the flat stone; D the arching stone, and E the recumbent ox stone.

The ten combinations mathematically possible with two of the basic stone forms used together. One grouping is shown in left and right positions.

Eight combinations are possible when combining together three of the basic stone forms. Two different ways of making one grouping are shown.

One way in which all five of the basic stone forms may be combined.

fore, would be to find five rocks in approximately these shapes. By the time they have been discovered, of interesting color and texture, a considerable step forward in awareness of stone forms will have been taken.

Using these five forms, Akizato then proceeds to combine them. It is mathematically possible to get ten combinations by using two at a time. These ten are illustrated here, with one pair showing a right and left arrangement. It is likewise possible to get eight combinations by using three together; however, when three stones or more are combined, it is possible to put them together in more than one way, so that the illustration of trios does not cover all the possibilities. As the number of stones in a group increases, the ways in which they can be arranged increases also; a single grouping of the entire five is illustrated.

By running through these combinations and then improvising new ones, a novice will quickly arrive at a new appreciation of the infinite resources of stone and the possibilities inherent in its arrangement for balanced, harmonic relationships of great beauty. And when, to this is added the realization that such easy and simplified forms are almost never found in actual gardens, some idea of the infinite resources of this art will be comprehended.

To return to the story of the Tokugawa gardens, we must know that formalism did not smother the life of the country without being protested. From the beginning of the Tokugawa regime, there were individuals who, in their life and work, stood out against the oppressive currents of conformity. As any attempt at political protest was quickly suppressed, these endeavors took place mostly in literary and artistic fields. Certain parts of the country, notably those belonging to the great daimyos who had been conquered by Ieyasu and only submitted to force, never forgot that the Tokugawas were usurpers. And as time went on a slow public opinion grew up that the Emperor should be restored to temporal power.

Leaders of this movement expressed their protests against the dominant powers and conformity in guarded ways. One minor method was for them to build their gardens in styles differing from the prevailing modes. Since these leaders were usually scholars and literary men, the style of these little nonconforming gardens came to be known as literary men's style, or *Bunjin-zukuri,* which was no style at all.

One of the first men thus to protest was the poet, scholar, and tea man, Ishikawa Jōzan, who lived in the early part of the Tokugawa period. He expressed his defiance of the formalism then beginning to restrict the tea ceremony by advocating the use of steeped tea instead of the powdered and frothy beverage of the classical ceremonial. The steeped-tea school, known as Sen-cha had, under Jōzan, many followers. In the words of Dr. Harada[2] this school "despised formalities and adored unreserved frankness in men and art. In an easy, quiet leisurely way, its devotees sought to enjoy serene quietness." In this, it is plain, they were attempting to get back to the feeling that had inspired the original tea ceremonial.

Jōzan built himself a small hermitage in the hills back of Kyoto, called Shisen-dō, where he spent the last forty years of his life. It became an object of pilgrimage to other literary men and has remained a shrine to Jōzan's memory ever since. Today, the little house and garden have been converted into a temple. This garden may be considerably changed from the way it looked in Jōzan's lifetime, but it still holds its feeling of informality and nonconformity with any style. The house stands on a hillside, with a view out through distant trees to the valley and the city spreading in it below. No fences or other visible boundaries shut it away from the surrounding hills, into which it blends easily and naturally. The level foreground near the house is a stretch of white sand suggesting that the place is a Zen temple; this sets off in a pleasing way the background of hills, trees, and distant valley.

In one angle of the building is an arrangement of plants not like that seen anywhere else. Large old azaleas grow into evergreen mounds which are kept clipped into smooth, rounded contours suggesting miniature hills and valleys. Above them rises a small stone pagoda two or three feet high, while a tiny arched bridge cut from a single stone spans the rill which flows

[2] *The Gardens of Japan.*

around this area. The whole is a suggested picture of the green hills which surround the hermitage.

Another of the small literary men's gardens surviving in Kyoto is that of Rai Sanyō, a historian who lived near the end of the Tokugawa period. He wrote guardedly against the regime in power, pointing out the true place of the Emperor in the nation's history and leaving the inference clear that his powers had been usurped. Rai Sanyō's house stood on the banks of the Kamo river, looking across the stream to the wooded folds of the Eastern Hills, fading to misty blues on the north. His study he called the House of Purple Mountains and Crystal Streams from the old tag of poetry. Back of the study is a tiny garden which he built; its chief feature today is a wide depression, its walls lined with stones in which grow small ferns and moss. In the bottom of this depression, reached by stone steps, is an old wooden wellhead brimming with water which induces a growth of emerald moss on its ancient wood. Here, it is said, Rai Sanyō purified his body and spirit by pouring many dippers full of the cold water over himself before beginning his daily tasks.

XVIII. *Gardens and Flowers of the Modern Age*

THE great change which has taken place in Japan since the mid-19th century has been, in reality, an explosion of the internal forces which had been accumulating pressure during a long era. For nearly two hundred and fifty years the country had been tightly shut against foreign intercourse, and every effort had been made to keep its internal conditions static and unchanging. This, of course, is an impossibility in human affairs as events in Japan itself have proved. But the effort at suppression had been like a closed steam vent, holding down the energies of the people. By 1854 a limit had been nearly reached, and the era initiated by the Tokugawas had almost run its course. Forces within the nation were moving rapidly and inevitably toward a change, a movement which was simply hastened to its logical conclusion by the coming of the Westerners for the second time.

Chinese had not been barred from Japan, and a few Dutch traders had been allowed to remain at Nagasaki, as already mentioned. Through the small door they kept open had dribbled a surprising amount of knowledge of the West; a few Japanese scholars had taught themselves to read Dutch books, and other books translated from European languages into the Chinese also circulated. Many European inventions, particularly firearms, found their way into the country.

From time to time during the closed period, various European powers had attempted to reopen trade relations with the "hermit nation," but the old fear of conquest by the West had repulsed them all. This fear had become a deep-rooted obsession which, even today, has not fundamentally disappeared from the feeling of the people. It can be imagined, therefore, with what consternation, in 1853, news swept over the nation that a flotilla of foreign, armed "black ships" lay at anchor in a bay near Kamakura, its commander demanding politely but firmly that a treaty of trade be made between Japan and the United States—a nation which had come into existence since the days of Ieyasu. The smoking "black ships" went away for a year, and Japan had a chance to consider its helplessness as a nation which had remained in the feudal period while the world had moved into the modern age. When the ships returned, the treaty was signed, and several ports were opened to foreigners.

These foreigners assumed, at first quite naturally, that the Shogun was king. Only slowly, as they became familiar with the language and history, did they discover the Emperor secluded in his palace in Kyoto. When they did, their insistence on dealing directly with him as the real ruler was one of the main, but indirect, causes of the Tokugawa downfall. The end of the shogunate was simple yet dramatic. Keiki, last of the Tokugawa shoguns, was a man of high mind who realized, apparently better than most of his countrymen, that a new day was at hand. When an opportunity arose, he suddenly, without persuasion, handed back to the Emperor the commission of generalissimo which had been given to his ancestor, Ieyasu, two hundred and fifty years before.

A few of his followers would not accept this sudden end to their prestige and power, and several brief battles were fought with the imperialist forces, but there was no important struggle. Keiki is not a popular hero, for the Japanese seldom admire a failure, even a glorious one. Yet, his act saved the nation what might have been a period of strife with nearly fatal consequences had it come at this critical time.

The very year of this resignation, 1868, the young Emperor Meiji moved to the city of Edo which then was re-named Tokyo, or Eastern Capital. The old city he left behind had been known for over a thousand years as simply The Capital—Miyako. In the new period it became Kyoto, or Western Capital, for it was, and still is, one of the two head cities of the nation. To it, the Emperors return on the most important occasion of their lives, the enthronement ceremonies.

There began then that remarkable period of change with the adoption of foreign ideas which finds its best parallel in Japan's own history thirteen hundred years before when the island nation was first coming in contact with Chinese civilization. In both periods, the Japanese desired, at first, only material things from abroad, swords and mirrors from the T'ang; guns and ships from the Victorian. At both times, however, it was found impossible to take these and escape entirely the foreign ideology which had produced them. Yet, though Chinese philosophy and art have deeply affected the Japanese, they never became Chinese in spirit; likewise there is no reason to assume they will ever become one of the Western nations in personality even if, in time, they should be as deeply affected by Western philosophy and art as they were by the Chinese. Any such time seems to be far away, however, for, in spite of an outward appearance of Westernization in the cities, Western philosophy, that is, the way in which Westerners think, has made almost no impression on the fundamental mind and feeling of the people, nor has there yet been shown any noticeable ability to create outstanding art in Western forms.

With the acceptance of the changed order, prejudice against Westerners disappeared, and there began a period of enthusiastic and wholesale adoption of Western materialism, with houses and gardens among other objects of curiosity. Most of these things were copied without understanding of their use and in ignorance of what lay behind them. "Foreign style" houses and gardens, as Dr. Tamura notes,[1] were frequently "wedged, as it were, into spacious Japanese gardens." The two styles were kept so distinct there seems hardly to have been a realization that Western parks and parterres were really forms of the same craft as the native landscape garden.

A number of these early houses were designed by Dr. Conder himself during the years when he was gathering the materials for his book on the old daimyo gardens. Among other places, he designed one for Baron Mi-

[1] *Art of the Landscape Garden in Japan.*

tsui, head of the great concern which bears his name, and for Baron Iwasaki, head of the vast Mitsubishi interests. For the latter he made a fine Tudor castle and another house around which were built extensive parterres and a rose garden which are still maintained.

The Tudor castle was built in one of the old daimyo gardens in Tokyo which was centered by an extensive tidal lake. This was improved in the Japanese manner by bringing in many large stones from all over the country, made possible through the extensive transportation facilities of the owners. The stones were placed around the lake in the old lavish Kyoto style and, as in earlier times, constituted a fine display of wealth. This castle and much of the estate were totally destroyed by the great earthquake of 1923 but part of the lake with its rockwork was left. This part was afterward given to the city of Tokyo and has now been converted into a public park, called Kiyosumi Kōen. The rockwork is a fine example of the survival of rock artistry in the modern age. But it is here a copied art, based on the study of old forms and not on any inspiration from a new period.

By the nineties, enough understanding of Western gardens had been achieved for certain gardeners to conceive of fusing their details with the native art. The best surviving example of this attempt, probably, is in the imperial garden of Shinjuku in Tokyo, which also was originally a daimyo garden. In making this over, the broad lawns of the European gardens and their wide, tree-shaded paths were superimposed on the old landscape outlines, while stone groups beside the path and occasional clipped shrubs and trees were details from the Japanese side. The effect is not displeasing, for it was done with artistic understanding.

Shinjuku is best known as the garden in which the Emperor holds annually those two large parties, the cherry blossom and the chrysanthemum, which were originally planned as entertainment for foreigners but are now attended largely by Japanese. The cherry blossom party, like the long succession of such affairs which has preceded it, is held on a glorious spring day when the petally pink masses of the flowering trees make incredible canopies against the blue sky. The chrysanthemum party is held on a mellow afternoon in November, when the sun shines warm and golden and the gardens hold the last late glow of beauty.

The guests, who number thousands, wander about the paths of the immense estate which is so large that it never appears crowded. They gather at last on a vast lawn and form two long lines with an avenue between them. Followed by his suite and her ladies, the Emperor and Empress walk slowly up the length of this lawn to where refreshment tables have been set out. When the imperial hosts are seated, the other guests also take their places at tables set on the broad lawn.

The chrysanthemums, which are the ostensible excuse for this party, are displayed in small bamboo shelters which have been built at intervals along the path. These are quaint little structures with oilpaper roofs and open fronts. Chrysanthemums are grown almost entirely in pots in Japan; only in a cottage dooryard or sometimes along the dykes of a rice field will the plants be found sprawling on the ground. The imperial gardeners, like thousands of amateurs and professionals all over the country, take great pride in the beauty and variety of their chrysanthemum blossoms. But to them sheer size is not so important as perfection of leaf and petal. Some plants are grown as brilliant cascades of a thousand tiny blossoms; others are trained into conical shrubs, like miniature Christmas trees, each little flower on the end of a branchlet glowing like a candle. Others again are grown for single large blossoms, three plants in a pot, each of the three perfect in every way.

Another imperial garden in Tokyo, built in the Meiji period, carried over interestingly into the modern age the old tradition that garden planning was worthy of the attention of the most exalted personages. At the same time it reveals the one way in which the West seems to have influenced, fundamentally, modern Japanese gardens; that is, by introducing to them something of the West's own interest in plants and flowers for their own sake. The way in which the Japanese had limited their interest in flowers to a few like the "plum" and chrysanthemum which had received conventional Chinese endorsement and to the native cherry with its ancient spring associations is one of the striking features of their garden history. But from the Meiji period onward, an interest in plants as an important part of the garden becomes very evident.

This imperial garden, in which the trend is plain, is now called the Inner Garden of Meiji Shrine. It was planned originally, it is said, partly by the Emperor Meiji himself for the pleasure of his Empress. The unique feature is that, while it makes use of landscape for a background, its purpose is the glorification and display of a single flower, the water iris. In late June, when this plant blooms, the Meiji iris garden becomes a gorgeous and breath-taking river of flowers, flowing in a rolling purple flood down a small green valley.

There must have been a natural little valley once where the garden is now, with a small streamlet wandering through it. To prepare it for the iris flowers, its sloping banks were planted with Japanese maples whose delicate lacy foliage, bright green in June, makes a perfect frame for the flowers. Using the technique of rice field terracing, the stream was broadened and flattened by creating a series of shallow water terraces, each supported by a dyke of small poles driven into the ground endways. Each terrace is about thirty feet across, as long as the contour permits, and a few inches lower than the one preceding it. The succession of these terraces forms a broad, shallow flow of water which meanders in graceful curves down the valley, never straightening, nor yet turning for any but an apparently natural reason. Halfway up its length the valley bends abruptly, so that its full length cannot be seen except from a rustic summer houses which has been built on a height beside the curve.

The banks of the stream are sodded, and a path follows along the water's edge, crossing the stream on a rustic bridge. It is made in the ancient zigzag fashion called the "Eight Plank" style, in which the ends of the boards are laid side by side on the support in midstream, not end to end in a straight line. The iris clumps grow close enough to appear a solid mass of color at a short distance, but the shadowed surface of the water

Ishikawa Jozen, a protestant against conformity in the early Toku-
gawa period, built this small garden around his house in the hills
back of Kyoto. It follows no rules of form—a characteristic of these
"literary men's gardens." Huge old azaleas clipped into rounded
contours and crowned by a small pagoda simulate mountains.
(Photo from Board of Tourist Industry.)

Water lilies in the garden of Heian shrine show the new interest in growing flowers, now widespread in Japan. It is, perhaps, the one way in which the West has fundamentally influenced Japanese gardening. The rounded stepping stones in the background are the foundation stones which once supported one of Kyoto's old bridges. (Photo from Kyoto Municipal Office.)

between them is revealed closer at hand. Every available color of this flower grows here in happy confusion, from palest lavender and violet through deep purple with linings of pure gold. There is even a pink and a maroon, while an occasional pure white plant is like a fleck of foam on the flood. Crossing the bridge, we stand knee deep in the gorgeous stream of color.

Indicating likewise the new interest in flowers is the waterlily pond which is part of this garden. The iris stream flows into a small lake given over to the growing of Nympheas. These Western flowers are cultivated here with skill and artistry. Each plant is given the large area of lake surface it needs for perfect development, so that the broad pond is covered by the immense polka dots of pads and flowers made up of separate plants, each one a different color.

Private gardens were made in the new era, as they always have been, by the men who had risen to wealth and power through control of the forces dominant in that era. In the modern age such men are the merchant princes who have become wealthy through finance, foreign trade, and manufacturing. As in the rising days of Ko no Moronao, who, it will be recalled, brought cherries from Yoshino and rocks from distant provinces for his garden in Kyoto, there is today a disposition for such newly successful men to bring into their garden items of sentimental or historic interest. An old stone lantern or water basin, a round rock which has served as the foundation under a temple pillar, a tea room that belonged to some master, or even larger buildings of historic association may become the chief treasure of a garden. In recent years it has been a popular fad to move ancient farmhouses from their native fields to Tokyo estates. The garden around these architectural treasures is designed to show them off in the best and most appropriate way and is of secondary interest to the building itself.

Perhaps the most notable of such collections is the group of buildings which has been moved to the spacious Yokohama estate of Mr. Hara. His oldest building is a pagoda dating back to Nara and the 8th century. Another treasure is a chapel built at Kamakura in its heyday. There is a pavilion which was part of Hideyoshi's Jūraku-tei, the Palace of Pleasure, and another from his Fushimi Castle. Still another pavilion came from Nijō Castle where it was constructed for the third Tokugawa shogun. All these have been placed in appropriate situations and given surroundings in keeping with their style and feeling.

But for the truest development in Japanese gardening in the modern period we must return to Kyoto, the old city which throughout the years has gone its immemorial way, a way whose pattern was laid down by the Heian court on a T'ang model, which was strengthened by the warrior's vigor, given depth and meaning by Zen thought, and finally, was perpetuated by the tea ritual. Kyoto still clings to old forms and ceremonies, prefers restraint, subdued colors, and subtly balanced occult forms to more showy ways, loves nature and its ancient beauties, and is still largely unswayed by modern fancies and foreign fads.

When the Emperor Meiji left the town where his forebears had lived for over a thousand years, it seemed destined to become a city of the past, old and proud and in time—shabby. But once again those canons of taste formulated by the aristocrats exerted their subtle influence on the rising *nouveau riche*. "Kyoto taste" which is now the taste of the whole city is today the final term of excellence anywhere in Japan, a synonym for all that is best in design and craftsmanship. Things made in Kyoto's studios and handicraft shops, its kilns and looms, the textile designs worked out by Kyoto artists and applied in the city's dye vats are eagerly bought by the whole country. The town has thus achieved a new and solid prosperity on the foundation of its old ways and has grown today to greater size than ever before. Every traveler, native and foreign, visits it if possible, going away influenced by its ancient beauties and leaving behind substantial sums.

As 1894 approached, when the city would be eleven centuries old, it was felt that something appropriate should be done to mark the date. The Emperor Kwammu, that active and able ruler who had caused the capital to be removed from priest-ridden Nara, had never been properly honored by the town he founded. It was decided, therefore, to build a great shrine to his spirit, a shrine constructed in the form of the Hall of State which had been the finest building in his capital, Heian-kyō. The annual festival of this shrine was inaugurated that year as a splendid pageant through the streets so that people lining them might see again, for one brief afternoon, some of the stately processions that have taken place in them down the centuries. Annually on this day, Heian courtiers ride as on that New Year's morning in 794 when they first paid their respects to Kwammu in the new palace; Nobunaga and Hideyoshi with their glittering trains pass through the streets; a Tokugawa daimyo is carried in his palanquin, enroute to Edo and the Shogun, and the imperial forces which aided the great restoration of Meiji march once more.

Kwammu's great Hall of State whither they are bound is called Heian Shrine, and is, as nearly as possible, a reproduction of the enthronement hall in the City of Peace and Tranquillity. It is a lofty structure on a stone foundation, its red-lacquered pillars upholding complicated Chinese eaves and blue-green rooftiles crowned by formalized golden dolphins. On either side of the main hall stretch arcaded wings ending in ornate little end-pavilions. In front, a stately two-storied gateway incloses the broad, graveled forecourt.

The original Heian palace had had no place beside it for a large garden, it will be recalled, but Shinsen-en lay just outside the inclosure. Heian Shrine, however, has a garden around three sides of it. Unfortunately, no attempt has been made in this garden, as with the building, to reproduce a Heian landscape. The only thing this modern one has in common with those of Heian is a large lake, large enough to float dragon-headed boats were it ever desired. This is not done, but, instead, the garden is given over to strolling with the new interest in flowers strongly predominant.

The ground around the lake is landscaped in naturalistic Japanese fashion, with winding paths, shrubbery, trees, and occasional rocks. Stones are used because they are part of the traditional formula but no longer do they carry significance nor even much interest; they are now only a decorative detail. A touch of the historical sentiment so popular in modern gardens

271

is introduced by a row of rounded stepping stones crossing a corner of the lake. They are old, circular, foundation rocks which once supported one of the city's main bridges, now rebuilt with steel and concrete. Another part of the lake is crossed by a long, roofed bridge which holds a Chinese cupola in the center. Seen across the water, this structure is suggestive of the way the end-pavilions must have looked overhanging the waters of Heian lakes.

But it is the flowers in this garden which the crowds come oftenest to see, for at almost every season the traditional blossoms may be found. Earliest of these are the snow-flowers, for snow is regarded as part of the cycle of blossoms. It clings like white petals bursting from the bare stems, while fluffy masses on broadleaved evergreens seem to be sudden masses of white bloom.

Sometimes the waxen blossoms of the Japanese apricot appear through a late snow, for this tree is the earliest to bloom and is called, in consequence, the "elder brother" of the other flowers. Its hardihood, joined to its delicate refinement, early caused the Chinese to regard it as the symbol of the superior man, and its fragrance to be likened to the influence of such a man, touching all who come near. It is the only flower scent the Japanese ever mention or seem to be aware of.

Not long after the snow-flowers have melted, the trees look as if they had again caught a fall of snow, but this time of palest pink. The cherries of Heian garden are today the finest in the old capital. Masses of bloom on the Yoshino variety of tree crowd the branches like an old-fashioned feather boa; these tall trees grow around the lake and are hung at night with soft pink silk lanterns and flooded by hidden lights which throw them into cameo relief against the dark sky. They are doubled in the polished black onyx of the water, a vision of enchanting loveliness.

Near the main hall of Heian Shrine stands a row of the weeping variety of cherry tree, their small, bright flowers strung tightly on pendant branches which seem to flow downward like a fountain of delicate color. Sometimes the branches seem to have caught a storm of pink confetti which flutters gently, bit by bit, to the pool of fallen petals on the ground.

The fresh new foliage of spring is regarded also as part of the flower cycle in Japan, and people go out to see and enjoy it as they do blossoms. At a distance, the buds of the pendant willows are like a green haze and, nearer, are like freshly carved jade. The tiny hand-like leaves of the Japanese maple are like fine and delicate lace and often as brightly colored in spring as they will be again eight months later. But the spring colors are warmer and glow more softly; they are pinky apricot and terra-cotta instead of the sharp gold and scarlet of autumn.

Camellias are a spring and winter flower too but are never grown in a pleasure garden, unless it be that of a modern skeptic who plants improved varieties as an up-to-date hobby. The older kinds of camellia flowers usually fall from the branch while still fresh and perfect. This fact was long ago seized on by Buddhist priests to illustrate their preachments that in the midst of life we are in death. The Japanese, who love life and gaiety, do not want to be reminded of death, hence the camellia is found only in temple gardens. But in them the trees often grow very old and large, sometimes forty feet high or more, or, as spreading old shrubs, cover an area many feet wide.

Azaleas of all varieties are planted in Heian Shrine garden, as everywhere else. They are grown, however, not for their flowers, but for their adaptable green forms and ability to withstand clipping and adverse conditions. For most of the year they contribute demurely to the atmosphere of green peace and quiet which pervades the Japanese garden, until, suddenly, in May, they break their green bonds and become rowdy floral ragamuffins, rioting in flaming scarlet, magenta, and crimson. The Japanese people, who themselves like to throw off restraint once a year and go on a little binge under the cherry trees, hide their smiles behind their sleeves and enjoy secretly the brief period of gaudiness, forgetting for the moment their traditional disapproval of all but quiet greys, greens, and browns in the garden.

The proletariat openly enjoys the sensation of color intoxication which the azaleas bring and goes annually to the hillside around the municipal waterworks in Kyoto, which has been solidly planted with these shrubs. Here, with babies and baskets, they joyously scatter orange peel and waste paper, forgetting the necessity of being politely decorous and conventional. In the garden of Heian Shrine, the azaleas seem to have been planted in both roles, that of green background and for bright color; certainly there are more of them and better massed for color effects across the lake than mere background would require.

Visitors to Kyoto are told of a garden which existed some years ago in which the blooming azaleas were used to enhance a classical setting; but only the white ones were planted. These grew along a dry cascade and stream bed, so that, when the flowers opened, their bloom seemed to be foaming and tumbling masses of water among the cascade rocks.

In May also comes the wisteria blossom, a native flower which can be found growing in wild purple masses on the walls of quiet green canyons. From this flower—the *fuji*—came the name of the Fujiwara family synonymous for centuries with aristocratic nobility. In Nara the shrine to the deity-ancestor of this family stands in an ancient park where wisteria vines lift huge, gnarled trunks into old pines and tall cryptomerias to hang out banners of purple bloom in spring.

The wisteria is usually cultivated on trellises built out along the edge of ponds; sometimes it forms a roof over small platforms overhanging the pond, where tea is served. The length of the wisteria streamers from such a roof may be as much as six feet but usually it is nearer three. The flowers hang overhead in pendant lines which sway in unison with the breeze. Seated on such a platform we seem to be floating under a floral canopy, with big black bumblebees roaring softly in it while the swaying flowers swing back and forth, back and forth, in a rhythmic, intoxicated trance.

Midsummer finds the garden luxuriantly green and pulsing under the heavy tropical beat of the sun. The cicadas, true voice of summer in the Far East, shrill in earsplitting complaint as the sun mounts. On these torrid days the flower lover rises early in the fresh dawn to see what the night has brought to his morning-glories. Usually this flower is grown in pots for forcing but it may be found making a tangle of glorious color in cottage doorways. Raising morning-glories in pots is a hobby of rich and poor alike, for even the poor can afford a few seeds and room for pots. Pot-grown plants may be made to produce a few magnificent blossoms eight or ten inches across; or a plant may be induced to shoot its entire force in a single morning with a floral broadside of bloom that completely covers it. Such a display, lasting a few hours, is considered well worth the weeks of effort needed to produce it. Shows of such flowers are held in cool summer dawns, the proud growers displaying their great velvety blossoms in rows set on red-covered shelves. The flowers may be in plain colors or rimmed and throated or shot with white; there are tones of deep royal purple, light, azure blue, rich sapphire, palest pink, snowy white, gorgeous crimson, and even the brownish color of tea.

In midsummer, too, the lotus blooms, but these flowers, like the camellia, are seen only in temple gardens because of their association with death. Artists and laymen alike, however, love the great blue-green waxen leaf-bowls with the inevitable crystal ball of dew rolling around in them. Esthetes used to go out early to the lotus ponds to hear, as they thought, the slight pop made by the opening lotus buds until, a few years ago, a group of scientists took gleefully to the role of iconoclast and maintained that the pops could only be made by frogs leaping into the water since the lotus buds are not sealed. On this, the country seethed with dissension, and to settle the point a large national newspaper arranged a nation-wide radio hookup, setting a microphone in a lotus pond with mechanism to magnify sounds five hundred times. The whole nation listened in breathlessly on the appointed morning but heard only the papery rustle of the stiff petals unfolding in the dawn.

September is a month of spent quiet after the heat, when the insect chorus begins to wane. Viewing the moon, not blossoms, is the traditional pastime of this season, with only small, late-summer wild flowers on the floral calendar. These, first grouped and named in China, are called the

275

"Seven Grasses of Autumn," but six of them are little wild flowers and only the seventh is a grass. It is a species of pampas grass which lifts its sparse plume in every swampy spot. Seen against the full harvest moon, this plume becomes the recognized symbol of early autumn in poems and pictures.

In November comes the burst of flaming foliage, maple and sumach, while every little town or big city park holds its chrysanthemum show. This is the second most favored season for outings, a last moment of mellow relaxation outdoors before fevered preparations for the New Year must begin.

For the New Year season, the "Three Friends of Winter," pine, bamboo, and "plum," are the favored decorations. They are usually arranged in tubs on either side of the outer gateway. Huge segments of giant green bamboo, sliced obliquely to form a decorative white oval or rim are used as a support for branches of the pine and plum. While the latter is not in bloom on the modern date for the New Year, its message of hardihood and long life is carried in old lichens on its bare branches.

The sentimental regard which all the nation feels for Kyoto joined to its ancient beauties of "purple mountains and crystal streams" have made it the most favored spot in the nation for villas of the successful. At the foot of the Eastern Hills, where for a millenium were built temples and hermitages, are today many fine estates, show places of the wealthy. Most of the owners' names are new, but at least one, that of Marquis Hosokawa, is familiar to history. The green hills behind these estates are as charming today as ever they were down the centuries, and now their views are often pricked by the roof of an old pagoda or temple rising above the trees.

Many of the modern estates were started about the turn of this century when real-estate developments in this district followed the building of a tunnel through the hills which brought unlimited water from Lake Biwa. About the same time, Nanzenji monastery sold off part of the land which had once been occupied by its subtemples. The finest of the estates now

cluster near this historic institution. On this ancient site is occasionally preserved some relic of a former temple which gives flavor to the estate. The
plentiful supply of water from Lake Biwa, rushing through the cascades and
streams of these estates, is one of their special features. Noticeable too, is
their generous size of two or three acres, as compared to the gardens built
in Kyoto for long before. During the Tokugawa period these older gardens
had been limited in size by the resources of the privileged few who had
been allowed to construct gardens. When business men could put their
money into estates, size immediately became a feature once more as it had
been, for instance, in the days of Prince Katsura.

The best of these Kyoto estates seem to have been made by one man,
Ogawa Jihei, a garden craftsman and designer who is the most recent outstanding figure in that long line which stems from Michikō, the Ugly
Artisan of Korea. For seven generations the Ogawa family has had its garden building establishment on the site where it stands today, and for
something over two hundred years its members have been making gardens
in Kyoto for court nobles, daimyos, temples, and shrines. The Ogawa establishment occupies a generous bit of land with the family residence in one corner; the place is shaded by tall trees and piled with rocks and stone lanterns
which gather moss until such time as a purchaser shall be found. Plants are
not raised here, however, but left to the nurserymen who have their estab-
lishments on the edge of the city.

Ogawa Jihei was born about the time of the great change of Meiji, and
growing up in its quickening decades, was filled with its new spirit. He
threw off the conventions and rules which had hampered his craft for so
long, but being a true son of Kyoto, he never became deeply interested in
the new "foreign style" gardens, never copied them, and was never directly
influenced by them.

Nevertheless, changing times brought changing architectural styles
and changed modes of living. Men of the modern age, while they might
not wish a "foreign style" garden, desired their estate to provide the setting for modern life, influenced as it is by various contacts with the West.

Thus, the new estates usually have somewhere about them a wide lawn, well hidden, not simply to copy the Western lawn, but as a place where large garden parties may be held, like those given for the Garden Club of America in 1935. There are entrance forecourts for two and three-car garages and often service gardens for growing vegetables and flowers for cutting. These modern features, however, are all hidden from the main garden which remains a landscape picture in the traditional fashion, using woods and water, hills and streams as its pattern.

In laying out these estates, Ogawa functioned not only as the contractor but frequently as the designer also. Yet, in a few gardens the old tradition of the gentleman planner lingers, and they are said to be the work of their owners. The individuality of these owners is evident, even, sometimes, to lapses in taste, though these lapses are less frequent in Kyoto with its old permeating "tea taste" than elsewhere. Some owners have created grand and impressive show places, typical expressions of the *nouveau riche*; others reveal a finer and more intimate understanding of garden artistry. As a rule, the men who have planned their own gardens are those who have cultivated an interest in the tea ceremony and been influenced by its canons of quiet simplicity.

Yet, however much the owners may have planned, overlying their personality is Ogawa's hand, for he did the actual work, and his technique could not but be everywhere evident. Often he planned the entire garden from bare hillside to finished landscape. After these places were finished, they were generally left under his supervision, so that some of them show the accumulated effects of his attention for over thirty years.

An Ogawa garden may almost always be identified by its plants; their freshness and variety and the way in which they become an important factor in the garden's interest is outstanding.

"In the old days only certain plants were allowed in the garden and these in certain places," he told me when I interviewed him in 1931, about a year before his sudden death. My interpreter and I sat in the small office where he received his clients, a rustic Japanese cottage in the grounds of his establishment, surrounded by the mossy stones and lanterns, and shaded by old trees.

"But," he continued, "I decided there was no reason why any plant should not be used, even a foreign one, provided it was harmonious with its surroundings."

Holding this opinion, he abandoned also the Tokugawa style of clipping trees and shrubs into grotesque "arty" shapes, as seen in Conder's photographs. Nor do his gardens hold those highly trained little pine trees, forced into stilted forms of agedness, which were so popular with an older generation. He did not, however, abandon the vigorous pruning and thinning by which a Japanese garden is kept always within the bounds of its original proportions. Unless neglected, these gardens are never allowed to become oversized and stuffy with growth. But pruning nowadays is directed toward obtaining the most graceful natural form of the plant—not necessarily, or even usually, a symmetrical form—or toward keeping the plants in their relative place in the composition. The clarity of line which results from such vigorous cutting back is one of the most conspicuous attributes of a Japanese as compared to a Western naturalistic garden. The latter often seems frowzy in contrast; the Japanese garden, like a well-groomed woman, is never hairy or unkempt, no matter how informal and natural it may be.

While staying close to the traditional landscape pattern, yet freed from constricting Tokugawa conventions, the best of modern Kyoto garden art has turned back in the old, and apparently inevitable, way to naturalism. Gone are the spiritual qualities of the esoteric gardens, and vanished is the soaring artistry of the painting gardens. But there remain today, apparently as strong as ever, the ancient love of nature and its beauties and the desire to have them close.

This feeling and the forms which are its expression survived the Tokugawa centuries because of the tea ceremonial. Or perhaps it would be more accurate to say that *cha no yu* survived because of this feeling. Whichever the case, the tea ritual still clings outwardly to its tenets of rustic simplicity, although, inwardly, real simplicity and naturalness have too often become a travesty of themselves. During the long centuries of peace, when the gentlemanly warriors turned for something to do to the tea ceremony, the precepts of Rikyū were minutely studied, codified, and set into hard and fast rules. Following these rules became an end in itself, not the means to an end. The tea room and the tea garden became something so complicated and expensive that only the well-to-do could hope to possess them. Beautiful wood, exquisite joinery, fine artcraft in woven reed ceilings, along with many other items which an outsider might never notice, are required of the modern tea room. It is said that a small tea cottage will often cost almost as much as the mansion on an estate.

In the modern period the tea ritual has come to have a tremendous renaissance of popularity until today it is more widely practiced than ever before. No girl but must take lessons if she is to be considered at all a finished young lady, and every adult of either sex with any pretentions to the old culture must be able to take part in a ceremonial when required. Men who study it usually do so very seriously and often professionally as do men who study music in the West. Yet, of all the thousands who perform the rite today few, one ventures to believe, have much idea of its original meaning and deeper significance. Study of it covers the ritual movements and some knowledge of its canons of taste. Those few persons who are capable of discovering more in it are probably the same few who have always found its deeper meaning. Yet, it has been this very study by the many, no doubt, which in the end has widely perpetuated its tastes and given it the influence which it exercises today. "Tea taste" is still the standard by which Kyoto measures the good and bad in design and craftsmanship.

Tea influence may be seen in many phases of modern life. In domestic architecture, for instance, interior woodwork remains in its natural state, unpainted, as in the tea room; plastered walls are left the color of the natural sand; paper on the dividing screens is either plain white or shadowed with diaphanous designs in silver or powdery gold. In ceramics the most artistic pottery is held to be that crudely fashioned in cottage style and finished in rough glazes and dull colors. Practice of the tea ritual has probably increased ceremoniousness of manner and lent a slow, careful grace to women's hands. Mentally, the way in which the ritual has been minutely prescribed and followed, leaving almost nothing to individual interpretation, has probably contributed much to that tendency toward regimentation, so noticeable to one remaining long in Japan.

The influence of the ceremony on gardening has been as pronounced as on architecture. Little home gardens all partake in some degree of the tea garden's qualities, possessing the same feeling of seclusion and privacy, the same atmosphere of quiet greenness. Stepping stones appear often and the water basin and stone lantern are frequently present.

House lots in Japan are usually quite small, so that even residences of the better class have, as a rule, but little ground around them. The houses are placed so that the ground left for the garden is all on the side overlooked by the living room, usually the south side, which is sunny in winter and coolest in summer. In good weather the sliding doors are pushed widely back, and it is but a step down from the house into the garden. Around such property there is usually a wall several feet high and often topped by a hedge. The section opposite the living room is usually developed by piling soil from the house excavation against it to make a small slope, a rudimentary hillock which forms the basis for naturalistic planting. Trees and shrubs grown in this slope more or less conceal its small size and increase privacy. They are never allowed to become so large as to crowd each other or shade the house unduly. In the narrow, sunny space left between the slope and the house, a winding path of stepping stones is usually placed and, for accent, in a curve of the slope, a stone water basin and lantern. Appropriate planting frames these objects, moss and ferns around the basin, a lacy shrub partly veiling the stone lantern.

The modest little house which cannot afford a wall and stone ornaments and has only a few square feet of land outside its door uses a high fence to secure privacy. Though often of plain boards, this fence usually manages to be artistic by having its boards placed alternately on opposite sides of the horizontal supports and charred to remove glaring newness. Or, if planed smooth, the wood may be left to weather to a soft grey and become mossy around its posts. The ground so inclosed usually holds one or two half-buried rocks framed by ferns and low shrubs. In the corners a tree and a few larger shrubs complete the setting. Even in such a modest place there is the tea atmosphere of quiet greenness.

Homes of the better class will often have one room which can be used for the tea ceremonial if desired. This room usually opens into a corner of the garden set apart from the rest by a hedge or small bamboo fence and developed in rather more direct tea fashion with its own stone basin, lantern, and green plants.

The detached tea house and its surrounding garden is to be found only on the large estates where space and expense need not be considered. Under modern conditions the presence of several of these tea places—and sometimes there are three or even four—can only be regarded as a way of showing off wealth. While many tea room owners, no doubt, get sincere use and pleasure from them, one has the feeling that others are frequently owned because it is the proper thing to have them as an item in the cultural show window.

The little tea gardens around the tea houses on an estate are usually quite charming in their sophisticated simplicity. Since Rikyū's day, however, they have acquired a number of features which the earlier gardens did not have. One item is a covered waiting bench or summer house placed near the garden entrance, where guests may sit until called into the tea room. Near this there used to be built a privy, but after a while the practical purpose of this building was neglected and for long it was included only as an ornament. Humor, however, has asserted itself and such buildings are now seldom seen.

Another feature from the Tokugawa period is the division of the garden into two parts symbolizing the nearer and more distant portions of the path which led, by convention, to the retreat in the hills. A light gate of woven bamboo usually marks the division between these two parts. The outer portion is the transition area, while the inner portion is more simple, intended to suggest the distant wildness of the mountain path as it approached the hut in the hills.

The interest in antique things also finds expression in the tea garden. Wealthy collectors, when they can, put water basins and lanterns associated with old gardens and old masters into their tea gardens. Or, lacking these, other significant antiques are used. One estate in Kyoto conducts water to the stone basin of its tea garden through a rill cut in the edge of an old rock which was dug up near Nara. The rock is believed to have been part of a prehistoric *sake* press.

Within its extremely limited pattern, infinite ingenuity is used to make the tea garden different and pleasing. An example of this and of Ogawa's unconventional use of plants is found in the tea garden on the Ichida estate in Kyoto, regarded as one of the finest in the old capital. A small stream of water flowing along the border of the tea garden has its banks deeply overgrown with moss, while pushing up through this are short rushes of the "horsetail" type. Their slender, parallel, green stems marching beside the flowing stream suggests vividly the atmosphere of a natural watercourse. Simulating "flood control" on the little stream are long tubular baskets filled with stones, just like those which on a very large scale are laid along the margin of rivers, taking the place of the sacks filled with sand which the West uses, but infinitely more picturesque.

In addition to the tea house and its garden, the modern estate usually includes several special parts as previously mentioned. A forecourt takes care of entrances and exits, leaving the rest of the garden entirely private. One of the most attractive of these forecourts was made by Ogawa for Mr. Inabata. This estate like most others is inclosed by a wall made of natural stones and topped by a hedge. The main gate into the forecourt is made of fine polished woods, with a roof and solid doors. A wide central entrance admits automobiles, while small flanking entrances are used by pedestrians. The ground of the forecourt is covered with fine gravel and bordered with well-trimmed shrubbery in naturalistic groupings. The garage is an inconspicuous building at one side.

Flowing directly across the forecourt is a small stream which carries off the generous amount of water which flows through the estate. One must cross this on a bridge in order to reach the front door of the residence. In having this stream cross the forecourt an extra touch of interest is added.

Modern estates are stroll gardens, their various parts reached by following a path which circles through them. On the Inabata estate the path wanders through a landscape garden lying in front of the house with a pool and cascade, then leads up a hillside which serves as it background. During this woodland stroll the path crosses the incoming stream as it dashes down the hillside to the pool below. Sometimes the path becomes a series of broad steps, each upheld by a segment of tree trunk. Lichens have found a foothold on the tree bark, and little ferns grow in the corners. Sunlight falls in golden shafts through the tall trees overhead, lighting up the glossy leaves of lower shrubs. The path comes out at the top of the hill onto a lawn used for entertainments.

From here a wide view of the valley may be obtained, for this hillside is really a spur of the Eastern Hills. The roofs of old Nanzenji monastery rise near at hand with the folds of the hills receding beyond. It is a view to delight a Western person who might be a guest at a party on this lawn and quite different from the Japanese view upward against the hillside which forms the background for the landscape garden below.

On the Ichida estate the party lawn possesses an interesting detail in the way two paths cross each other. Instead of making a mere right angle, they run together for a few feet, then separate again, making a pattern like two Y's laid stem to step. An unusual detail on Mr. Nomura's estate is a private *nō* stage built in the classical style for presentations of this special type of Japanese entertainment.

If we continue on the path through the modern estate, we usually come to the service garden, where flowers and vegetables are grown for use. This is an entirely Western idea but on these estates it is often carried out in an original manner. On the Inabata place, the geometrical beds are raised behind inclosing curbs of small logs driven closely together into the ground.

Masses of the Yoshino variety of cherry bloom crowd the lake shore in Heian shrine garden, making the finest display in the old capital. A roofed bridge crossing the lake suggests, perhaps, how the end-pavilions of Heian mansions may have looked in early days. (Photo from Kyoto Municipal Office.)

The garden-making establishment of the Ōgawa family has occupied the same site in Kyoto for over two hundred years. The place
is shaded by old trees and piled with fine rocks and stone lanterns
which gather moss until such time as a purchaser may take them
away. (Photo by Okamoto Toyo.)

The tea cottage in Mr. Hirai's garden in Kyoto is typical of many. Made out of beautiful woods with exquisite joinery, it still suggests the rustic pattern of a retreat in the hills. (Photo by Okamoto Toyo.)

The garden of Mr. Watanabe's villa in Kyoto occupies a comparatively small space. Earth piled up along the outer boundaries forms a suggested hill slope in which grow trees and shrubs. Behind it show the distant hills. A tiny pond curves around the foot of the slope, while between it and the pond is a path of stepping stones set in gravel and framed in low azaleas. This garden was but a few months old at the time the picture was taken. (Photo by Okamoto Toyo.)

Water is conducted to the hand-washing basin of one of Koyoto's tea gardens by a trough in a stone dug up near Nara and believed to be part of a prehistoric sake press. (Photo by Okamoto Toyo.)

A touch of adventure is given to the walk around the Ichida garden by having the path go on stepping stones right under a corner of the house where it overhangs the water of the lake. (Photo by Okamoto Toyo.)

The large lake on the Nomura estate holds a boat and boathouse, sometimes used for the tea ceremonial. The large stone in the foreground was broken into several pieces in order to move it into the garden, then reassembled. Only small cracks now indicate this adventure. (Photo by Okamoto Toyo.)

In Marquis Hosokawa's garden in Kyoto, a brook flows out of the pond in the rear and, curving down past the doorstep, must be crossed on stepping stones in order to reach the rest of the garden. (Photo by Okamoto Toyo.)

The last garden made by Ōgawa Jihei is in the grounds of the Miyako Hotel in Kyoto. This part of it, facing a small Japanese cottage, forms a modest garden picture showing the return to naturalism in the placement of its stones.

This is the same garden in the grounds of the Miyako Hotel during its construction by Ogawa's men; note the same three-cornered stone in the lower right of both photographs. In spite of the apparent simplicity of the finished garden, the size of the stones as revealed here shows that garden making of this kind is not simple. (Photo by Okamoto Toyo.)

GARDENS AND FLOWERS OF THE MODERN AGE

A small runnel of water flows down the center of the four main paths; when the garden needs extra water it is lifted from these small canals with a dipper having a handle as long as a rake, and poured on the beds.

The service garden on the Ichida estate, in addition to its flower beds, possesses what might be called a Japanese service garden. In one corner is a small, wet paddy field in which a few sheaves of rice are grown each season —purely, it must be, for atmosphere. A path on the dyke through this field is bordered by iris which flourish in the swampy ground, while an old wisteria covers an arbor. In one corner lotus is grown for its edible roots and seeds, as it is in many country wet-fields. A little farm hut with a thatched roof and brown mud-plastered walls gives point to the farm atmosphere. Beside it is a huge old water wheel slowly turning. Inside the hut this wheel moves an old fashioned rice polishing pestle which thumps slowly up and down in its bin of golden grain. The dripping, old wheel, slowly turning behind the trees becomes a romantic part of the outlook from the main landscape garden just beyond the service garden.

A landscape picture is, of course, the main feature of a private garden. It is always arranged to form an outlook from the house, bringing the two intimately together. Some of these landscapes are large and formal, made up of a spacious lake, a cascade, and hills in the background. Others are more intimate, with a little stream and a pool coming down into the foreground. An example of each is found in the Ichida estate, which is really a double garden. The best view of the lake is obtained from a corner of the house which overhangs the water or from a small summer house at the lower end of the garden. From here the lake stretches up to the foot of a cascade which seems to flow down from the green Eastern Hills behind. The flow of the water itself is here of chief interest, not the rocks which form the cascade; indeed, they are almost concealed by planting. The water glides in a high fall directly into the pool, while a branch of a maple tree, in traditional fashion, extends half across it. All around the lake the planting is of interest, gay with azaleas in May and bright with berried shrubs in winter. In autumn tall reeds push up through the pond water beside some of the

285

"floating stone" islets; on a secluded bank the small wild flowers of September are grown. Where the corner of the house overhangs the pond, a touch of adventure is given to a walk through the garden by the path taking to stepping stones in the lake, laid under the overhanging corner. It is quite high enough to walk under, the floor supported by a stout pillar resting on a stone in the water. The stone wall which holds the embankment under the house has small plants growing in its shadowy crevices.

A modern lake quite large enough for boating in the old manner is on the Nomura estate. There is, indeed, a boathouse on the farther shore with a barge moored under it, but this is not one of the dragon-headed boats in old Heian style. Instead, it holds on its deck an inclosed room, shut away with paper-covered lattices, in which the tea ceremony can be held if desired. Sometimes, on moonlight nights the boat is poled out into the middle of the lake and used for moon-viewing parties. Around this large lake, some of the stones are so immense it was impossible to transport them intact, so they were broken and reassembled in the garden. One very large one now shows only a few cracks as evidence of this adventure; they can be seen but would never be noticed unless attention were directed to them.

A garden with a smaller and narrower lake which winds interestingly along the foot of an inclosing hillock to form the middle ground of the picture is that on Baron Sumitomo's estate. Rising close behind this garden is a flank of the Eastern Hills which here become the center of interest as they do in the Silver Pavilion garden not far away. A grove of maples on these hills burns brightly in autumn, and the color is brought down into the garden itself by skillfully extending the same planting.

For the more intimate garden picture, a favorite device of Ogawa was to bring a small streamlet down almost to the doorstep. Standing on the edge of the water seems to be an almost universal human desire, and this plan satisfies it. Marquis Hosokawa's estate holds a good example of it on a larger scale. The pond lies well back at a level slightly higher than the house. A brook flowing from its right end swings in a wide curve and flows past the front of the house; it is so close that it must be crossed on a couple of stepping stones to reach the rest of the garden. A little cascade in the brook near the house chatters musically, while the edge of the brook is lined by low plants and occasional rocks in a natural way.

From the living room of the Ichida residence, the little stream which starts invisibly among trees at the back tumbles in four low falls on its way into the foreground. Near the living room, it flattens into a shallow pool, the opposite side of which is inclosed by a mossy bank shaded by trees and shrubbery. A few lazy golden carp scratch their bellies on the bottom pebbles of this pool and cut a wake with their tails across its limpid surface. When such fish live in pools as shallow as this, a deep hole is provided for them in winter so their tails will not get caught some cold night in a crust of ice.

These huge carp are found in most of the modern garden pools. They are not the ordinary, chubby, lacy-tailed goldfish, but slender, clean-lined creatures, often two feet long. Most of them are a dazzling orange color, but some are mottled boldly in black or white and some are a pure silver. A pool designed especially to show off the beauty of these fish lies outside the Carp Room of Mr. Watanabe's residence. The water is crystal clear, due to a modern cement bottom carefully concealed under pebbles and water moss. The dozens of great fish flow together through the clean water in gigantic whorls, like the slow turning of some great gold and silver nebula.

The streamlet flowing into the foreground is seen on a very small scale in the setting for a Japanese cottage in the grounds of the Miyako Hotel in Kyoto. This was part of the last garden laid out by Ogawa Jihei and finished after his death. In the little garden around this cottage, a landscape picture is formed by a high thread of water pouring down from the hillside to form a pool surrounded by rocks and plants. Out of the pool a streamlet flows forward to the very doorstep of the cottage, then past the side of the house, and so out of the grounds. The rockwork around the pool and the stream is very naturalistic, for, while the stones were put in with evident human artistry, we have the feeling they could hardly have been placed otherwise had nature itself done them. This is typical of the rockwork in modern gardens which has gone back to the ever recurring theme of nature as the model, more so at the present day than for many hundreds of years past.

For gardening has gone through a cycle in Japan and is back now to what it was in the early days—and still is in other countries—a park or a setting for a home. In following this course, it became a fine art, was swept up until it touched the stars, and then came down, eventually, to the depths of pedantry. Today, no artist draws a symbolism from all nature, nor does any mystic express his feeling about the Infinite in his garden. But still the Oriental garden maker sees nature and sees it whole, its rocks and hills and streams as well as its trees and flowers. And, when he makes a garden, he puts into it all of these things to create a little picture of the outdoors, a corner of nature as it is.

Notes

The quotations following are translations from the *Bulletin of the Society for Research in Chinese Architecture,* an article on *Collected Biographies of Master Craftsmen,* Part 2, Landscape Architecture, edited by Liang Chi-hsiung, in Vol. IV, Nos. 4 and 5, June, 1934. The translations are by A. C. Soper through whose kindness excerpts are being printed here for the first time.

B

From a commentary by an unknown writer on the *Ch'ang-anshi* (History of Ch'ang-an) quoted by Kosugi Kazuo in an article on antecedents of artificial garden hills in the Asuka period, in *Ho-un Magazine,* July, 1935.

C

I am indebted to Mr. A. C. Soper for permission to use a translation of the *Sakuteiki* made for him by Mr. Hogitarō Inada.

Selected Bibliography

IN JAPANESE

Nihon Teienshi Zukan (An Illustrated History of Japanese Gardens), by Shigemori Mirei, 26 vols.   Yukosha, Tokyo, 1937-38.

日 本 庭 園 史 圖 鑑
重 森 三 玲

Kyōto Bijutsu Taikan; Teien (Kyōto Fine Arts Survey; Gardens), by Shigemori Mirei.   Kozando Shoten, Tokyo, 1936.

京 都 美 術 大 觀　庭 園
重 森 三 玲

Muromachi Jidai Teienshi (History of [Japanese] Gardens in the Muromachi Period), by Toyama Eisaku.   Iwanami Shoten, Tokyo, 1934.

室 町 時 代 庭 園 史
外 山 英 策

Nihon Teien Shiyō (A Short History of Japanese Gardens), by Tatsui Matsunosuke.   Yusankaku, Tokyo, 1937.

日 本 庭 園 史 要
龍 居 松 之 助

THE ART OF JAPANESE GARDENS

Nihon Teien no Shuhō (The Technique of Japanese Garden Making), by
Saitō Katsuo. Seibido Shoten, Tokyo, 1933.

日 本 庭 園 の 手 法
齋 藤 勝 雄

Rinsen (a landscape garden magazine), edited and published by Shigemori
Mirei and associates. Vols. I, II, III.
Kyoto Rinsen Kyokai, Kyoto, 1935.

林 泉

Teien Geijutsu (Garden Crafts), edited by Tamura Tsuyoshi.
Seibido Shoten, Tokyo, 1936.

庭 園 藝 術
田 村 剛

*Teien Hisho Kudenkai (Analysis of Secret Books and Oral Traditions on
Garden Making)*, by Saitō Katsuo. Seibido Shoten, Tokyo, 1934.

庭 園 秘 書 口 傳 解
齋 藤 勝 雄

IN ENGLISH

Landscape Gardening in Japan, by Josiah Conder. 2 Vols.
Tokyo, 1893.

The Gardens of Japan, by Jiro Harada.
The Studio Ltd., London, 1928.

Art of the Landscape Garden in Japan, by Tsuyoshi Tamura.
Kokusai Bunka Shinkokai, Tokyo, 1935.

Gardens of Japan, (a pictorial record of famous palaces, gardens, and tea
gardens with an explanation by M. Tatsui, edited by Naoya Shiga and
Motoi Hashimoto.) The Sauho Press, Tokyo, 1935.

Index

Note: Italic figures indicate illustrations on or following page.

INDEX

INDEX

298

INDEX